RESURGENCE OF RELIGIOUS INSTRUCTION

BY THE SAME AUTHORS:

BY DIDIER-JACQUES PIVETEAU

L'Actualité des langues vivantes, 1955
Le Vrai problème de l'école, 1968
L'Ecole chrétienne, pourquoi?, 1969 (with E. Vandermeersch)
Jeunesse européenne d'aujourd'hui, 1970 (with G. Lutte)
Guide pour votre école de promotion collective, 1970
Attention école!, 1972 (with contributors)

BY J. T. DILLON

Catechetics Reconsidered, 1968 (with contributors)
Personal Teaching, 1971
The Nature of Giftedness and the Education of the Gifted. in
Handbook of Research on Teaching, 1973 (with J. W. Getzels)

RESURGENCE
OF RELIGIOUS INSTRUCTION

*Conception and Practice in a World of
Change*

DIDIER-JACQUES PIVETEAU
and
J. T. DILLON

RELIGIOUS EDUCATION PRESS
NOTRE DAME INDIANA

Printed in the United States of America

Library of Congress Catalog Number: 76-55588

ISBN: 0-89135-007-1

2 3 4 5 6 7 8 9 10

Religious Education Press
Box 364
Mishawaka, Indiana 46544

Religious Education Press, Inc., publishes books and educational materials exclusively in religious education and in areas closely related to religious education. It is committed to enhancing and professionalizing religious education through the publication of significant scholarly and popular books.

TO MICHAEL AND AUGUSTA LANG

CONTENTS

viii   Contents

INTRODUCTION

This is just the time, so it seems to us, for fresh thinking about religious instruction in the United States. A period of calm appears to characterize the field at present, giving pause for sober reflection now that recent tumult has given way to relative tranquility, and giving cause for timely reflection as well, before repose gives way to lethargy.

Contrary to what could have been observed a few years ago, religious instruction does not seem to be in a state of crisis today. After a time of shake-ups, changes, trials and errors, the enterprise has settled down once again to take its customary course. Those who had announced the imminent demise of religious instruction would thus have proved false, or at least premature, in their forecasts: in Catholic high schools particularly, religious instruction remains robust enough to make some three appearances per week over a long four-year engagement. We might stand to profit from this period of calm by trying to grasp the events of recent years and put them in perspective, for happenings are hard to assess in moments of crisis—outlooks tend to be strained or foreshortened, evidence elusive, and significance misplaced. But a moratorium of sorts having descended upon the field, conditions seem ripe for an examination of past efforts, an understanding of our prospects and the reasons for past errors such as they may be.

On the other hand, this calm might be only the harbinger of lethargy. For instance, this past year has seen the closing of the Department of Religious Instruction at Notre Dame, founded only in 1967; the same fate had already been visited upon programs in Detroit and St. Louis. And where are the prophets of yesteryear, one wonders. They have either stilled their voice and activity or now lecture in wider pastoral fields, leaving to us apparently to sow the good seed for religious instruction. That is not to say that nothing is happening. It is to say only that it is now happening peaceably and at some far remove. Could this betoken insignificance of a field formerly of crucial endeavor? For religious instruction is no longer at the center of practical concerns, nor heads the priorities, nor crests the waves of the mainstream of church life. On this hypothesis, thoughtful study of the enterprise might reveal some of the heart of these matters and compel conclusions which might easily have escaped consideration only a few short years ago: withal, to bring us back to life. We have taken such a study upon ourselves and now venture to offer it in form of this book.

1

The merit of this venture in particular is a matter on which judgments will surely, and reasonably, diverge. Yet we presuppose agreement as to the appropriateness of some such a try—on all of our parts, according to one's lights and experiences: in response to no mere inner prompting but to the urging of the times and the task, to the call moreover of that public, church-wide engagement of voice and action elicited by documents such as the National Catechetical Directory; and we make a point of referring to these texts. Of special note here (since unavailable at the time of writing) is the agenda for the synod of bishops in 1977. We have shared its theme, "Catechetics in our Time,"* and we have shared its purpose:

> The purpose is to reflect on catechetics, with a view to a useful exchange of information and experiences, and for a united commitment to renewal. . . . The purpose is to reflect on the catechetics of the church in our time (p. 1).

Further, the agenda sets for study a series of pointed questions which we happen to have pursued as well; indeed, this book might even be viewed as a contribution of some part of the answers to these very questions (some of which are listed in the Appendix). Hence this book may be situated within a growing compass of thought, and dialogue, that envisage the renewal—or *resurgence,* as we would hope—of religious instruction in the United States of our day.

The structure of the book supports inquiry into our history, conceptions, and practices. We propose in Part One to gather lessons from the past two decades; in Part Two to adduce conceptions from the present world of change, and then on this foundation to erect in Part Three programs for application in the immediate future. Care has been taken to provide that the structure parallel the content in some wise, so that the succession of parts and chapters within accords a sense of movement, achievement, and culmination: decline over yesterday; confused stirring of present day; resurgence to new life and shape of tomorrow. If the book would be read as it has been rendered, as a symphony in three movements, one would mark the themes of past decline *marcia funebre;* the themes of present stirring, *andante cantabile;* the themes of coming to new life, *allegro vivace.* The leitmotif is change and resurgence. The whole is meant to build to a flourish, as resounding and splendid as all of us can make it.

How did these two people come to write this one book? In our case it was easy, in the main. And yet, while our manner of proceeding was at no time in doubt between us, it remains curiously difficult to describe. To our mind, both of us are responsible for the whole as it stands. But the book takes its original

---

*Synod of Bishops, "Catechetics in our Time with Special Reference to Catechetics for Children and Young People." For the use of the Episcopal Conferences. Theme for 1977, International Synod of Bishops. Washington, D.C.: United States Catholic Conference, 1976.

conception from the senior author, who invited collaboration; one French and two English manuscripts were completed between August 1975 and August of 1976, when we confirmed the present form of the book. In two cases the text represents, apart from mere form, the singular authorship of DJP: the last section of chapter 4, and the design of the programs in Part Three. The writing of the text, the siting in American scholarship, and the technical apparatus of footnotes, quotations and references were assumed primarily by JTD. We realize that further details may be of legitimate interest but these might better await more precise inquiries than we can speculate here. For ourselves an appreciation of such questions has not as yet risen to formulation since we have enjoyed both fraternity of thought and mutuality of commitment to the task.

Devising this book has been an exciting and happy effort and, in the end, we hope a fruitful one for our readers and our enterprise. It remains for us now but to make our acknowledgements and then leave the field clear for your plucking.

> - Didier-Jacques Piveteau,
> Paris, France.
>
> - J.T. Dillon,
> Chicago, Illinois.
>
> January 1977.

ACKNOWLEDGEMENTS

It was by the kind invitation of James Michael Lee and Harold William Burgess that I was permitted to spend a summer at Notre Dame writing without distraction. My thanks go also to Helen Cohan and Elizabeth Fowkes, foundresses of Pius XII Institute, for having introduced me to the world of religious education in America, and to Vincent Ayel for having brought me into the field in the first place. These religious educators have freely given of their scarce time and prolific insights to help clarify my own thinking: Trinita Schilling, Marcella Regan, Joan Witucki, Clement Pribil, Robert O'Gorman, Christiane Brusselmanns, and Ernest Flusche. And to all my American students at Detroit, Notre Dame, Oklahoma City, and Louvain go my thanks for their stimulating attention and questions.   -DJP.

Humdrum facets of scholarly pursuit which never fail to excite my feeling of good thanks, now gladly offered, include the privilege of access to university libraries and expert librarians—at Chicago, Loyola, and McCormick-Bellarmine-Lutheran School of Theology; as also the ready scholarship of colleagues in reply to harassing queries—gentlemen and scholars all. In special protection against my ignorance, Ronald Cervero kindly read the chapter on adults and permitted use of his unpublished researches. I appreciate too Anne Chaplin's efficient typing of the manuscript. More than anyone Juanita Peñuela sustained me through this writing and, as she does so well, thus quickened also the prose. Lastly I record my pleasure in association with the accomplished Monsieur Piveteau.   -JTD.

PART ONE

Procession to Impasse: 1955–1975

CHAPTER 1

EMERGENCE OF CHANGE

To start our history of recent developments in religious instruction we may reasonably search out a year when in fact developments began to occur. The year 1955 would seem one appropriate choice.

That year represents a kind of watershed in the enterprise. It marks the end of an epoch that may be seen to stretch beyond pre-war times to the turn of the century, during all of which era the enterprise had not sensibly altered in important respects. The year 1955 marks as well the start of a period during which developments, as opposed to mere events, can be observed and things began to change rather than just happen. Moreover, around that time the generation that is now entering upon young adulthood came to birth while today's established generation was coming to maturity. Constituting the adult church of our times is a mature generation formed by a religious enterprise that had remained fundamentally the same for half a century. It is a generation formed by an enterprise that had already begun a transformation still in hesitant process to this day. This emergence of change and merging of generations into a renewed community of faith offers us a provocative perspective from which to review the past and to preview the future.

Our first task is to get a sense of the state of religious instruction as it once was. From what base did the enterprise we know today set forth on its path to change? What kind of shape did it have to start with?

An observer of the American scene[1] around 1955 would have had no trouble at all discerning the main features of religious education. We can imagine him to have seen a systematic undertaking on the part of American priests and religious to teach, with pronounced European accent, lessons in theology to youngsters in school. What might our observer have concluded? Twenty years later, at a conference in Detroit, the question was to become, Were we taught wrong? Let us postpone the answer until we have situated the question in terms of yesterday's world.

One context is within a wider issue, one which always faces religious instruction and which has posed a special difficulty over these twenty years. Broadly put: How are God and we to come together? How to relate revelation and experience, divine word and human questioning? The resolution of this vexing matter is reflected in the position which the church assumes in relation to society. Two favored positions have been over above society, and

7

alongside against it. These have been confounded with transcendence and immanence, respectively; but whether the world of God is superordinated to the world of man or whether it is subsumed with the society of Christians, the divine and human are set at a distance; society and divinity and Christianity are in worlds apart. To be sure, there are other resolutions to be made. But what was the case in 1955?

This was the time when Catholicism in the United States was said to have a "ghetto mentality."[2] Catholic communities still led the sheltered existence of an ethnic minority turned in upon itself and its own concerns; to establish ties with neighboring communities and the overall society was a matter viewed with alarm when not with indifference. Within these specifically Christian walls the world of man was subordinated to the world of God, while without there stood American society, viz., "the world." This was the world to guard against. This was the world one forsook for a higher world, and into which one sank on forsaking God. This was the world that schemed to imperil Christian souls and society. But this also was the world in which Christian adults had perforce to live and work. Human existence was to be endured with an eye to eternity and human pursuits carried on with both feet on a foundation of Christian life. To point out this end and to lay this foundation early and permanently constituted the labor of religious educators.

In undertaking religious instruction, teachers took on a task that was never light yet by no means exacting at that time in that world. For, although the divine and human were set apart they were not unrelated: there was nature and then there was supernature; there was the human way and then The Way. The situation could not be clearer. There could be no question as to who was to follow Whom and what What. Therefore, there could be no thought of accommodating religious instruction to the shape of human experience. For the Christian, adult as well as child, only one factor counted in the end: the Word of God. If the child was to say anything, it would be to echo or respond to God's Word. If the child did not understand it as spoken, it was for not having listened; if heard but not echoed, it was for hardness of heart; if echoed and not lived, it was for weakness of flesh and the effect of passion. Not to respond to God's Word as invited was to have bad manners and thus be guilty of faulty humanity. The Word of God was clear, as was the catechism. And so catechists, once delivered of the message, could consider themselves in the clear.

Were we not, then, taught wrong? No. To the contrary, when we were young we did indeed receive a remarkable religious education. It gives us little call for regret or apology. Few societies can have devised a system of introduction to schemes of language, conduct, and values as coherent, attractive, and encompassing as the education which we were privileged to enjoy. We must take the case on its own terms, affirming its success for the times and the world in which it operated. That is not to gainsay the case for our present day.

If we ought to respond to the question with "Yes, we were given a good education in the faith," we must not follow up with "—and what was good for us should be good for our children." The affirmation of our own youthful experience should in no wise stand in the way of our examining with a generous spirit other educative efforts that might better be provided for generations that follow our own. Things that were good enough yesterday are bad enough today.

In our own time everything was in its place, all was more or less of one piece; so it surely seemed to us. Nowadays it is apparent to everyone young and old that the times are out of joint and things are not "together," as idiom has it. But howsoever, the two cases are at the very least not equivalent. Someone else now lives in the ghetto, and the church has moved to open to society and contemporaneity (cf. *aggiornamento*). The world has surely undergone dramatic, even cosmic, changes: humans now trod literally in what was once the super-world; the man on the moon is us. Instruction in Christian life has become a task of increasing difficulty and decreasing sureness. In response, the enterprise has become far different from what we once knew it to be. And what was that? Let us rejoin our observer whom we left stranded in 1955.

Three features stand out at the start of change: European influence, clerical personnel, and scholastic paradigm. In peering closer at these we discover implications for the enterprise not only as it came to be today but as we might also make it to become for tomorrow.

EUROPEAN INFLUENCE

Religious instruction in the United States of 1955 was strongly influenced by European thought. This influence extends back many decades and was to continue for yet a decade and more. It appears clearly enough in the transatlantic movement of European books and authors to America.

Even as the enterprise began to shift from its long-settled base, its first call for direction went out to lands overseas. Prominent catechists arrived here from Germany, from France, from Belgium to give lectures and courses. Goldbrunner came, and Jungmann, together with Babin, Van Caster, Audinet, Hofinger, and others still. Theirs was the message to listen to—and read; for if one inquired after a few good books on religious instruction likely as not he would be handed translations from these same thinkers. A representative list appears in Table 1. These books were influential at the time on American thinking and writing; whether they also influenced practice is a separate question.

When in 1958 Gerard Sloyan published a pioneering American volume, *Shaping the Christian Message*,[3] of the thirteen contributors he assembled, eight were non-Americans. One would have had to look long and hard to find

Table 1. SELECTED ENGLISH TRANSLATIONS
OF INFLUENTIAL EUROPEAN WORKS

Date	Author	Title
1959	Josef Jungmann	*Handing on the Faith*
1961	Johannes Hofinger	*Teaching All Nations*
1962	Johannes Hofinger	*The ABC's of Modern Catechetics*
1963	Pierre Babin	*Crisis of Faith*
1963	Josef Goldbrunner	*Teaching the Catholic Catechism*
1965	Pierre Babin	*Faith and the Adolescent*
1965	Josef Goldbrunner	*New Catechetical Methods*
1965	Marcel Van Caster	*The Structure of Catechetics*
1966	Marcel Van Caster	*Themes of Catechesis*
1967	Pierre Babin	*Methods*
1967	Pierre Babin	*Options*
1968	Jacques Audinet	*Forming the Faith of Adolescents*
1969	Jean LeDu and Marcel Van Caster	*Experiential Catechetics*
1970	François Coudreau	*Basic Catechetical Perspectives*
1970	Marcel Van Caster	*Values Catechetics*
1971	Hubert Halbfas	*Theory of Catechetics*

a parallel volume in Europe, for the borrowing was unilateral and American thought remained largely unknown overseas.[4] Indeed, American theology at the time was already Germanic, its catechetics already Gallic or Flemish. For a century and more Sulpician methods had been practiced in American schools and seminaries. One thinks of the number of Catholic schools in this country staffed by various congregations (e.g., Christian Brothers) whose spirituality and pedagogy were informed by Sulpician methods, and until not long ago one could still hear American seminarians joke, "All the Way with Olier!"[5]

What were the implications of this European influence? A receptiveness to various trends of thought could have gone some way in indicating a desire for change. However, it rested on two assumptions which invite criticism. It presupposed first that religious instruction was to be practiced the same way throughout the world; second, that the theories of prominent thinkers either reflected or influenced practice at home and abroad.

The view whereby religious instruction the world over would proceed along identical lines had always been favored by Rome. Out of this city arose at the beginning of the century a plan envisaging a "Catechism for the Universal Church."[6] In our own day we have the General Catechetical Directory[7] to reinforce this version of things. To be sure, the Directory politely invites national synods to make the appropriate local adaptations, but it nonetheless advances a series of propositions as if they were thought desirable and valuable everywhere on the surface of this planet. Such projects flow from a theology of Church Universal, not church as constituted here and there locally. These and the vision which they embody tend to retard the effort of local churches to take stock of their responsibilities in face of local problems in educating to the faith. In consequence, the moment is delayed when members can feel responsible, autonomous, and full of confidence in themselves, thanks to the knowledge that they too share in the Spirit. They are prevented as well from acting on a conception of this world in which men live in the most widely-divergent societies, each seeking in its own diversified way to respond to its own particular problems, challenges, and opportunities.

The view on the second assumption is that thought reflects or affects practice. No case is less assured than this. The writings of French thinkers imported by the United States, for example, were certainly a clouded mirror of French practice as a whole. Nor did they always succeed in having much to do with the state of affairs as these developed in their own country. No wonder they had the time and eagerness to accept invitations abroad. But the ideas they brought, quite apart from intrinsic merit, were far from having been shown tried and true. Sociologists and philosophers had pointed out even at that time the fragility of assertions that a culture is one big open market where ideas are exchanged all on one level; where trends in theory and practice, in town and university, pass easily from one to another; where an idea appears in one and the same garb on all occasions.

The error behind all efforts at Christian renewal between 1955 and 1975 might well have been to believe that each and every idea could generate action. This is an error proper to intellectuals. It permits them to elaborate theories of unassailable worth and then lay on the shoulders of those in charge two weighty burdens: the duty to put the theories to work, and the blame for their not working. But the truth of the matter is that a society is changed by ideas which are conceived within the bowels of a society already pregnant with them, and which await only one mind and one voice for their expression in reality. Thinkers perceive these nascent ideas, seize upon them, clarify, refine, and formulate them in terms which leave the populace at large in no doubt of recognizing their own aspirations within. Agents of change and development who worked in the Third World countries and the industrialized world's corporations were familiar with these imperatives and resistances behind change and innovation. But those in charge of renewal in religious instruction in this country proceeded apparently without this familiarity. An undiscerning application in America of suggestions and formulas coming out of a country like France, for example, simply flies in the face of protruding realities: (1) the history and mentality of the two peoples; (2) the privileged situation which Catholicism has enjoyed in France for the last thirteen centuries, and the prejudiced American reaction; (3) the extreme divergence in official church-state relations as constitutionally defined; (4) the differing emphases on schooling, church schools, mass education, national system; *usque ad nauseam utique ad absurdum.*

Where was the thought for indigenous concerns? In 1967 a survey of materials for religious instruction came to conclude as follows.

> Perhaps the greatest criticism that could be made of the catechetical movement in the United States is that it still draws too heavily from European sources. . . . There is very little around that could be considered an American approach to religious education based on American culture and educational needs (p.166).[8]

Criticism continued into the 1970s of the "almost childish dependence" that prevented basic change: "in many ways the American religious instructional enterprise still suckles at Europe's breast."[9] No doubt it slowed the enterprise down on its path to renewal and maturity.

CLERICAL PERSONNEL

During all of this time religious instruction was given principally by priests and religious, not by laypeople. Catechetical formation figured in all seminary programs[10] often as part of training in homiletics. The preface to a manual from 1941 stated:

> The purpose of this volume is to provide instructors with a comprehensive outline of religion. . . . It will also be of use in the instruction of converts and in the preparation of sermons.[11]

Seemingly endless waves of youngsters surged into seminaries and motherhouses of every kind. Only towards the end of our period was it evident that this flowering of grace had succumbed to dystrophy. In the meantime all seemed proper and assured with only religious in religion class and more on the way.

When a pope accorded the dignity of "Apostles of the Catechism" it was to a congregation of religious, not layfolk. Yet service of a kind and some recognition were indeed paid to the place of the laity: they were urged to "associate" themselves in the work of priests and religious. For the one thing that was not assured in those days was the unredeemed world into which numbers of Christians were observed with alarm to be slipping away. Then as now one could always count on morals to be decadent, duties to be neglected, family life to be endangered, the voice of truth, righteousness, and hierarchy to be insufficiently heeded. Forces of secularity, in sum, were widening the breach; into it could be thrown the footmen of Church Militant, the laity, confirmed Soldiers of Christ. A text from 1935 perceived thousands "who are quietly slipping away from us," names appearing on records of baptism but not rolls of catechism, "100,000 children are lost annually in this country through mixed marriage alone."[12] But the humble souls called to combat these perfidies were not to be given much say in the action. They would be guided, directed, supervised and commanded by clerics who continued to run the schools, devise the programs, propose the methods, and write the texts, aids, and summaries for their lay executants and assistants as well as pupils. The CCD Manual of 1941 calls "active" members those men, women, and youth of the parish enrolled as layteachers, "who shall assist priests and religious in catechetical work."[13]

Two general factors may be seen to have attached to the religious education enterprise under the circumstance of its being pursued largely by clerical personnel. Whether these factors are in the manner of assumptions at base or implications in consequence is not always clear. The first is that the enterprise came to be a matter of passing on a certain body of theological knowledge. The second is that its objective came to be to prepare and sustain participation in the sacraments.

If clerics were assumed to fit so deservedly in religion class, it was by reason of the view that to teach religion was in essence to transmit theological knowledge. It was to the evils of ignorance that a stream of papal and epis- copal pronouncements would regularly attribute the responsibility for declin- ing belief and practice. With their years of training, including several in theology, priests especially seemed well-armed against this foe; it was they who could combat ignorance, enlighten obscurity, and redress error. Those of the zealous but unordained and unprofessed faithful who would join in this work were urged to acquire a level of theological competence in some sort analogous to that of the clergy. They would "be examined and certified by ecclesiastical authority" and then "undertake the precious work of religious instruction."[14] From a widely used text of 1955 comes a description of this work:

> The child has a right to the knowledge of religion that will enable him to live a full Catholic life at his present age level, whether that age level be four or fourteen. . . . The catechism should provide a secure foundation on which the catechist builds the presentation by means of which doctrine is made concrete and vital and the child is led through understanding and appreciation to live what he learns.[15]

Behind such a conception, or perhaps constituting it, were several elements. For one, there was an enormous collection of things known about God, the sacraments, grace and prayer, heaven and hell, the saints, and so on and on. So much known gave so much to be said. It was normal that people wanted to say them, all the more because these learnings had behind them the force of tradition and rightness, not to mention infallibility. Today we still seem anx- ious to talk but are somewhat more cautious and confused about what we have to say. But in those days things were known with a clarity and certainty that fairly compelled their utterance before the neophyte. Further, as we have seen, convention held that thought generated action. Memorizing the ten commandments would entail obeying them; explaining the conditions of prayer would lead someone to pray. To this point the famous syllogism of Descartes had become: "I know, therefore I teach; wherefore they learn, therefore they do.'' A last element is the fact that many teachers of the time knew either little else than theology or few other modes of discoursing than in didactic theological terms. The prominent presence of priests in religion classes easily led to the view that their task was to teach what they knew best, and that was theology; wherefore education in faith undeservedly came to be instruction in dogma.

In addition to holding theological knowledge, the clergy were ministers of the sacraments. Religious instruction under their tutelage began to take on more and more clearly the objective of preparing for and sustaining in regular reception of the sacraments. The criterion of successful religious instruction hence became the pupil's faithful attendance at Mass, frequent reception of holy communion, and regular confession. It never seems to have occurred to anyone's mind that such a cycle of sacramental participation represented an ideal fixed for adult Christians in periods of intense spiritual life. There was little if any reflection on the capacity of the Holy Spirit to accommodate delays or irregularities of religious rhythmicity such as may arise during adolescence. Despite texts in adolescent psychology already available for half a century since G. Stanley Hall's famous and monumental inquiries—despite too the pioneering studies on religious psychology of adolescence published by Clark and Starbuck early in the century—it was not until the mid 'sixties that Catholics began to suspect, thanks to works by Pierre Babin and Ronald Goldman for example, the existence of a spiritual moratorium in adolescence during which it appears unwise to draw conclusions about a youngster's state of faith from his manner of practicing its pieties.[16] Nor did historical reminders seem to strike home, that the early church gave one part of its instruction on sacraments only after their reception. Finally, this emphasis on reception of sacraments may have led to a certain violation or at least disregard for student conscience. Numbers of students were well enough disposed to inquire into the faith without necessarily wishing to end up receiving a sacrament on a given date, occasion, or schedule.

SCHOLASTIC PARADIGM

The locus of religious instruction in 1955 was everywhere a scholastic institution and its focus was uniquely a scholastic being.

The champion American volume at the time, Sloyan's *Shaping the Christian Message,* restricts the subject of instruction, namely humans, to those in scholastic states. That emphasis not only excepts adults to treat of youth alone but also excepts youth as it figures in life to stress students, i.e., youth-in-school. An alien descended upon this planet with no prior experience or conception of the sort of thing that transmission of faith might be, would have been forced to view it as a kind of activity engaged in for the benefit of beings exclusively between the ages of five and eighteen. Not until 1973 would the order followed for centuries be reversed. In their pastoral on education, *To Teach as Jesus Did,*[17] the American bishops treat of the educational ministry first to adults, then to youth; they treat of youth first outside the school, then within the school. But that was not the case in 1955.

The scholastic character of religious instruction decades ago was revealed by the vocabulary used to describe it, the place where it occurred, and beyond all else by its feature of age-graded courses. It was never a question of anything but religious schools, religion classes and religion lessons; of teachers and students, textbooks and tests. In this regard we have an entry dating from 1909, a guide to educational success[18] that aims to apply the principles enunciated two years earlier in a papal encyclical on the teaching of Christian doctrine. Because of special significance, two passages deserve quotation in full.

> Ever greater effort in this must be had in order to bring the methods employed in our Sunday schools up to the high standard which modern education requires. A more thorough system of grading than that now found in many of our Sunday schools is not only a thing to be desired, but a necessity, and there is no adequate reason why it should not be had (p.11).

> A more systematically graded course of study is demanded. The benefits from this are almost countless. It includes a study of all Christian doctrine and imparts a practical, comprehensive, and even scholarly knowledge of the same. . . . Such a course of study, lifting the children every year to a higher plane of life and thought, would make the teaching of Christ known as never before (p.24).

Now what could be less remarkable than these familiar notions? The significance of these passages lies in showing that there once was a time, not so really long ago, when religious instruction was not assimilated into a school system. Compare now this passage from a manual of 1963, *Catechetics Today.*[19]

> *Grade-group the children,* preferably *a teacher for each grade.* Failure to observe this fundamental principle may lead to regrettable consequences. . . . Where dearth of teachers does not permit this ideal grouping, the following combinations may be made: grade one on the basis of psychology of first-graders, grades two and three together, grade four alone, for psychological reasons—this period is a transitional one, grades five and six together, grades seven and eight together (p.79).

Here psychology as well as education has been invoked to justify making of catechetics a school affair, assumed without question. But as the earlier text demonstrates, to assume so once took deliberate effort of thought. Today it requires a like effort to put this assumption into question.

What lay behind this effort to insert religious instruction into a paradigm of systematic schooling? What followed from it in consequence? The effort appears to have rested upon assumptions about the nature of human development and the worth of the school; the consequences seem to have included a certain loss of opportunity and perspective in the enterprise. A child's social development to maturity was presupposed to be marked by smooth and stable progression.

Now, one can imagine such an assumption to be the case in a society which itself exhibits the same sort of development. The accumulation of adult experience creates what is called a state of maturity, distinguished by an equilibrium in the face of diverse tensions and solicitations to which the human is subject as a being susceptible of assuming a variety of forms and expressions of his "nature." The relative states of childhood and adolescence take their form and meaning by being set against the model of adult maturity particular to the society. All of this was certainly the case in the society which existed before the Second World War. A relatively stable model of adult maturity had found definition; in its light, the periods of childhood and adolescence were viewed as preparatory to entering upon that stable adult state in which one was to spend the remainder of life, more or less successfully equipped to rebuff whatever blows might befall.

A religious education was good, then, if it succeeded in setting the youthful human into a higher orbit of adult awareness and responsibility; a poor education was one which failed to raise the child to required heights. The thought at the time was that the child would scarcely enjoy a second chance thereafter to change orbit or direction, save in the always exceptional and rare case of religious conversion in later life. This view was disputed in psychological works of the time[20] but represented nonetheless the reigning version. One may consider it normal that in the course of things the church's work should have conformed to the mentality of the age. One has less understanding over the failure to apply the church's demonstrated capacity to be worldly-wise: to grasp the relativity of this scheme; to keep a safe enough distance from it in practice; and finally to divest itself of its traces once the scheme had showed itself impracticable over the decades.

But the church did none of these. It divided its catechumens in two stages and put both of them in school. Children were thought malleable and docile. Religious formation at this age would therefore consist of a kind of impregnation: planting the seeds of truth for future flowering. Pupils were drilled in prayers, rules, mottoes, and formulas in the confident expectation that they would memorize these without too much trouble, and in the full knowledge that they would do so without very much comprehension. Children could be counted on to show tendencies toward imitation and suggestibility—the uncritical acceptance of ideas.[21] There would ensue at any rate the period of adolescence when the child was known to experience a sort of second birth, acceding this time to conscious life. Then he and she would make the teachings their own, expunge them of generality and banality, and apply them to their personal experience in the world. A high school series in widespread use would provide that each lesson and chapter end with the student's recording in a notebook his daily "practical application" of the points made; thus was he prepared for Living with Christ.[22]

This assumption viewed the human being as making a relatively steady passage to adult status of equilibrium and maturity. Childhood and adolescence were preparatory stages on the way to that enduring state of life. By concentrating on these two periods, then, one could provide the young Christian with all that was necessary to fight the good fight unto death in this world and life everlasting in the next.[23]

Another implication of this assumption viewed the school as constituting an enviable model to imitate.

After World War II the school appeared as an institution capable of banishing forever the assorted evils we had known. It would abolish racism and establish equality among men; it would abolish illiteracy and establish parity among nations. National and local budgets for education swelled to proportions hitherto unimagined even in the West, and international agencies lent prestige and resources, as when UNESCO set apart the decade of 1960–1970 for an international struggle against illiteracy around the world. From this time forward the enterprise of religious instruction was directed less to a search for structures and procedures appropriate to its own given ends than to an occasionally frantic and certainly concerted effort to bring itself up to what was deemed the higher level occupied by school systems of education.

Religious schools were aimed to be as grand as public schools, as beautiful and imposing, as commodious and equipped, as competent and certified. Within the Christian school itself, departments of religion were aimed to be as respectable as the academic departments, with a budget as considerable, a staff as professional, a schedule as expandable. If math is taught five periods per week, can we tolerate that religion has only three? Will students take us seriously if we can't even get as much room/money/time as biology and modern languages have? Finally, the CCD moved into the school lest it be exposed as education at a discount.

For a decade and more since 1955 we were therefore to assist at the spectacle of wholesale abandonment of thoughtfulness in favor of a simple attempt to emulate developments in the school, without ever questioning these or giving thought to their befittingness for religious instruction. One cannot help but marvel over this fruitless alliance with the school. It was a waste of time and more. One wonders whether a little more pride and distinctiveness on the part of the church in this country might not have enabled her to avoid this sorry state of affairs.

The distinctiveness of religious instruction in the United States of 1955 did not at all lie in its magnificent network of schools. After all, countries like France, Belgium, and Holland had also built similar systems at the time and enrolled a comparatively greater percentage of the school-age population. What seemed both important and original in America, rather, were the CCD programs.

Consider that of the eighteen thousand Catholic parishes in the United States fully ten thousand had no school building in 1955. Clearly the youth of this country could not all be attending parochial schools nor could they all be receiving instruction in the faith by clerical tutors alone. In scope, in program, in personnel the CCD might have constituted in this country the base for a new church such as we dream on about today.

One is indeed struck by the inventive spirit, the flexibility, the forward concerns which this aspect of the enterprise showed before 1955. Take for illustration the diversity of roles conceived necessary to put the parish on a footing for teaching the faith. The CCD Manual of 1941 distinguished these six: teachers; "fishers" (home visitors); helpers; discussion-club leaders; parent-educators; and "Apostles to Non-Catholics" (p.21). Consider also the concerns and suggestions of the CCD 1946 National Congress.[24] Entire sections were devoted to religious education of adults, and of parents; adolescent religious education was conceived less in terms of classroom procedures as in retreats, clubs, intensive week-ends, and the like. The overall impression is of a distinctive and authentic pastoral effort, adapted to the specific situation in which thousands of parishes found themselves throughout rural and small-town America. If ever a new concept of pastoral education in faith were to rise to prominence, one would think it to take much the same shape as these insights that appeared in the CCD of an earlier time.

But what in fact was made of this promising situation? It was overlooked in the rush to school, a rush which eventually carried with it the CCD itself, programs and personnel, together with an important part of opportunity and perspective. The programs of the CCD were aligned to those in the school, as somewhat less ambitious perhaps, and its youngsters were lined up as students, somewhat less serious ones perhaps. The personnel were trained in academic theology and then treated as second-rate or second-rank clergy. A discussion of the training they needed appealed to lay devotion and self-sacrifice.[25]

> From the point of view of the lay catechists, great self-sacrifice is unquestionably required. Only this spirit will incline a person to undertake a course of some sixty hours and at the end submit himself to examination before beginning his catechetical labors. Grateful acknowledgement must be made of this spirit of sacrifice (p.223).

These thanks from one of the leading thinkers of the time for enduring a program of training in need of which no lay personnel in fact stood. Why was it thought that lay catechists in the CCD required the same competence in theology and pedagogy as had the clerical scholars? As originally conceived the CCD had not even required a school. On the contrary, its structures and activities could not possibly have proceeded within a school. Better might it have been for the school to acquire traits of the CCD rather than the rueful reverse that occurred in reality.

Yet education in faith was thought an activity for schools and for Christians alone. To be sure, when one zealous for the faith starts to talk of it among adult acquaintances it becomes licit to address as well the non-Christians who happen to be among that company. But teachers in classrooms can have neither the same venturous spirit nor even the opportunity. Here also the CCD had once shown a broader concern, more kerygmatic and missionary than did those immured in the framework of Christian schools. One preoccupation of a text from 1936 likely appeared quaint to the en-schooled.

> The problem of instructing the children in factory centers, immigrant districts, and rural areas, children who live far from church, and children who come from careless parents, calls for organized action and intensive effort.[26]

The school clientele at the time was heavily concentrated, deeply religious, and virtuously sacrificing to send their children to Christian schools. "Organized action and intensive effort" was already being expended on a select population supposedly attached to Christianity as to Christian schooling. We had lost for a time a good part of our mission, spirit, and clientele in favor of less venturous pursuits.

The prestige of institutional schooling won out over every sensible consideration of religious instruction. It swept up within a single paradigm all the possibly divergent, alternative, additional manners of educating and types of learners. It made of everyone a school teacher or pupil. It made of the faith a lesson and of education in faith a matter of classroom technique. This literal imitation of the school as model might well have caused religious instruction in this country to lose a decade and more on its distracted way to achieving its own paradigm. To document such peregrination we may now follow the doleful traces of the enterprise as it set off from this starting point around 1955.

CHAPTER 2

TRACING A PATH

Since 1970 an increasing number of attempts have been made to distinguish the phases through which the enterprise of religious instruction has passed in recent decades. The very fact that such attempts are undertaken suggests that we have arrived at a crossroad.

In an effort to situate the present and identify options for the immediate future, attention is turning to an analysis of the recent past. Sensing that we find ourselves in a problematic situation, we seek first to identify and situate the problem, asking: How did we come to the present situation? What steps or developments might be discerned which have brought us out of a comfortable past to the point of present malaise? How might these developments help define present experience and at the same time point to the various steps we might possibly consider next? For we sense that we must now watch our step.

Questions like these in all likelihood underlie reflective analysis of the past. They are not explicitly asked. But when we see a search for historical answers, we may presume that the present is in question. For this reason we realize that an era has come to an end. A page has been turned and a new one is about to be written. What shall we enter on the new leaf of religious instruction? Let us first pause to read the entries of days just past, reviewing first the schemes that others have proposed to trace the path taken.

TRENDS IN THEORY

Six trends may be selected from current literature on religious instruction. Table 2 summarizes these in a form convenient for discussion. The bases or criteria for distinguishing these various trends are generally the same in all analyses. These include: the key underlying assumption or principle; goal, aim, or purpose of instruction; content or curriculum; roles of teacher, student, and environment.

In the first listed, Richard Rummery,[1] an Australian educator, reviews the evolution of religious instruction between 1930 and 1970. Among several analyses, he makes a diachronic distinction among five principal phases: the traditional, pedagogical, and kerygmatic periods; then an existential, life-centered one, and lastly a group-centered phase. He points to a number of new positions assumed by prominent thinkers which appear in his view to have influenced the later stages he identifies: provocative articles in which Joseph

Colomb contests the enterprise of religious instruction, Pierre Babin announces his departure from religious instruction, and Gabriel Moran announces the departure of religious education itself in "Catechetics R.I.P."

Rummery's work is filled with original insights and useful suggestions. It may well become a classic in the field. But however that may be, it nonetheless does not entirely satisfy our purposes here. For instance, the later stages in this trend do not apply to the situation in the United States; the group-centered emphasis would appear to characterize European developments.[2] Further, Rummery seems to attribute too great an influence to theology as promoter of change in religious instruction. But this enterprise is not run on theology. One cannot hope that developments in theology will of themselves entail changes in religious instruction, although they can serve to validate desired changes. Theology does not cause change but can do the enterprise a service by not preventing it. Moreover, the analysis bears on theoretical rather than practical developments. It reflects the perceptions of thinkers in the field rather than the lived experience of those engaged in daily practice of religious instruction. There is no fundamental difference between the traditional and the pedagogical nor even the kergymatic phases at the level on which they evolved in practice. Whatever differences may appear are in fact only superficial: at bottom the aims were identical, the assumptions similar, respecting revelation, institution, and teaching function. Between these three stages and the fourth, called "life-centered and situational," there is a genuine difference. This fourth stage marks a passage from one encompassing viewpoint to another, a change in conception of God, man, and the world, of revelation and church. But even here we are dealing with a change in conception more than in practice; new positions were taken by thinkers and writers but not by teachers and administrators.

Two American educators, Catholic and Protestant, make what amount to parallel distinctions in their analyses. Robert R. Newton[3] usefully distinguishes among approaches according as they aim at the fulfillment of person, acquisition of knowledge, or change of behavior. For his part, Wayne Rood[4] lists different terms for somewhat the same elements: personalism, essentialism, and experimentalism. To these three Rood adds a fourth which in his view represents the new direction to take, and which appears to take personalism one step further—or, if you will, to take personalism and strip it of the presence of a God standing outside of humanity, substituting in its place a God personally and immanently present among men. These categories are certainly useful, but not to our purpose. They are made on a synchronic analysis, evidently without aim of showing succession or interrelation, or of indicating on what basis practitioners might have been led to adopt one or the other position over time. Moreover, it is not clear to what degree these terms represent schools of thought only, or options actually put into practice. Insofar as they are taken to describe application in practice, they must be said to

Table 2.   SELECTED ANALYSES OF RECENT TRENDS IN THEORY

Source	Trends	Representatives	
		Protestant	Catholic
A) R. M. Rummery "Catechesis and Religious Education in a Pluralist Cociety" (1975)	1. traditional	Ninian Smart, *Secular Education and the Logic of Religion* (1966)	Conciliar documents Catechetical Congresses (Cf. L. Erdozain) Articles—
	2. pedagogical	Ronald Goldman *Religious Thinking from Childhood to Adolescence* (1964)	Joseph Colomb, "Catechetics Contested," in *Lumen Vitae* Vol. XXV, Nr. 3 pp. 369–386.
	3. kerygmatic		Pierre Babin, "J'abandonne la catéchèse," in *Catéchistes*, No. 76, October 1968, pp. 415–428.
	4. life-centered		Gabriel Moran, "Catechetics R.I.P." in *Commonweal*, 18th December, 1970, pp. 299–302.
	5. group-centered		
B) Robert R. Newton, "Current Educational Trends and Strategies in Religious Education" (1972)	1. individual fulfillment	*	Carl R. Rogers, [*On Becoming a Person* (1961)]
	2. scholarly discipline	*	Jerome S. Bruner, *The Process of Education* (1960) *
	3. [behavioral change]	*	B. F. Skinner, [*Science and Human Behavior* (1953)] *

*

*

*

continued

C) Wayne R. Rood, *Understanding Christian Education* (1970)

1. experimentalism

William Clayton Bower, *Character through Creative Experience* (1929)

Ernest J. Chave, *A Functional Approach to Religious Education* (1947)

Ernest M. Ligon, *The Psychology of Christian Personality* (1935)

2. personalism

Edgar Sheffield Brightman, *Person and Reality* (1958)

George . Coe, *What is Christian Education?* (1935)

Lewis J. Sherrill, *The Gift of Power* (1955)

3. essentialism

Emil Brunner, *Revelation and Reason* (1946)

A. Campbell Garnett, *A Realistic Philosophy of Religion* (1942)

A. Victor Murray, *Education into Religion* (1953)

Table 2, *continued*

Source	Trends	Representatives	
		Protestant	Catholic
	4. new direction	Wayne R. Rood, *Understanding Christian Education* (1970)	*
D) Harold W. Burgess, *An Invitation to Religious Education* (1975)	1. traditional theological	Frank E. Gaebelein, *Christian Education in a Democracy* (1951)	Johannes Hofinger, *The Art of Teaching Christian Doctrine* (1962)
		Lois E. LeBar, *Education that is Christian* (1958)	Josef A. Jungmann, *Handing on the Faith* (1959)
		Harold Carlton Mason, *Abiding Values in Christian Education* (1955)	Marcel van Caster, *The Structure of Catechetics* (1965)
	2. social-culture	William Clayton Bower, *The Curriculum of Religious Education* (1925)	*
		George A. Coe, *A Social Theory of Religious Education* (1917)	
		Ernest J. Chave, *A Functional Approach to Religious Education* (1947)	

3. contemporary theological	Randolph Crum Miller, *The Clue to Christian Education* (1950)	Gabriel Moran, *Catechesis of Revelation* (1966)
	Lewis J. Sherrill, *The Gift of Power* (1955)	
	James D. Smart, *The Teaching Ministry of the Church* (1954)	
4. social-science	*	James Michael Lee, *The Shape of Religious Instruction: A Social Science Approach* (1971)
1. transcendist	James Stuart	Johannes Hofinger, Josef A. Jungmann
2. integrationist	Randolph Crump Miller, Lewis J. Sherrill	Marcel van Caster
3. immanentist	George A. Coe	James Michael Lee, Gabriel Moran
E) Ian P. Knox, "The Natural/Supernatural Relationship as a Determinative Factor in Religious Education Theory," (1976)		
F) Luis Erdozain, [0. pedagogical	*	Munich Congress (1928)]

continued

Table 2, continued

Source	Trends	Representatives	
		Protestant	Catholic
"The Evolution of Catechetics: A Survey of Six International Study Weeks on Catechetics" (1970)	1. kerygmatic 2. anthropological 3. political	* * *	Eichstätt Congress (1960) Bangkok Congress (1962) Medellin Congress (1968)
G) James Michael Lee, The Flow of Religious Instruction (1973)	1. Authenticity 2. Blow [Holy Spirit]	* Sara Little, The Role of the Bible in Contemporary Christian Wayne R. Rood, The Art of Teaching Christianity (1968) Roger L. Shinn, "Christian Education as Adoption" (1962)	Christianne Brusselmanns Gabriel Moran, Catechesis of Revelation (1966)
	3. Dedication	Wayne Rood (1968)	*

4. Dialogue	*	Reuel L. Howe, *The Miracle of Dialogue* (1953) David R. Hunter, *Christian Education as Engagement* (1963) Wayne Rood (1968)	*
5. Personality		*	*
6. Proclamation		*	Johannes Hofinger, *The Art of Teaching Christian Doctrine: The Good News and its Proclamation* (1962) Josef A. Jungmann, *Handing on the Faith* (1959) Albert McBride, *Catechetics: A Theology of Proclamation* (1966)
7. Teaching		*	James Michael Lee, "The *Teaching* of Religion" (1970)
8. Witness		Wayne Rood (1968)	Gabriel Moran (1966)

*No data or does not apply.   [ ] = change or addition to original refer more to Protestant than Catholic efforts. Given the weight of Catholic structure it would seem a rare find to discover ventures having other than in rhetoric the aim of individual fulfillment and of grounding revelation in personally-lived experience.

More ambitious in scope is the analysis made by Harold Burgess[5] in an attempt to encompass trends both Protestant and Catholic, American and European, theoretical and practical. Burgess articulates theological trends into the traditional and contemporary, and trends in social studies into the cultural and scientific. For example, in the first category, traditional-theological, are placed Gaebelin, LeBar, and Mason from the Protestant tradition and Jungman, Hofinger, and Van Caster from the Catholic. One category is reserved for James Michael Lee as having opened an approach strongly characterized by a social-scientific mentality.

This entire volume, as Robert O'Gorman remarks in the preface, "marks a new level of scholarship in religious education" (p. xii). It is particularly enlightening to see Christian thought conceptualized for once according to similarity of principle rather than rubric of tradition; Burgess draws our attention to the fact that under different names certain Catholic and Protestant studies are informed by the same spirit. Despite these merits however, Burgess' categories cannot be used to organize our own recital of recent developments, for these categories are not developmental but synchronic. On this order of analysis, Burgess, like Rood, discerns rather than relates differences, giving a list rather than a history, ordering elements on another basis than succession, development, or evolution. This is his purpose. Our purpose requires a *history* of steps as they have been taken. We might better understand the impasse we are presently in if we can follow the steps by which we came to it. This much said in uncritical spirit, we might reasonably question the classification of certain authors. Why not for example save Lee from splendid isolation by adding the company of other scholars in the same social-science approach to religious instruction?[6] On the other hand, putting Van Caster in the company of Jungmann and Hofinger seems to make rather light of his efforts to break new ground in *Values Catechetics*. Moreover, the entire enterprise of work on values and teaching,[7] so evidently influential to daily practice in the past decade, is nowhere represented in this scheme.

Burgess was a graduate of the now defunct Notre Dame doctoral program in religious instruction. From another graduate of that program comes a different analysis. Ian Knox[8] distinguishes theories of religious instruction according to their view of the relationship between the natural and supernatural. Two basic answers to this question have been given. In its pure form, the transcendist theory gives absolute priority to grace over nature, while the immanentist gives the reverse—or more accurately, does not distinguish the two. Between these two extremes is what Knox terms the integrationist position. Taking mostly the same authors as Burgess, Knox then allocates them to the two opposing camps and the no-man's land in between. The value of this scheme lies principally in the caution it affords us against the ill which F. H. Underhill diagnosed as ''hardening of the categories''; the limitation of the scheme lies in its imprecise definition of the middle term, seemingly classifying by default all those who cannot clearly fit into the other two. In this view, for example, Van Caster appears as a middle-grounder, whereas he occupies a traditional-theological place in Burgess' scheme—hardly qualify as being intermediate between transcendent and immanentist positions. Categories are useful instruments of thought, often rising to interesting hypotheses. But they rarely can claim to express or exhaust reality in the concrete.

The last analysis to capture our attention is that offered by Luis Erdozain[9] in a survey of catechetical congresses from 1959 to 1968. He sees these as reflecting three successive periods, the kerygmatic, the anthropological, and the political. There is no fault with this classification. Moreover, its first category, uniting as it does the traditional and pedagogical phases to the kerygmatic, lends support to the demurrer entered against Rummery for having distinguished these separately. Nevertheless the international subject of this analysis makes it too general for our purposes, only two American educators (Moran and Sloyan) figuring in a host of others. Additionally the theoretical character attaching of necessity to the author's subject, makes it important to inquire after the reflection in practice of the trends adopted by thinkers in congress. Erdozain himself is quite sensitive to this issue, remarking that insight is often distorted in working practice. He cites in particular the case of biblical renewal, which caused a lot of sound and fury in catechetical circles but eventually came down in practice to nothing more than replacing a series of meaningless dogmatic formulations with a series of meaningless biblical recitations (p.26). We see how a given notion proceeding from one version of things is misconstrued when approached with another mentality altogether. The same fate thus befell scripture as had earlier befallen dogma; the bible became a Baltimore Catechism, put to the same dreary use with the same deadening effect. A dimension of religious education simply was taken as a novel teaching technique, and faithfully prostituted.

There is a lesson in all of this. But we shall not even have noticed it, much less learned it, if we have not so much as asked the question. How has theory fared in practice? Have these lofty trends wafted through school corridors as well as groves of academe? When we know whether certain notions have been received in practice and what has thereupon become of them, when we know as well the practices themselves and the thinking which proves to have supported them—when we know these answers we shall know the history of religious instruction in such a way as to throw light on our confused days, enabling us to clear the way for purposeful action.

EVENTS IN PRACTICE

Events, one may suggest, never do proceed according to the pronouncements of pundits. Let us take some examples. In 1970, Gabriel Moran announced the death of catechetics: "R.I.P."[10] But as happened in the case of Mark Twain's obituary, this report proved to be an exaggeration; current indications are that the enterprise has survived and is bearing up fairly well, thank you. In 1967, on the other hand, Moran and a number of others affixed their signatures to a manifesto urging among other points that competent catechists devote their primary efforts to adults, especially parents, rather than to children.[11] Here we are a decade later and no closer to realizing that ideal. In that same year of 1967, Matthew Fedewa[12] foresaw a radical change in the practice of religious instruction, concluding that Vatican II called for a new approach to working with teenagers, and that this approach would take the form not of instruction but of youth movements, groups and weekend encounters similar to his own Teens Encounter Christ (TEC). Today as we look about that future into which Fedewa had peered we find the Vatican declarations ignored, traditional structures upheld, instruction pursued, teens and Christ estranged, the TEC movement dissipated, and Fedewa himself, founder and erstwhile promoter, nowhere to be seen. The point to be made is that the history of ideas in religious instruction is not sufficient for the history of developments in the field as a whole. This circumstance is not unique to religious instruction but applies to every branch of human endeavor; witness the relationship between scientific research and technological application; or between the philosophy and practice of education—all the textbooks extol the ideas of Plato, Rousseau, Froebel, Pestalozzi, Montessori, Dewey; and none of the schools embody their virtuous models. This is not said to minimize the influence of ideas and theories, but to highlight the historical lapses in their realization in practice.

What happened to insights and suggestions which flowed from researchers, scholars, and theorists? They have often as not in practice been put to a use which could only thwart original intents. Certain ideas from group dynamics or encounter-experiences might have led to an altogether revised religious instruction if their tendency were given result. But they were mis-taken and put in the service of a mentality counter to their origin and purposes, namely a transcendental view of God and the world. Practitioners received these views from their own religious education in youth and continued to use them in their later instructional efforts. Approaching from this viewpoint suggestions emanating from a radically different view, some practitioners succeeded in making of these a pedagogical gimmickry rather than a basis for educational renewal.

From the manner in which certain analytic schemes have categorized theoretical trends and represented each of them as a collection of practices gathered about a body of thought, one is left with the impression that we educators have a free choice to make among them. The picture is of a catechetical consumer browsing through a furniture mart inspecting ensembles which are clearly on display, precisely tagged, and wholly within his budget. Not so. By reason of temperament, training, and circumstance, teachers furnish their rooms bit by bit with period-pieces, modern plastics, second-hand buys, all refurbished, replaced, and rearranged from time to time. Teachers, that is, improvise rather than adopt wholesale. To one theory they give their allegiance, to another they give over their practice; one they use to set their objectives, another they use to evaluate the same; and so forth. Scenarios of change have not unfolded according to script, whether written by a theorist or catalogued by an analyst. Four considerations come to mind as factors to help one understand this phenomenon.

First, as we have come to understand better the process of change we discover that it does not come about as result of any single consideration but is in fact a product of multiple factors. To be effective, therefore, a theory must embrace, provide for, and interact with, a number of other facilitating factors of political, social, and economic nature.

Secondly, the belief in all-powerful theory carries with it the supposition that theories, like the universe, are created out of nothing as if by the hand of God. But in truth, theories and facts have a common source in the changing environment and the stimuli which these changes create.[13] As ideas react to environmental stimuli more rapidly than facts and structures do, it frequently so happens that thoughtful suggestions remain for years without practical effect; when results do follow thereafter they prove as much the product of changes in the environment as the consequence of intellectual insight. Theories and facts are correlated but not in a properly causal sense. Brought to bear on our own enterprise, these remarks would translate to the effect that changes occurring in the decade of 1960–1970 might be laid more to the influence of factors such as the war in Vietnam, racial tensions, and student demonstrations than to the determinations of theorists, books, and articles. These last served above all to give clear voice to sentiments which all the world found confusedly excited within them by the stimulant of widespread unrest and change. By some curious omission, this idea that changes in the outside world have more to do with changing the church than has the historical unfolding of theories elaborated from within the church herself has been studied from various angles throughout the religious literature in America with the sole exception of writings on religious instruction.[14]

Further, studies of organizational change in the school[15] have shown that if research findings are not endorsed by school authorities within two or three years of their being proposed they lose both their allure and their efficacity by reason of the prevailing influence of the authority principle so strongly held in academic circles. Now in catechetical circles, at the level of teachers and their highly-developed sense of duty, the voice of prophets stands no chance whatever of being heeded in practice if credence is not forthcoming from episcopal authority. Teachers who act prematurely just as quickly find themselves on the outs, in that marginal state of quasi rebellion reserved for those of precipitate will.

Lastly, theory cannot be embodied in practice without suffering inevitable distortion. It is obliged to come to terms with factors of resistance, opposing theories, and institutional compromises.[16] Thus to write the history of educational practice, public or religious, can be viewed as recording the successive adulterations of theory.

We may retain from these considerations the view that change is attributable above all else to stimuli arising from environmental mutation and modification, and that each segment of a given world's population is most responsive to those aspects of change which touch it directly in its everyday life and work. For those engaged in religious instruction, the most compelling stimuli arising from the changing world were the growing difficulties they experienced in accomplishing their daily tasks among the young, especially adolescents. In recording their response to these stimuli, we find ourselves writing a sorrowful history, not as to the outcome of these tasks, be they bungled, managed, or whatever, but as to the fate of those who attempted them.

What became of our religion teachers these past years? In all the concern that we have shown for various aspects of religious instruction we must admit to an embarrassing neglect, on the part of hierarchy and theorists alike, of the lot of those men and women who willingly gave themselves over to the Christian instruction of our young. As phase succeeded phase, trend replaced trend, and issue surmounted issue in the quest to adapt to changing times, numerous victims fell by the side. Not all of these were unworthy notions or negligible practices. Among the victims were numbers of virtuous, enfleshed human beings who had essayed to serve as teachers of religion. At times more attention may seem to have been paid to the failure of cherished programs or to the distortions visited upon theory-in-practice than to the attrition and demise of many a religious educator. When Gabriel Moran in 1970 wrote the article entitled "Catechetics R.I.P." he may not have formulated the situation exactly. But whatever its accuracy in describing the state of the enterprise, truer would it have been to read "Catechists R.I.P."

The slow death of religion teachers transpired in several stages. The first two arose from experiencing external difficulties and consisted in turning upon one's students or one's tools; the last two arose from internal troubles and consisted in turning upon one's self, and then upon one's task.

As difficulties began to appear, the first tendency was to throw the blame back upon the students. The present generation had become corrupted by money, distracted and deadened by television and movies, materialistic and egoistic one and all. As it proved increasingly difficult to sustain the belief that an entire generation of youth could have been thus abandoned by God and sunk to a man and woman in depths of evil beyond the capacity of other generations, a second tendency arose.

This response was to turn upon the instruments of instruction at hand and to find them unsuited to the present task. Thereupon commenced an outpouring of: beautifully printed, handsomely illustrated, and fulsomely phrased texts, booklets, posters; technically superb films, cassettes, and slides all seductively engaging and one more determinedly relevant than the other; summer workshops, midyear institutes, weekend retreats, conferences, and conventions ever more exciting in promise of finding those methods which, finally, would really get 'em involved. As however in spite of these efforts an everwidening breach continued to separate teacher and students, an insidious thought would begin to take shape in the teacher's mind. "Suppose these youngsters are just as good as any others, only different, and suppose these methods and materials are perfectly all right . . . what then?" Then came what Savio Warren[17] called "a crucial moment of truth" for the religion teacher:

> Standing in self-assurance before a class, he suddenly realizes that the voice echoing off the back wall is merely being tolerated by his students. Clearly, they are not absorbing a single syllable of his lesson; it dawns on him that in fact they couldn't care less". . . (p.191).

His search to make them care, listen and get involved "is sure to entail much agonized frustration." For the question of failure had by now become a question of *my* failure, flowing from insufficiency of self, not deficiency in students, method, or materials. The third tendency was therefore to turn upon the self. The teacher began to torture himself with doubt as to his competence and skill. He would take courses in adolescent psychology to increase his knowledgeable understanding of students. She would plunge herself in the study of group dynamics and even into the midst of assorted encounter groups to learn how to interact with others and lead group discussions. Everything within their power they would undertake in the hope of "getting their head together" and emerging with a new, improved me.

But withal there remained one step more to take in this descent into hell. The teacher had arrived at a point beyond which a number of religious educators had already passed, meriting the claim to every bit of our attention. For it is simply not with the power of any human being to endure life in the misery which comes with acute, unremitting awareness of one's incompetence, insufficiency, and helplessness. There would ensue a moment when the last question would come to mind. "Suppose after all that I myself were no more to blame than the students or methods? Then could it be that failure is due to the very task I am trying to accomplish? What about this message of Christianity I am supposed to be passing on? What if the 'good news' is not really good, after all? Why should these kids listen, then? Why should they pay any attention at all? Who cares? Maybe they're right.''

And thus it transpired that during the years 1960–1970 one could meet teachers who had lost not only their heart for teaching but also the essence of their faith.

The greatest source of activity in the practice of religious instruction between 1960 and 1970 was unfortunately the indifference and even hostility which students showed in face of their teacher's ceaseless efforts to win them over. This is hard enough to admit. Far nobler were it that evolution proceed on vision. However it did nothing of the sort. Our history must duly record not only progress made but also what it was in practice that stimulated the progress. This proves to be the difficulties which religion teachers faced from within and without. If every one of them deserve a historical footnote, then for many the notice must also be necrological. For the events of recent past constitute a history of religious educators handing on the faith and also losing hold of it.

A number of events may be traced to the role that money has played in past practice of religious instruction. This ignoble circumstance may be repugnant to high-minded spirits without on that account losing a whit of its importance.

One aspect to this question is rarely discussed. We are ready enough to talk money when it comes to salaries, budgets, subsidies, and outlays. But how many of us have given thought to the considerable financial interests which lay behind the publication and promotion of those texts and teaching devices for which we yearly handed over more than a princely pittance? Many a colleague comes to know new religious conceptions solely through the texts and materials he is to use in his task. Now, according to widespread convention these publications are to represent a translation of theory into practical form. But they do not.

Theories can afford to be novel, provocative, and controversial, but textbooks cannot. Texts and materials are printed to be sold in large numbers to a wide market. If a printing of twenty or fifty thousand copies is to sell, the product must be pleasing to a great number of educators and parents of every stripe, who must be able to adopt the text without finding in it anything offensive to anyone. Publishers have been known who rashly incorporated a certain novel view, persuaded some high-level functionary to adopt their text system-wide, only to find themselves in midseason forced to buy back, emend, reprint, and then try to resell the entire issue, at enormous loss of money and face. One such case occurred in a large urban diocese during the kerygmatic heydays when, due to wholesale revision of texts, money could be made hand over fist by the first publisher to issue decently postconciliar materials for teaching religion. The offense in question was to print a photo of a certain Negro civil rights leader *en marche,* with caption to the effect that he, like Jesus, worked for justice and brotherhood. Such mistakes are not often made, since other publishers are eager to profit from the awful lesson taught. Their own texts would henceforward present novel views with circumspection, if at all.

Moreover, there are a number of theories that publishers simply will not print as conceived, for these would entail abandoning the use of textbooks in favor of, for example, relying on the flow of student experience as it occurs, or making the teacher create his own "text" day after day. The consequences of these views, if allowed to pass into practice, would be catastrophic for the publishing concerns. Hence they do not pass into practice, at least in pure form. What appears is a parody of practice pretending to pass for applied insights. When once a textbook claims to aid the teacher in proceeding on the presently-lived experience of his students, what one has in hand is not experience but a caricature of process-reality, affixed, arranged, programmed and presented with "exercises" to match. If the content is now to be experiences, well then the manual will show you how a few of these can be created to order in three easy steps, giving your students an experience calculated to drive home the point you wish to make with far more telling effect than all those messy, unorganized ones which students might just happen to be feeling at the time with no thought at all to the curriculum. Perhaps things could be moved along if teachers assigned a few experiences to be had that night for homework—written of course, preferably in the workbook provided by the same publisher (who also offers standardized tests?). Actual cases, unbelievably enough, can be cited. One theory of "value-teaching" stresses great flexibility of approach on the part of the teacher, who is urged to keep alert at all times to the possibilities of the moment, to disregard factors of schedule and curriculum, to provide training in the valuing process at every likely turn, and to give helpful responses in conversations with students wherever and whenever he meets them, even downtown.[18] This theory proved vastly popular among humanistic and religious educators. What has happened is that now a decade later the market teems with truly astonishing texts and manuals which have taken up this theory, given structure and organization to its free-flowing flexible methods, provided teachers with well-thought-out techniques of proven creativity and innovativeness, the whole timed to be finished by the end of the class period, facilitated if need be by timely lectures and assigned readings, no less.[19]

In like manner will the good news of Christianity be adapted to the needs of our great publishing houses. The textbook will win out every time, giving system and order to everything it touches, even life itself.

In consequence, those theories that have been translated into texts and tools have been the best-known and most influential ones of all. The views of Pierre Babin enjoyed great success thanks to the ease with which they found their way into texts, techniques and teaching aids: *Methods, Options,* and *Audio-Visual Man* successfully entitled his views to apply in practice.[20] The views of

Gabriel Moran and James Michael Lee, on the other hand, have met with resistance—the one because of its pointed refusal to prescribe any applications whatever, the other because of its equally pointed insistence on prescribing them in every detail. On neither account are they easily put into practice. Teachers and publishers alike pall before the task of translating Moran's theology of revelation into humble procedures—it is enough just to grasp the conception! Or, equally, of executing in all its exquisite and exhaustive specificity Lee's trilogy on religious instruction—it is enough just to wade through the tomes![21]

Teaching materials have served now to promote progress, now to prevent it. They have promoted religious instruction considered as an enterprise of transmission, centered upon a given content. They have prevented progress of the enterprise considered as an active response to and utilization of present experience. Finally they have served to filter a number of theories, preventing their appearance—or pure appearance—in the practice and minds of many teachers, together with their students, leaving all in a confused state of thinking they think anew while unwittingly toying with minor novelties. There is no risk in appearing to change. Decorum over daring change seems to have been the rule, so much so that it invites the question, what came of it all?

FRUITS OF CHANGE

Passing between his own country and the United States over the past ten years or so, one of the authors could not help but notice American flurry in contrast to French quiescence. And what is most striking is the disproportion between the liveliness of energy and effort put into religious instruction and the apparently cadaverous results obtained.

Never has any enterprise in any other country produced in so short a time such myriads of books, articles, devices, proclamations, demands, suggestions, movements, programs, experiments. Each visit to the United States once or twice a year was an adventure to look forward to. On every return one would step off the plane to find the entire field changed from top to bottom. Useless to inquire after last year's prominent figures or promising experiments—new prophets had suddenly arisen, new programs had been launched, new devices put on the market, new techniques were being tried. Arriving from a land where far fewer changes take place, and these at far more leisurely pace, one simply stood in admiration over all of this.

The speed and ease with which changes were made especially impressed the visitor. Each new experiment or suggestion rapidly succeeded in finding widespread acceptance and application. In France, happiness consists more in talking about change then doing something about it. But, ah, les Américains! Here a change is no sooner conceived than it is proposed, applied, tried, and tested. And with what amazing facility did people engage themselves successively and totally in various different and even opposing directions: one year Montessori would have taken over, and teachers just have discovered how fascinated children were by mobiles, so nearly every lesson would end by their making a mobile—of dangling fish after the story of the miraculous catch, of dangling loaves after the miraculous feeding of the multitudes; another year the artists would have triumphed and walls would be covered with collages, while in still another year the weavers would win out and colorful banners would hang from parish ceilings.

On the other hand, one is brought to make one sobering observation. This change was so facile that it touched only the trappings and failed to attain the substance of things. It is something like what we see coming out of Detroit year after year. The new models are certainly a change over the old ones, not by reason of a transformation of the motor, general design, or overall conception but only for decorative alterations in bumpers, grilles, tail-lights and chrome finish.

Take for illustration two recent booklets for use in religious instruction in the earliest grades. Entitled *Live* and *Act*[22], these purport to embody in title alone the honored theory articulated by Dewey among others, whereupon children are to learn by doing. But the only hint of activity is in the titles and the only change is accordingly. The names have been changed, one darkly suspects, to protect the guilty. Open the third-grade booklet, *Act,* and behold the ''activity'' proposed under explicit heading of ''learning by doing'':

- explain the threefold promise of God to Abraham (p.147).
- explain the chief purpose of the Church, the Kingdom of Christ on earth (p.192).

Now open the first-grade booklet, *Live,* and read under ''home-school activity'' the sole and repeated suggestion for action:

- have the children take home their artwork and tell their families about its meaning (pp. 69 passim)

How do these modern materials represent a change over the catechisms of yesteryear? In what respect do they incorporate the theory of learning by doing? This is not learning, and certainly not doing—it is listening, repeating, and explaining of abstractions beyond the reach of child's mind to grasp. As to the suggested activity repeatedly urged upon children, what child has to be told to bring his drawings home, and what child in his right mind would thereupon proceed to explain, of all things, its meaning? What family would receive such precious personal expressions with demands that they be construed? Out of what world, in sum, do these texts arise?

With these and like changes we are by all appearances dealing only with appearances. The more frenetic and spectacular the change, the more we have dispensed from the risk of taking on the essential ones. Today in spite of manifold innovations religious instruction fairly remains the enterprise it was a decade ago.

CHAPTER 3

TURNS FOR THE WORSE

As teachers of religion wended their way through daily lessons what was it, we may ask, that in point of fact prodded them to mend their ways? Trends in theory, we have suggested, merely wafted o'erhead; trends in theology, on the other hand, had simply not been seen to be brewing, in Catholic circles, since The Council (of Trent) or thereabouts. In any case, it was not so much the promptings of theorists or theologians as the perplexities presented by pupils that seem to have led catechists to change their ways, starting them off on a search of paths that might lead to effective accomplishment of practical tasks.

From time out of mind these tasks had been based upon a "traditional" model of education that, as with most idealizations, invites caricature as well as admiration and sympathy. The teacher was seen as possessing authority, a quality conferred upon him and her by Higher Authority, enhanced by possession of knowledge or secret access thereunto, confirmed by a presumed embodiment of model Christian conduct, and supplemented by prestige accruing from age and function, not to say size. The pupil was seen as possessing none of these. The task of the teacher was to transmit truths of the faith; to learn these was the pupil's duty, not solely by reason of ignorance but especially as these truths emanated from Authority, of church as well as teacher, that is, of a depository of faith and guide infallible to that which was True and that which was to be held as Error. More pointedly, to know or not to know these matters was thought an issue fraught with eternal consequence, and so also the issue to teach and to learn, or not. It was this consequence that weighed upon high-minded and good-willed teachers as they undertook to instruct their charges, and it was that same consequence which figured ever so disproportionately little, as it seemed, in the concerns of youth, who, docile or no, mysteriously remained unreceptive recipients of faith's message and hence increasingly endangered *sub specie aeternitatis*. All the more, then, to press forward with the catechetical task, achieved, it was thought, by activity on the part of the teacher and passivity on the part of pupils. These would listen as the teacher talked and would receive the lesson that the teacher gave; they would read and retain and repeat, in proof of having learned; and, having learned, they would believe and behave according to the formulations of faith thusly passed on.

During much of the nineteenth century, then, while Roman Catholic children under religious instruction were busy memorizing the lessons of the catechism, Protestant

38

children in Sunday schools were busy memorizing the bible. *When a child could repeat what was true and right, he would believe the truth and do the right thing as the Holy Spirit worked within him through the lessons that he had learned—or so the prevailing theory went.*[1]

It was not long—mere centuries—before this model, in recognition of intractable events that proved it impracticable, came into some question and a search began for more effective ways to do the same thing as before, only better.

At the turn of this century in the suburbs of Munich was undertaken the paradigmatic search to be replicated several times over by the enterprise in modern America. Dismayed by the fruitlessness of current catechetical methods—something of a reading and line-by-line *explication du texte*—and impressed by the seeming success of modern methods in secular education, a society of catechists led by Dr. Heinrich Steiglitz appropriated the psychopedagogy of the Herbartian school and devised a three-step approach whereby the abstract, so unappetitive to youthful minds, would be encased in the concrete, as follows: first a story would be told in illustration of a certain "truth"; next the truth itself, object of the lesson, would be arrived at in a process of pondering and explaining; lastly, the point would be applied to action. These three steps of observation, thought, and action constituted the Munich, or Psychological, Method, as it was called.[2]

In various ways and under various forms the Munich Method made its way to America and worked enormous influence on teachers. Josef Jungmann gave it a tremendous boost in the thirties by adding to it the "activity principle" and "personal experience principle," suggesting that learning by doing be applied to the joyful announcement of *The Good News* in the mission of *Handing on the Faith*.[3] The Munich method of three basic steps—presentation, explanation, application—was refined or elaborated to the five-step "kerygmatic method."[4] There had also developed out of the Munich method, from work at the Catholic University of America, the "integrated activity method" and the "adaptive method."[5] The Integrated Activity Method had six steps:[6]

1. *preparation* - to arouse interest in the lesson;
2. *presentation* - to appeal to the senses;
3. *explanation* - to appeal to the intellect;
4. *application* - to appeal to the will;
5. *assimilation* - to exercise the lesson through study;
6. *recitation* - to unify the lesson.

All of these methods appear to be variants of the popular Herbartian method which had also made its way to America and was enthusiastically taught and practiced by the greater part of American teachers up to World War II or so.[7]

Some such approach, then, remained for a time the model of instruction which practically all religion teachers, not to say all teachers, know to this day. They had likely themselves received such instruction, been formed in it as fledgling teachers, and had gone on to practice it in their own classes. As various practical difficulties began to arise, teachers tended to respond by adjusting rather than replacing this model. On all accounts but one, this model represented an impressive, indeed astonishing achievement.

Since the model was on the face of it a blend of psychology and pedagogy, and since none were about to abandon wholesale in favor of entirely different approaches a method with which all had been familiar since youth and which continued to be practiced all about, the natural tendency in face of mounting difficulties was to turn to those two branches of study in order to take from them the very best and latest developments and fit these into the basic model of instruction.

It was in this turn to psychology and pedagogy that the enterprise of religious instruction found itself taking a turn up blind alleys. Into these it penetrated with unique persistence until reaching the deadends of the mid-sixties.

TURN TO PSYCHOLOGY

This turn seemed to hinge upon an illusion that the problem was due to an inability to talk to children. It was an illusion, for if we had had before us a situation where forty adults were plunked into a classroom five times a week for a period of an hour there to provide audience for monological discoursing upon kerygmatic matters, we would have experienced in response that very same lack of appetite, enthusiasm, and energy. Nevertheless, our problem was thought to be that we did not know how to talk to these strange beings called children. The enterprise thus wheeled about on the slogan of the day, that to teach Johnny you had above all to know Johnny. The aim was to get to know him so well that our trouble with speaking to him, and his difficulties in listening to us, would vanish. Teachers therefore betook themselves to whichever psychologists could claim to have learned something about children as might affect their schooling. Professors Freud and Piaget, Dewey and Montessori astonished with discoveries about how children in truth speak and feel, think, learn and act.

Of all the branches of psychology encountered in this search, none held more promise or had more recourse or offered more relief for teachers than did developmental psychology, especially for its allocation of children into appropriate stages, ages, and phases. Considerable interest can be found in following the development of stage-models as they appeared in the thought of religious educators. Writing in 1955, Jungmann[8] proposed a model based upon the rough divisions made by canon law. This ancient scheme divided early life into a triplet of seven-year periods: infants (to age 7); prepubescents (7–14); minors (14–21). In Jungmann's version, the triplet was retained but the ages varied. Another scheme[9] from Europe showed up in American translation in 1958 to articulate five stages before age seven: the newborn, the baby, the toddler; the child from 3 to 6, and 6–7 years. This chapter constituted the sole appearance of psychology in the text. But a sequel heralding itself as modern contained six chapters, all by Americans, devoted to the psychology of children now divided from K through 12, by school grade.[10] Evidently religious instruction was to follow a school-age model. Children were viewed as beings who distinguished themselves according to the yearly grade they occupied in a school system. Even the CCD, long more flexible in its practices but now suffering inferior status, fell prey to this model and aped the school—lest consequence be dire, as a CCD manual warned in 1963:

> *Grade-group the children,* preferably *a teacher for each grade.* Failure to observe this fundamental principle may lead to regrettable consequences. The child who is placed in a group too far above or below his mental level is a potential failure or drop-out because he does not understand what the teacher says, or is bored by unnecessary repetition and explanation.[11]

The very same had been recommended, with more fervor, by another text from 1950:

> Learning and attention depend in large measure on teaching that is adapted to the child at a given grade level. Interest is aroused and attention held when the religion lesson is suited to the child's present stage of mental development. This adaptation can be made only when grading follows regular school grades as closely as possible. When it is necessary to combine two or more grades, this should always be recognized as a temporary expedient, and catechists should always work toward the ideal of having every child in his proper grade for religious instruction.[12]

Both texts direct that where this "ideal" cannot be achieved, the children should be grouped, "for psychological reasons," into grades 1; 2 and 3; 4; 5 and 6; 7 and 8. Once embarked on such a path we find no end to fineness of divisions. The ideal sought was so precisely to discern what was thought to be the reality of the matter that it could no longer escape our clutches. Action would follow naturally once we knew in detail what we were up against in the children we were to teach. Not lofty visions of the mission, form, or future of religious instruction, but down-to-earth exposés of the child's secret inner workings were what practitioners wanted from the theorists. Could a list be made, could a table be erected, could a scheme be drawn giving for each age all the information needed for unfailing diagnosis, prescription, and action? What are the needs, interests, and abilities of each age; the dangers, possibilities and potentials for education in general and religious education in particular?

Of all the schemes proffered in response, none seemed more attractive than those constructed after the epigenetic model of the child psychoanalyst Erik Erikson.[13] One of the attractions of this scheme was its articulation of eight stages of psycho-social development throughout the span, or cycle of life as Erikson called it, representing an extension of Freud's originally conceived stages of psycho-sexual development to adolescence. Religious educators Protestant and Catholic went on to an even finer articulation, resulting in a panoply of stages and dimensions. Wayne Rood,[14] for example, arrived at a scheme of spiritual development for ages four to seventeen, encompassing various traits relating to the child's experience of God, his sense of worship, discovery of love, awareness of dialogue, areas of tension and problems of personality. The evolution of intellect is given in seven stages: security (ages 4–5); curiosity (6–7); skepticism (8–9); adventure (10–11); idealism (12–13); materialism (14–15); empiricism (16–17): Catholics arrived at a similar scheme in the Green Bay Plan,[15] specifying for each school grade a unifying theme (e.g., development of sense of moral responsibility in the seventh grade); a triplet of goals for the teacher (human, faith, and theological); an attitudinal focus (moral responder); behavioral and/or intellectual objectives for the student (again under the same triplet of headings); and a variety of core units to be given (success, failure, and forgiveness; Jesus, redemption, and baptism).

Such undertakings were blessed by the hierarchy. None less than Pius XII stated that the teacher was obliged by office not simply to explain the faith but to do so in a manner which would accommodate the level of the pupil; the teacher, so ran papal recommendation, should therefore study psychology:

> He should accordingly apply himself intently to the study of *psychology* to determine accurately their *intellectual ability;* and moreover, he ought to give serious attention to their *needs* in order to meet them.[16]

The General Catechetical Directory later endorsed this approach by drawing attention to the importance of infancy and childhood as stages, and by the distinction between preadolescence, adolescence, and early adulthood, together with the traits marking off each one.[17] In its present tentative form, the National Catechetical Directory undertakes a similar approach to directing efforts of religious instruction in this country.[18]

Of all the stages thus delineated for instructional effort, none received so much and so anxious attention as adolescence. This was the stage above all to understand, and the one which most defied understanding. Protestants were led to its study long before the Catholics, perhaps by reason of their stress on the individual dimension of religion. Pioneering works by Starbuck and Clark,[19] in particular, had drawn attention to the phenomenon of conversion in adolescence (a shocking notion at the time). For Catholics the work of Pierre Babin stirred interest in the religious psychology of adolescence, the English title of *Crisis of Faith*[20] serving to jolt everyone's attention. The content was even more disturbing than the title. Basing his reflections on a sounding of several thousand French youth, Babin found them naturalistic, even pagan, in mentality, moralistic and individualistic in mode of thought, insecure in the extreme, thirsting for life, perspective, and interpersonal relations. Of special significance was his discovery that adolescence itself was in process of evolving, that the youth of today were simply no longer what we had known in the past. Equally startling was the work of Ronald Goldman, *Religious Thinking from Childhood to Adolescence,*[21] based on Piagetian research on the development of cognitive structures.

Theorists of religious instruction seemingly remained aloof from these developments, as nary a reference to genetic psychology may be found in the body of their work. But teachers of religion were quick to show their interest. In response came a flood of books and research projects aiming to help the teacher in every way and by every means to gain understanding of the young people in his charge.[22]

What came of this immense effort to salvage religious instruction by turning to psychology? Some teachers of religion doubted from the beginning that their task was as simple as the stages, charts, tables, and figures seemed to make it appear. Others concluded that research had not as yet gone far enough, wide enough, deep enough to resolve the matters presenting daily difficulty. But certain others began to suspect that hopes had been placed where they had no chance at all of being satisfied. The psychological solution never worked to satisfaction. We ought to be glad it did not. We have now come to the point where we have a chance to discard these models, however fancy, in favor of facing the realities before us.

Three general considerations may explain the failure of this turn to psychology. In the first place, our knowledge in this domain is simply deficient, while, secondly, the knowledge that we do have has been misapplied in an undertaking prompted, thirdly, by murky and misguided motivation.

The simplistic presentations to appear in teachers' manuals and journal articles fly in the face of the complexities of the problem. Teachers of religion must have been duped into thinking that psychology would be capable of resolving the issues involved so as to make their task easy and automatic. No specialists in the area would let themselves be caught asserting suchwise, save unawares. In discussing developmental tasks in Christian education, André Godin[23] states flat out that no one yet knows in fact how to effectively transmit a truly adult Christianity. In discussing the development of religious understanding, David Elkind, one of the nation's most distinguished authorities on child psychology, clearly enough describes the state of the field as follows:

> There is, however no cause for complacency. Our methodologies in this area as well as our conceptualizations are still relatively primitive and need to be made much more precise before we can really generalize and build upon our findings.[24]

The present state of our knowledge is therefore not sufficient to respond to the problem even as conceived, however unfruitfully, in the first place.

Secondly, even on condition that research and knowledge become perfected, we would still have no guide at all to applications in practice. Science, as may be recalled, is descriptive rather than prescriptive. In no case can it substitute for decision-making in actual circumstances according to the situation in question, the dictates of conscience or the religious requirements at hand. If psychology informs me that an eleven-year-old is incapable of understanding a certain scene from the gospel, it is not thereby directing me to withhold that scene from him at all costs. Description is the work of the scientist, prescription is the work of the educator, and intervention is the work of the teacher. The tendency is well-known whereby prescription or application is first made and then support for it sought afterwards. Psychology is cited when it seems to support preferences in practice; it is otherwise indicted or simply ignored. A case in point is the approach to "meeting the needs" of students, which is a prescriptive act based ideally on a descriptive one showing the actual needs of students. But teachers have been known to set themselves resolutely to the task of meeting their students' needs whether or not these are in fact needs of the very students before them; whatever these needs may be and howsoever students may represent them to be, teachers will already have ascertained what their Real Needs are, or failing that, what they ought to be.[25] There is further confusion in the use to which the findings of psychology have been put. There is no question but that it is a good and wise practice to adapt instructional materials so as to reflect validated findings about given age-groups. What may happen, however, is that, in the case where it is found that 70 percent of thirteen-year-olds would rather not see the question of the sacraments raised during that particular year in school, publishing companies will print textbooks in which the sacraments will accordingly find no mention. But the whole procedure is entirely without value for any one given class. The teacher may even risk failing to see the students before him in the flesh, favoring rather the picture given of them by the circumstantial views of a particular study or manual. Suppose that in his own class that year, 70 percent of the students are in fact receptive to dealing with the sacraments. How will he know that? And what will he do once he finds out? Without a certain amount of cautious skepticism regarding the application of generalized findings to the particular case at hand, we can easily reach the point of faulting our students for not being what they should be if matters are to proceed smoothly and according to norm.

None of this is meant to criticize every last effort to distinguish stages of development. The contribution which Lawrence Kohlberg[26] for example makes on the stages of moral development, continuing the earlier work of Piaget,[27] is certainly of the highest interest. What is to be criticized is rather the effort to transpose these stages to satisfy practical demands of the classroom, or even of the publishing market, when in themselves these stages point only to a sequence of development roughly approximated to, but in no wise fixed by, concurrent with, nor dependent on, chronological age or scholastic grade. Sequence of stages, not ages, is fundamental to these models. They are mis-taken when the age of the students is consulted first and their supposed stage thereon tagged to them, willy-nilly.[28]

Finally, if salvation will not be found at hand in the perfecting of psychological models of development, lamentation may yet be spared. For what after all was the motive behind this effort? In brief, it was the desire to adapt our teaching to the level of the student where we found him and her. This motive appears praiseworthy enough until we inquire into its source and flavor. These are given by the usual tag, nowadays politely left tacit but universally understood, to the effect that we must especially adapt *down,* to the lower levels of those students who are slow (or slower) to comprehend. Now, we are simply not sensitive enough to the attitude of literal condescension belied by this language under pretext of the best intentions in the world. For this sort of adaptation means to stoop down, to dilute and debase, to simplify and popularize, to weaken, cheapen, deaden, soften and lessen. With good heart, gentle manner and kindly voice we shall deliver a message condign to the diminished of intellect. And so we shall be teaching that to be Christian requires the understanding of religion and a certain standing of cognition. That runs counter to many tenets of spirituality.*

The point here is that however true it may be that a young child cannot grasp the whole of what, after all, *we propose* to give him and her it is not true that they need a particular intellectual development in order to grasp religion or to be Christian. If the man in the street and the child in school cannot enclose their faith in Christ and church with words of their own everyday experience, and language they use to wend their way through life, then something is very much awry, and that something is not to be found in them nor laid to their door. We should be most wary of any religion which requires for its expression a certain level of intellectual development or linguistic expertise. In any event when it comes to affairs of human experience the things which a twelve-year-old cannot understand will rarely be understood by the majority of adults. What differentiates the two ages is that the youngster has the forthrightness to evidence his boredom or confusion, while his elders and wisers have perfected the skill of dissembling and often enough only feign to grasp what in truth they have not the slightest idea of.

*I recall being mystified by this in my schooldays. Before sending us off to home in the afternoon the Brother would remind us that we had better learn our catechism lesson well lest our faith vacillate. Before starting us off to recite in the morning he would treat us to stories of the faith, pounding home the moral that the Curé of Ars had been saintly but none too bright at seminary studies, that the Virgin had appeared at Lourdes to a little peasant girl who scarcely knew her catechism but was beloved for her humility, and that the Apostles were men of good hearts despite remaining untutored in the Law. I was only nine years old at the time, but allow me to assure you that I wondered to myself just when it must have been, morning or evening, that the good Brother was trying to make damn fools out of us! (-DJP).

TURN TO PEDAGOGY

In addition to turning to psychology for a refined knowledge of students' differing characteristics according to age, religious educators also turned to the study of pedagogy to acquaint themselves with the most effective methods available for carrying on their instruction in practice. To write the history of practice of religious instruction thus entails recording the story of a search for the best means of teaching.

This aspect of recent history is no more to be found in the writings of theorists of religious instruction than is the turn to psychology. For the majority of theorists, the question of teaching method remained secondary; their attention was as ever directed to fundamental questions of the nature, sources, and objectives of religious instruction. Not until the Congress of San Antonio in 1969 does the issue of means of teaching the faith figure in the deliberations of assembled thinkers. To that time, practical implications had been left on the level of theory. But to teachers of religion the question of method captured first place among preoccupations of the time, for it was they who were experiencing untoward practical difficulties in accomplishing the tasks set for them by those engaged in reflecting upon the more removed aspects of the enterprise as a whole.

Testimony to these practical concerns is given by those who ran workshops for teachers at the time when the content of religious instruction as well as the materials embodying it seemed to be undergoing wholesale revision with the appearance of every September. Charles Burke, representing one of the most important publishers of instructional materials and one of the most ubiquitous of workshop instructors, had this to say of his experiences during 1967:

> I am not a little disturbed by the eager faces that I often see before me as I begin the day-long workshop program. I often get the feeling that many of the pencil-poised teachers before me are expecting the solution to their particular running battles with religiously unenthusiastic teenagers. Methods and techniques are merely tools of a profession.[29]

Mere tools or not, teachers were politely but insistently requesting methods and techniques that "work." What they not unnaturally expected from prominent thinkers and writers were a number of specific practical suggestions for teaching the new content and reaching the new objectives. They did indeed want tools of the trade, and it was in hope of learning to master these precisely as *tools* that teachers turned to the science of pedagogy, for that is what they envisaged this field to represent and that is what they felt in need of above all. Teachers could work faithfully in the vineyard if only they possessed the best tools and someone to show them how to use these most simply and effectively.[30] There were plenty of educators standing round ready to give demonstrations; very few held back like Charles Burke in favor of more educative provisions for teachers. Tools, tips, and techniques were taught the teacher for application within and without formal school settings by authors Catholic and Protestant who set the word "tool" in titles of paragraphs, chapters, series of chapters, and entire volumes.[31] The more lofty thinkers broke silence on this question only to register their somber view of these developments, as when Jungmann[32] warned all concerned that "the catechist cannot expect salvation or indeed a lightening of his real task from these technical aids." Such sober thoughts of course failed to stay the search for perfected pedagogical instruments.

Techniques may be classified into two categories: those which strengthen the position of the teacher relative to that of the student, and those which by contrast strengthen the position of the student.

The first reinforce either the teacher's persuasiveness or his competence. It cannot be said enough that teachers feel fundamentally anxious and inadequate in performing their tasks. As "help for the insecure religion teacher," Savio Warren extends the following recommendation:

> Possibly, then, many teachers of religion should and can shake free of the shackles of insecurity and begin to relax, using the powerful resources they have within their grasp.[33]

But in their precarious position most teachers understandably prefer to tighten rather than relax their guard, casting about for those items which will afford protection, ammunition, and reserve in their effort to hold on. The underlying conception, conscious or not, is that they must give battle against the students. Moreover, that is why teachers keep one eye open for techniques of discipline at the same time as they search for techniques of instruction: together these constitute "teaching" method. Only on this view can one comprehend the occasionally extreme lengths to which publishers, bookstores, and professors go in order to secure the teacher's manual against falling into student hands—staff plans in the hands of the enemy as it were. For these contain not only examination questions and answers, but also a series of suggestions which must seemingly not reach student lines until sprung upon them by the teacher one fine morn.

But there is a second category of teaching techniques which by contrast seem to augment the power of the student. Examples of these are group discussion, activities based on students' experiences, values, problems, techniques for creativity of expression, and so forth. Unfortunately these are sometimes put in service of contrary ends, as when a teacher so arranges things that his own purposes are satisfied and students have only limited access or participation in the so-called freely-structured classroom situation. One is sometimes led to wonder whether the essence of these techniques has been grasped in spirit as well as in rhetoric. For example, one article on "Discussion Techniques" begins by saying that their proper use in religion class "can serve as an educative process freeing the power of personal thinking and deciding'' but it concludes later that ''discussions are necessarily limited because the content of revelation cannot be won through conversation, discussion, cooperation; it must be heard and accepted by a believing heart.''[34] This is to take back with one hand what is given by the other. Another example is the case where the teacher's conception finally breaks through all appearances as he puts an end to awkward silences, stilted or irrelevant exchanges and proceeds to lecture the students—haplessly seated in a circle—in those points to which they had been supposed freely to bring themselves in democratic give-and-take of the discussion. Is it a fear of failure? Perhaps. But failure in what task as conceived which way?

Perhaps a third category of techniques might be suggested in that certain ones may be put to either of the two uses mentioned. Audio-visual techniques are an instance. As Pierre Babin points out, in *The Audio-Visual Man,*[35] ''audio-visuals are often used in catechetics as gimmicks''; they are ''merely attention-getting techniques'' on a captive audience ''for 'getting the message' across'' (p.9). To the contrary, ''audio-visuals must promote liberty'' (p.48).

> Audio-visuals require a greater personal involvement on the part of the educator than the traditional approach to catechesis, in the sense of a more democratic relationship between students and catechist. We must not use the media as instruments for domination but as means for establishing interpersonal relationships (p.47).

Another, and very interesting instance, might be techniques of questioning. These are widely used to put people on the spot, to catch them out, and even in milder usage, to direct thought and attention as per the questioner's purpose. Here again Babin is an exemplar. He included in his *Methods* a full chapter on questioning techniques that aimed to form the teacher in the art of eliciting and responding to questions of *students.*[36] This use of questioning flows from an entirely different world than that of the ancient catechisms. The importance of students' questions is laid to their essential role ''in the discovery and deepening of revelation'' (p.104), and ''in making oneself heard, the first step in self-expression'' (p.105). This emphasis corresponds to the most advanced thought and practice in education today.[37]

Wherein was this historical turn to technique a catechetical dead end? On grounds of leading to the misuse of essentials, and to the abuse of religious instruction itself.

The search for tools and techniques of teaching reduced to instrumental status a number of realities of far greater importance which enjoy an existence of their very own. Nothing could resist this overwhelming push for instrumentation and implementation; before it toppled even such as liturgy and bible.

Admirable descriptions of the profound ties between liturgy and religious instruction were available in plenty at the time. William Scherzer called the two "inseparable partners"; Mary Perkins Ryan and François Coudreau stressed beautiful conceptions of catechesis through celebration of liturgy; Josef Jungmann discreetly suggested that the teacher provide opportunities for direct sacramental participation or observation in preference to describing or illustrating the liturgy.[38] What was made of these in practice? In a move which can only floor the observer, liturgy as dimension of religious instruction was used instead as a technique for making lessons more interesting. Of the dozen examples regrettably to hand we take up a manual from 1965 announced as "the new approach to teaching religion."[39] Here is found developed in detail a sample lesson on the incarnation, suggesting that it be approached from the refreshing angle of the liturgy, using a sign which the children will have experienced during Christmas Mass, viz., genuflection at the creed. A series of questions leads to the point of conclusion: "That's right. So why do we kneel down? It is because Jesus came down from heaven" (pp. 22 sq). And the lesson on incarnation is launched. This same manual tutors its unfortunate readers in similar misuse of the bible. In their splendid presentations of the biblical dimension of religious instruction, writers like Gerard Sloyan and Joseph Colomb[40] had elevated the bible to the level of warp and woof of faith's expression; in this manual however, the bible has sunk to the level of anthologizing factual details of geography and history guaranteed to fascinate the nine-year-old, who is to learn the theme "because God is our Father and loves us, he speaks to us" by being told of the Ziggurats of Ur (pp.120–121).

The majority of teachers continued to use bible and liturgy as tools for illustrating main points of the lesson, thereby placing them on the same instrumental level as chalk and pointer.

Similar indignities were visited upon art and music. Catechists approach art somewhat like sex, remarks Thomas Mathews in sardonic tones—quite suspiciously, only for its useful byproduct, and then with multiple safeguards:

> Only insofar as it can be made to carry a literal, didactic content can the contemplation of art be justified. . . . This narrowly utilitarian attitude toward art is not only poor pedagogy, it is poor theology and entirely inconsistent with the church's tradition in the use of art.[41]

As for music, one can only register a particular note of perplexity over how Americans could defy sense and sound by causing their little ones to chant the Gélineau psalms. The least cultured ear in Christendom could not have failed to ache at this admixture of thought from an ancient world cast into retranslated language from a European rendering of the original.

The search for techniques to engage the young whatever the cost led betimes to the prostitution of the very enterprise of religious instruction. Teaching in practice began to take on the flavor of those syrupy medicaments in which a plenitude of artificial sweeteners disguises the bitterness of the real thing. In like manner, a ceaseless parade of fetching devices and seductive activities appeared to distract attention from the piquancy of the Christian message—which in fairness could still after all be found in the religion class, slipped in by one corner or another no matter how reduced the circumstances. More than one teacher in those days must have reflected on how unseemly it was to proclaim the gospel only when no one was sure to be looking. Or they might have felt a certain shame over what after all amounted to selling-out. That is by convention termed prostitution, "rougeing the cheeks of lady theology," as Francis de Sales so colorfully rendered it.

To switch to somewhat less carnal metaphor, let it be said that, in their anxiety to feed their students, numbers of teachers took to lacing the intellectual and spiritual dishes they were to serve with quantities of exotic condiments. Student appetite jaded in consequence. Students became more and more habituated to the pedagogical panoply before them, less and less responsive to the increasingly interesting angles which their teachers were given to root out ever more despairingly and to jangle ever more frantically. By this time students had become addicts of the spectacular, no less. Certain classes could be stirred only by production of a miracle, and even then the reaction would follow, "so what's next?"

UP BLIND ALLEYS

These efforts were undertaken to save religious instruction by adapting its fundamental model in accord with selected borrowings from psychology and pedagogy. But as events turned out these efforts only left our enterprise in floundering state—up a creek, one is tempted to say.

These adaptations represent no progress because they failed to change the basic model of teacher-student relations in any significant way. Teachers essayed to get to know their students better and to acquire the means to teach them better. But each was an attempt to "get" the students. By gaining inside knowledge and technique teachers tried to win students over, all the while making sure they kept their proper distance.

Three types of teachers may generally be distinguished.[42] There is first of all the *dominating* teacher, whose authority seems to flow from some sort of charisma of role, status, virtue, erudition, or whatever. This sort of teacher is at his best in the traditional model of education, the earliest phase identified in Table 2. There is next the *accommodating* teacher, who tries to reconcile his authority with student freedom and dignity by dint of psychological insight and pedagogical skill. This teacher is at his best in the second, or pedagogical, phase which seems to have characterized religious instruction up to 1966 certainly, and probably continues to mark it despite progressive proposals. Finally there is the *liberating* teacher, who makes a genuine try, not to lead someone to a point determined beforehand, but to permit him to arrive at a point of his own choosing, to become what he can and will. In passing from the first to the second model of the teacher, religious educators thought themselves to be making considerable progress. But such was not the case. The fact of deigning to accommodate to the student changed nothing in what is fundamental to both of the models. Accommodation is made only in an effort to bring the student to the same basic point as had been chosen before. To be sure, the student is brought there somewhat more subtly, gently, and skillfully, but no less unwillingly.

We may therefore construe as error the proposition that methods had become child-centered or student-oriented. A great deal of talk current in those days used these terms in a faintly self-congratulatory way. But no reality lay behind either the phrases or the praises. The intentions of all concerned could not have been more worthy, but for one reason or another the child-centered movement in education lost momentum and never truly carried through to its proper end. Rather it stopped at the point which we have just finished describing for it. The fact of having begun with a concern for the child in order to end by being better equipped to pass along some specified content to him makes of this educational enterprise to all appearances a form of manipulating children even worse than the traditional model. This permits the judgment to be made more soundly that religious instruction in 1936 was better than it was in 1966 and even 1976. (What does it promise to be in 1986?)

The student who receives with initial surprise the concern which he believes to be proffered him without any other end in mind may well open himself up considerably, even unrestrictedly. But when he thereupon perceives that the strategy all along was to get him to open up so as to more easily wedge in some point or other, he will shut tight as a clam, and rightly so. From then on he will react to our kindly interventions with either hostility or indifference. To a fraudulent child-centered approach goes a lion's share of responsibility for the studied reception which students of today give to our every effort in religious instruction.

As pointedly as possible we declare exempt from this distemper the concept of child-centered education. We support the concept. Further, the practice of this concept ought to distinguish religious education. To this point it has not, generally and regrettably speaking. Our position is at one with the opinion expressed latterly by Pierre Babin: "The first task of a Christian educator must be to make of his person and procedures a circumstance of unconditional openness and regard for students."[43]

In order to take up the practice of such education the teacher must be taken by its spirit. What has proved to be the faulty case is that teachers have not adopted a world-view, a conception of God and humanity which would permit them to pursue such practice to its educational end. There comes a moment when the practice without the conception crumbles to the ridiculous, such as we have seen to transpire between 1955 and 1965. At that moment the realization dawns that the entire venture must be based on a wholly-changed conception of the teaching act, in turn inspired by a renewed vision of God's revelation and relation to man.

As it happens precisely this moment arrived in the history of our enterprise around the years 1965–1968. And just then there so appeared a series of conceptual and practical ventures which looked for a time to promise change—a true one, this time, and for the better.

CHAPTER 4

VENTURES OF PROMISE

The years 1965–1968 were years of promise. They seemed a time when religious instruction in America was about to come around and assume a genuinely renewed prospect. Throughout these days the United States was the scene of ventures far superior in excitement, daring, and imagination to anything Europe would know. Elements of conception and practice appeared to conspire in a framework for thoroughgoing change in place of minute scattered improvements.

Nevertheless, as we know from today's state of affairs, the enterprise as a whole did not emerge in promising shape. Aspects of theory and practice were pieced together to give the appearance of change without its substance. That was the story everywhere but in the events to be recounted here. This chapter relates the exceptional history of the period.

One scheme fair and true, so it seems, is to select a number of educators who gave especial promise to the enterprise in areas of conception, method, and practice. These may be so ordered as to cumulate, if you will, progressively revealing the framework for renewal articulated by their combined contributions. Thus, from

- construction of a basis in theological and catechetical conceptions; through
- appropriation of methodology conducive in both theoretical and pedagogical aspects; to
- application in practice of the whole,

runs the scheme of the chapter.

CONCEPTIONS

These were provided by two original thinkers. Against the confused thinking of the time, Alfonso Nebreda raised the catechetical question and Gabriel Moran formulated the theological response.

Kerygma in Crisis?—Alfonso M. Nebreda

The interrogative in Nebreda's title[1] sounded a warning as it raised a question. Where are we heading? Is our enterprise in danger of running aground?

53

Have we not then been pointed in the wrong direction? Must we not make a radical turn-about and work a radical turn-over if we hope to avoid disaster? These are the issues to which Alfonso Nebreda in 1965 invited the attention of religious educators. He proposed a rethinking of the context of catechesis and a revision of its fundamental approach.

Nebreda's book was a reminder that catechesis represents only one phase of the total educative process undertaken by the Christian community. In ancient practice this education comprised in all three phases: preevangelization, evangelization (kerygma), and catechesis (p.viii). In the first, the nonbeliever was brought to the point of being receptive to the Christian message; obstacles in the way of hearing the gospel were dealt with. In the second phase, the message was announced (kerygma); the person was invited to take a stand by embracing or rejecting Jesus the Christ whom he and she was faced with. Thirdly came the phase of catechesis proper, which then responded to the convert's desire to come to know more intimately the Jesus in whom he and she had just placed faith as Christ. With this reminder Nebreda advanced a comment on the recent movement to renew religious education due to Josef Jungmann's inspiration. Jungmann's work had had the merit of recalling that the faith entailed a movement, a dynamic—cf. *Handing on the Faith*—and that the enterprise of religious education ought accordingly be informed throughout by the proclamation of the good news and the call to conversion. His invitation was thus to resituate the enterprise by moving it out of the third phase, catechesis, to concentrate on the second or kerygmatic one, evangelization. This effort represented substantial progress. But in Nebreda's view it did not go far enough, for it presupposed a receptivity to the gospel message, and this was precisely the assumption which Nebreda sought to put into question. He therefore proposed to move one step further and situate the enterprise in the very first phase, preevangelization. It was to be a return to the circumstances of the early church (pp.94ff.)

But on what grounds? Such a proposal might be appropriate to areas of missionary endeavor like Japan, where Nebreda had done most of his work; yet little enough reason could be found to apply a missionary scheme to the United States or to Europe, for example, where a network of parishes and dioceses and even a long-standing Christian culture would seem after all to make preevangelization a somewhat redundant and useless undertaking. Nebreda was well aware that some such objection could be raised. In response he developed a long argument purporting to show that urbanization was in process of changing the mentality of men the world over, to the point where throughout those stretches called Christian there was being created an emergent zone for missionary concentration no less acute than in the times of Paul and the early church (pp.48,52,80sq).

Here we may interject the observation that the so-called Third World countries have something to teach us in this regard. Nebreda's book itself echoes the concerns raised at the Congress of Bangkok in 1962. In 1968 at the Congress of Medellin the South American experience was raised to reveal a new theology, of "liberación." The fact that we do not recognize ourselves to share in the plight of Asian and South American countries, in these respects at least, might go to explain why we have neglected to examine and profit from the lessons they could give for the progress of religious education in Europe and North America. Again we see the consequence of failing to incorporate a theory of change into postconciliar endeavors. The church continues to defy the incarnation by persisting in the belief that ideas alone are immediately and all-powerfully consequential: things need but be said for them to be accomplished in reality.

Nebreda concluded that we must prepare ourselves to make some far-reaching changes. "I want to make it perfectly clear that the approach in preevangelization is radically different from the approach used in catechesis proper" (pp.102–103). He was not referring to adaptation, adjustment, alteration but to total radical change. The reason is that catechesis is christocentric, (*not* "student-centered") whereas preevangelization is anthropocentric, wholly, unambiguously, and unreservedly.

> It is in contrast to this Christocentric approach that I say that preevangelization must be governed by an anthropocentric approach in which we take man as he is and where he is. It is man himself who somehow leads us at this stage (p.104).

Elements in this radically different approach are not hard to divine. Nebreda specified these, among others:

> - *facilitation of dialogue:* "more than anything else, the procedure here will be to let him talk and ask questions" (p.106).
> - *respect for the individual:* "we must take our hearer seriously, his person, his conscience, his truths even if they are fragmentary" (p.105).
> - *personal contact:* "we must have some sort of personal, individual contact with the person to whom we wish to communicate the message" (p.109).

We can recognize in these elements characteristics of a Rogerian approach to counseling and psychotherapy.[2] Preevangelization befits a paradigm of counseling, while catechesis befits one of instruction. We can further recognize that Nebreda was inviting us at the time to brave entry across that threshold to which we had brought our students but then hesitated to step beyond.

Nebreda had thus alerted us to a situation of crisis. His was a remarkable and timely warning, but beyond that he did not go. In retrospect we can see the limits of his effort.

For one, the term preevangelization is somewhat unfortunate, arising out of a conception of theology which separates the things of God and those of man. This difference is more accurately put in terms of implicit-explicit. All explicit reference to Jesus Christ is withheld at this stage but without prejudice to the individual's implicitly experiencing already the aegis and auspice of the gospel.

In the second place, Nebreda failed to articulate the passage from this first step to the next. He furnished no strategies or procedures for practice. Left to themselves, religious educators might tend to have recourse to a mysterious imperium of grace to cover the move, without at the same time trying to specify which human interventions in practice might be conducive to mediation.

Lastly, Nebreda does not seem to have realized the sensational implications of his view. He appears curiously naive and unsuspecting that to adopt a position as "radical" as he himself describes it to be must entail an institutional upset in school and parish structures, for example. Rather he relies for assurance upon the guarantee of the past in order to make his proposals come true. But history, even church history, never repeats itself. The dispositions made by the ancient church cannot provide for the practice of our enterprise in the twentieth century. If religious educators had been able to put proposals into effective practice with relative ease, then the recommendations of the Congress of Bangkok, out of which Nebreda's volume had arisen, would have long since passed into operation instead of passing away in publication. And what a surprise that would have been. The Council had after all already accustomed us to receiving dead letters from the Vatican, however lively the sender's style and intent.

Nebreda too had issued a message: religious instruction must become preevangelizational and anthropocentric. Why then did it not become so? In all likelihood, enough people were so frightened, resistant, or overwhelmed by the institutional overhaul they detected between the lines that the message was prevented from ever being translated faithfully into practical terms.[3]

Catechesis of Revelation—Gabriel Moran

Although Gabriel Moran is clearly a religious educator, he is primarily a theologian: *Catechesis of Revelation* is a sequel to *Theology of Revelation*. Both are fruits of an emerging conception the development and implications of which preoccupy his concern throughout other works.* This concern is in no wise to specify that practice of religious instruction but rather to provide

*Published by Herder & Herder, these include: *Scripture and Tradition: A Survey of the Controversy* (1963); *Theology of Revelation* (1966), hereafter cited as *TR; Catechesis of Revelation* (1966), hereafter, *CR; Vision and Tactics: Toward an Adult Church* (1968), hereafter, *VT; Experiences in Community: Should Religious Life Survive?* (1968) (with Maria Harris); *Design for Religion: Towards Ecumenical Education* (1970), hereafter, *DR; The New Community: Religious Life in an Era of Change* (1970); *The Present Revelation: The Search for Religious Foundations* (1972), hereafter, *PR; Religious Body: Design for a New Reformation* (Seabury, 1974).

for it the conceptual, theological, underpinning which in his view it most requires. "What has been most painfully lacking and what is most desperately needed is some intellectual seriousness and competence in the teaching of religion" (CR, 35). The contribution he intends to make is a conception of revelation which, if adopted, would eventuate in a wholesale renewal of religious instruction in practice.

In setting forth this one view of Moran's thought, a diagnosis-intervention model comes to mind as particularly useful. Having first noted a deficiency in the "body" of religious instruction, Moran gives a diagnosis, prescribes a remedy, and offers a prognosis. Lastly, a number of side-effects follow if, so to speak, we were to swallow the pill he proffers.

There is no question but that Moran early on spotted a deficiency in the field—and that is to put it mildly. At first, in 1966, he detected a "catechetical problem" (CR, 13). Two years later he proposed that "the fundamental problem of catechetics is that it exists" (VT, 19); the future would see the field either "alive in much richer ways" or else "the field will cease to be" (p.36). By 1970 he was "locating the crisis" (DR, 11). In that same year he was moved to pronounce (prematurely) our demise: "Catechetics, R.I.P."[4]

But, soft: how could the enterprise have thus declined when it was being tended by so many hopeful and energetic hands? What of all the signs of life, the activity, the change? Those who hoped for catechetical change, says Moran, must conclude that "at best it was not worth the effort, and at worst it has been a disaster" (DR, 11). What had gone wrong?

At the very outset Moran dismisses as etiological factors the twin concerns favored at the time: "the difficulty does not lie wholly or even primarily with pedagogy or psychology" (TR, 20). Rather it lies with theology, "the most fundamental question of the nature of revelation" (p.21). Moran's diagnosis-cum-autopsy revealed, as he had suspected, a faulty conception of revelation running through the heart and marrow of the enterprise. All the remedial efforts of recent years had amounted to little more than patchwork, serving only to distract or stall the ineluctable and well-deserved final collapse.

"The only thing which can save the catechetical movement from self-strangulation is to prepare teachers who have a theological understanding of Christian revelation" (CR, 151). Here therefore is the prescription, necessary and indispensable "if there is to be thorough reform of and lasting improvement in religious education" (TR, 20).

The prognosis is that the enterprise "is on the verge of its greatest breakthrough" and that its conception of revelation "will make or break" the movement (CR, 32, 151).

What is this conception of revelation that Moran recommends? What are some of its consequences for religious instruction?

In his early formulations Moran tended to use classic terms in somewhat unfamiliar contexts.

As the first community shared in this consciousness in the Spirit, so all Christians are to participate in the experience of the apostles, that is, the experience of Christ in the Spirit (*TR*,90).

Through a dozen publications Moran sought to explicate his view, yet people still found it obscure: either they did not understand it at all, or they thought his statements exaggerated or carelessly expressed (*PR*,20). He was later moved to plainer, almost informal expression. No attempt shall be made here to review the explications or to exhaust the subtleties of this conception. For our purposes his main view entails two key points. These may actually be put rather simply and then noted over and again in various contexts.

First, revelation is "present in the life of every individual" (*PR*,19). Whereas religion teachers appeared to be treating revelation as merely a collection of events in remotest times, on Moran's view revelation is a continuous, presently-occurring process (*CR*,44). Casting the concept in grammatical terms, we might put it that, while true that God did reveal himself to others in times past, God *is* revealing now, to me; God has spoken and God has saved—but also God is speaking and God is saving.[5]

Second, revelation is "neither doctrine nor message, but is a real, personal intercommunion" (*CR*,33). Knowledge of revelation would thus arise out of encounter and experience rather than from words and concepts. Moran will not equate knowledge with static entities cut off from the real world; to him it is a human activity of knowing-loving, a single act within which knowledge and love may be distinguished but remain joined in reciprocal inner union (*TR*,83,156). Revelation, again, "is a personal communion of knowledge, an interrelationship of God and the individual within a believing community" (*CR*,13).

This manner of viewing things evidently runs counter to a number of cherished concepts of salvation and education, requiring moreover a new articulation of how these are related. However simple the terms, understanding and applying this view is not at all a simple matter. The brunt of it is that educative effort must be grounded and guided in theological understanding. Precisely what instructional steps are entailed is a thorny question. What is Moran's answer?

Moran thinks this question is important but the answer not easily come by (*DR*,24–25). Nor will he try to find it. He is not unmindful of the problem but he is not responsible for resolving it, either. His concern is with theology, not pedagogy, and "the theology of revelation cannot solve the catechetical problem" (*CR*,40). He designedly restricts himself to enunciating the principles, leaving to others the task of discovering applications.

One can only regret that Moran has never taken the trouble to spell out the educative dispositions that might be made in practice to favor his conception. Yet he does make clear that religious education must in essential respects follow the manner in which God reveals himself to the person. We might hazard to identify four major implications, involving a sort of recentering of effort: upon the present experience and personal freedom of students; upon adult education and the human world.

Present experience. If God's revelation is continuously present in the felt experience of the individual, religious instruction must evidently deal with the present experiencing of students rather than recite the past experiences of biblical personages. Not: what happened to figures of yore and lore? but: what is happening within and around you, now?

Personal freedom. "Education must mean growth in independence and freedom" (*CR,* 123). Variants of this appeal to freedom recur throughout *Catechesis of Revelation.* Religion textbooks, for example, must show appreciation for "the giveness of God's revelation" in the life of each individual, and the person's need "to reflect freely upon that reality" (p.39). Parents should take care lest their child become "too dependent" upon them for his and her religious beliefs and practices (p.23). Teachers also: "A teacher has neither the right nor the power to determine the religious life of another" (p.117). As to methods, Moran spurns, on theological grounds, all "methodological gimmicks" (p.32). He argues that the teacher is a witness to Christianity.

> The witness is one who recognizes and accepts the values of freedom and personal autonomy. His only means for transforming another person is an appeal to the freedom of the other. If this appeal does not seem to work, it cannot be put aside in favor of some other instrument. The catechist, like every other Christian, succeeds by being a witness to freedom or else he does not succeed at all" (p.120).

If Moran can be said to suggest a method, it would be to appeal, as God does, to the student as a human person and to respect, as God does, the person's free response.

Adult education. When Moran speaks of religious education he refers to one "directed by an adult mentality" and "defined by an adult model" (*DR,* 121). Perhaps surprisingly, he recommends reducing attention on children while concentrating upon adults. Here are his *Vision and Tactics: Toward an Adult Church*—less money and effort, and fewer classes, for the young; more resources and focus upon the adult (p.145). As for the young, we are assured that "no great calamities will ensue" (p.145), whereas "we urgently need education by adults for adults to become more adult" (*DR,* 121). Moran argues his case as follows:

> I would question whether it is possible to overcome the obvious inadequacies of religion teaching so long as it is assumed that the teaching of Christianity is a child-centered endeavor. . . . I see no evidence to suggest that Christianity can be taught well to little children and I see no reason to suppose that one should try to teach it at all (pp.9–10).[6]

Thus quite in contrast to the emphasis of the time, Moran explicitly rejects "child-centered" religious education. By the same token he rejects "child-prolonged'' adult education—viz., extending to adults the same type of instruction given to children, or piling on yet another story to the already overbuilt structure.

Human World. In several senses Moran directs attention to the world we live in. Religious instruction must become ecumenical, in a special sense: "An ecumenical education is one that will be concerned with the world man lives in" (*DR,27*). Theology too must adopt this concern: to turn away "would be a wrong path even if it were possible" (p.44). The study of human sciences is important, "as indicated by the theology of revelation itself," which requires such study in complement to its own (*CR,16*). The enterprise of religious education, if it is to "complete and implement" the theology of revelation, must incorporate findings from disciplines of philosophy, anthropology, psychology, sociology, and pedagogy (*CR,32; TR,20–21*). Special emphasis is given to Christian community, which must be restored as a place of revelation and celebration: liturgy is a summit of continuing revelation, and Christian love is revelatory. The couple religious education-community has concerned Moran over the years, as his thought has turned to the foundations now of one (e.g., *Catechesis of Revelation*), now of the other (e.g., *The New Community*). Not to see these two in relation is "to have a distorted picture of both subjects."[7]

Here then is a conception of ample scope, solid from the point of view of theology, responsive to problems experienced over the previous decade, and extraordinarily promising for the fruitful pursuit and progress of religious instruction. Yet hardly anyone gave it the hearing which it deserves. Why?

First there is the evident consideration that Moran's views entail a profound and encompassing shake-up not only of thought but also of institutions. The same fate as befell the views of Nebreda was also visited upon Moran's, with all the more justification in the eyes of those who would not suffer change.

Then too there are those who will not suffer Gabriel Moran, on two accounts. He is not what many consider an inspiring writer; and he exasperates a good many more by his absolute refusal to enter into details of instructional renewal other than to dismiss the efforts others make. Far from exuding warmth and generating enthusiasm, Moran leaves a lot of readers cold. His style is aloof and lightly sarcastic. He ticks off high-minded principles with the regularity of a metronome, issuing a stream of encompassing pronouncements with the serenity of a pinnacled savant.

Many readers must occasionally be put off by Moran's merciless lucidity. To teachers who are so fond of hearing about ways and means, moreover, Moran presents a stony face. And he knows it. He warns in advance that his books may be disappointing to "those who want a detailed program of instruction," even stating flat out: "I have almost nothing to say on drawing up a program of instruction" (*CR,18*). The reader must extrapolate of his own wits. Fair enough, to a point. But then Moran is later heard to call these extrapolations dim-witted. Those who are first directed to sally forth as best they can then find themselves under relentless fire from of all places the rear echelon. Their attacks are trivial, showy, ill-founded, misguided, unplanned. That must rankle, considering the source. Here we are all good and humble Israelites, huddled 'neath the mountain top from which is floated down the vision of a Promised Land but no directions on how to get there.

Gabriel Moran's is a vision to behold. Better still to be held in practice. There were those at the time who followed through with his conceptions, difficult as this proved to be. But they were unfortunately not many and even some of these eventually quit the field altogether. As we will shortly see, this failure is not to be laid to their door, nor to Moran's, but to the intransigence and obduracy of certain circumstances and those who stood pat by.

METHODOLOGY

During the time that Nebreda was proclaiming the crisis of kerygma and Moran was declaiming the concept of revelation, a group of professional educators were detailing a tried and apparently true approach to the teaching of values. Their book, *Values and Teaching,** enjoyed enormous success among teachers, so much so that sequels continue to appear regularly to specify this and that application of the central approach.[8]

The significance of this book for our own enterprise is that it seemingly responded not only to the concerns of practitioners but also to the hopes of theorists. Whereas Nebreda and Moran had advanced conceptions of great coherence without in the least troubling themselves with questions of how to mediate them in practice, Sidney Simon and colleagues spilled over with suggestions for practice without much concern for the over-arching theory in service of which their methods might be pursued. Indeed, these might serve for the religious instruction of Buddhist and Moslem as well as of Christian. The approach is ecumenical, discreetly atheological, based in experience and dialogue, personalized, respectful, liberating, and student-centered. And it is practical to boot. It thus provided a bridge between the conceptions of theorists and the tasks of practitioners while satisfying a good many of the desires and demands of both.

Definitions

The method of *Values and Teaching* consists in teaching the process of valuing rather than any particular values. Values and valuing are thus importantly distinguished.

*Louis E. Raths, Merrill Harmin and Sidney B. Simon, *Values and Teaching: Working with Values in the Classroom* (Merrill, 1966). Simon's name will be taken to represent this approach.

Value "represents something important in human existence" and "show[s] how a person has decided to use his life" (pp.6,9). Valuing is "the process a person uses to obtain his values" (p.28). This distinction is of first importance because Simon intends to lay stress on process over product.

> We believe that it is more useful to consider the posture of a person facing his world . . . than to consider what he might find valuable at any one time or in any one particular circumstance or in a series of similar times or circumstances, for that matter. "How did he get his ideas?" is a more fundamental question for us than "What did he get?" (p.10).

The valuing process is specified as comprising three steps or acts, with seven traits in all (p.30):

CHOOSING: (1) freely
             (2) from alternatives
             (3) after thoughtful consideration of the consequences of each alternative
PRIZING: (4) cherishing, being happy with the choice
             (5) willing to affirm the choice publicly
ACTING: (6) doing something with the choice
             (7) repeatedly, in some pattern of life.

These collectively define valuing. All seven criteria must be satisfied for the outcome of the process to be called a value (p.28).

Even to this point, in barest outline, the approach can be seen to share in a number of current developments in education and other fields. The emphasis on process over product, for example, is echoed in titles like *Process Catechetics*—and theology, philosophy, etc.[9] Moreover the three main activities involved in the valuing process together constitute a spectrum of educational objectives, representing respectively, the cognitive, affective, and behavioral domains such as specified in the celebrated *Taxonomy* project headed by Benjamin Bloom.[10] In addition, the origin and flavor of the approach seem to owe much to Carl Rogers' theory of client-centered or nondirective therapy as it has been applied to education; Simon notes this similarity (p.9) in recommending Rogers' *On Becoming a Person*.[11]

Procedures

The pedagogical procedures involve both techniques and conditions for their use. All the techniques have for aim to evoke or to enhance a dialogue between teacher and student. There are two general sorts: techniques for avoiding obstacles to dialogue, and techniques for promoting it.

In the first, the basic attitude is to forebear persuading the student—selling, pushing, or urging him to this or that set of values. The list of such reprehensible methods (pp.39–40) is compatible with traditional and even honored practices but not with the process of valuing as defined by the seven criteria cited, nor with the emphasis given to valuing over values. "The approach seems not to be how to help the child develop a valuing process but, rather, how to persuade the child to adopt the 'right' values" (p.41). This list of contrary practices seems to have received a rather hurried reading among some educators; charity suggests that they may in haste have overlooked Simon's negative prefix. The practice in certain schools has been to entitle a course "Values and Valuing" and then proceed to embody the very list of tactics which infirm the valuing process. Religious educators would be well advised to reflect on the general context of their units on "values" as copied from this book. Some have been known to teach the valuing process in required courses, with required attendance, assignments, discipline, and other nonvalues; others have concentrated on limiting choice, appealing to conscience, and presenting cultural and religious dogma as unquestioned wisdom or principle—all of which figure in Simon's list as methods which "have not *and cannot* lead to values" (p.40).

The second set of techniques aims to promote teacher-student dialogue on values. This dialogue may be brief in the extreme, consisting perhaps of nothing more than a "value-indicator" from the student and a "clarifying response" by the teacher. Thus the teacher needs presence of mind to spot these indicators, namely: goals, purposes, and aspirations, attitudes and interests, feelings, beliefs, and convictions, activities, worries, problems, and obstacles (pp.30–32). Once he has spotted them, the teacher needs the ability to listen attentively and the fluency to respond precisely. Just what he responds with is not made clear, curiously enough. Simon gives a number of examples and describes the air about them but limits himself to stating that "clarifying responses are not mechanical things that carefully follow a formula" (p.54). At any rate the whole affair tends to be impromptu, arising at everywhich time and place that teacher and student bump into each other.

Additional techniques required of the teacher are thus agility to switch preoccupations and ability to extemporize. Simon repeatedly stresses that the dialogue should be very brief. After an exchange of two, the teacher is advised to break off with a "nice talking to you . . ." or some such noncommittal remark (p.53). The rationale is that the student thinks best alone, without having to justify his thoughts to an adult or defend himself against extended probes (pp.53,54). The unexpectedness of circumstance and the brevity and extemporaneity of exchange withal require literal agility on the teacher's part. "Sometimes we call these exchanges 'one-legged' conferences," note the authors, "because they often take place while a teacher is on one leg, pausing briefly on his way elsewhere" (p.55). Given this repeated insistence, one is at a complete loss to understand how some teachers can have studied this book and still proceed in classroom and classtime only, to stimulate—or worse, to *assign* —the production of value-indicators and then, having squared away and planted two feet firmly on the ground, to drive home the clarifying response for the next fifty minutes.

The other aspect of this approach is a triplet of conditions required to practice the various techniques. First, as with Nebreda's approach in preevangelization, the procedure is more individual than collective. This condition is evident from the nature of the subject, speakers, and their exchange. Secondly the atmosphere is permissive. A student may normally choose *not* to choose among alternatives offered, nor even "look or decide or think" (p.53). How some schools and teachers can require regular courses in the valuing process, assign grades and grant credit all the while fulfilling this condition remains a marvel of scholastic ingenuity. Lastly the role and aim of the teacher must be despoiled of all trace of transmitting a predetermined set of values—be they one's own or one's betters'. We cannot teach the valuing process if we conceive that our chief function with children "is to *tell* them things" (p.24), nor if all the while "we demand, even subtly, that the outcome of that thinking must conform to what we believe" (p.170). This last is of predictable difficulty for especially such as religion teachers. But well might they not even try to fulfill this condition if they construe their task as requiring exactly the opposite instead. In that case, why even give so much as a nod to the entire approach?

The oddity of recent history is that teachers of religion above all others welcomed Simon's methods. The question of recent history is: which teachers applied this method, in what form and based in which conception of theology and religious instruction? There are a number of truly thorny issues here which simply cannot be brushed aside.

We know our tendency to change technique rather than attitude or conception. Often enough we view our major problem, for example, as one of spending class time profitably and smoothly if possible, but in any event we must fill up the hour. The attraction of a Sidney Simon compared to a Gabriel Moran is that with Simon we may be confident of having something specific, and probably fruitful, to do with our students. But even with a Simon we may skim off the games, exercises, and activities while skipping the substance behind them. We can thus not only neglect to shuffle our underlying conceptions but keep our hands and heads plenty occupied—that is, distracted from any and every consideration of what does and should inform our teaching practices.

The basic question is whether these techniques can find due place in the teaching of religion. A considerable number of pages have been devoted to discussing or applying Simon's method to religious education.[12] But as long as this basic question remains unresolved, religious educators will be tempted to adopt either of two positions. One consists in the attempt to direct youth's way from the values it might be searching for to the values which elders have already settled upon. This position entails using a permissive and liberating method to manipulate the young. The other position consists in taking a stand on one side or the other, having first assumed a dichotomy to be in question.

Thus, one teacher or school forms students in the valuing process while a colleague or neighbor gives courses in kerygma. Such is the state of the enterprise as practiced in numerous schools and parishes today. This circumstance is not wholly disadvantageous, especially where thought has given rise to it.

A third possibility exists. This is the position based upon an understanding that to adopt Simon's method and to ally it to the conceptions of Nebreda and Moran would necessitate on both counts certain structural changes in the institution of religious instruction. Certain religious educators of the time had such an understanding and accepted the obligation of change. To the story of these venturous educators we may now expectantly turn.

PRACTICE

Certainly there could be found in those critical years of 1965–1968 a good number of outstanding religious educators who ventured to embark religious instruction on a path leading to the emergence of a new church. Of particular note among these were teachers caught up in daily practice. It was to teachers that fell the charge, after all was said and done, of integrating grand conceptions of theology, catechesis, and education; of discovering pedagogical approaches and methods appropriate to these; of acquiring the skills needed to practice the whole; and lastly of finding within themselves the courage and wit to restructure their immediate institutional milieu. This last charge in particular had to be filled in practice, so that the entire venture might proceed within a supportive structure rather than suffering collapse, distortion, or frustration in face of things as they were then and always had been.

The experience of two teachers, John Murphy and J. T. Dillon,[13] will serve to illustrate the general position adopted by doubtlessly many others at the time both here and, somewhat later, in Europe.[14]

The Catechetical Experience—John F. Murphy

In 1967, while writing the preface to his translation of Babin's *Methods,* John Murphy could already pronounce upon the sad state of our affairs: "We are aware that the traditional forms of religious education, formerly supported and strengthened by authority-centered cultures, are no longer truly effective" (p. 11). Not only did he announce the end of an old world but he went on to call for "a communal search, a fraternal undertaking" towards creating a new one. John Murphy had every right to speak on these matters, as he had himself engaged in such a search in practical experience, and would shortly publish the story of one year's undertaking, 1965–1966, under the apt title of *The Catechetical Experience.*

This experience had been not so much one of careful preparation and execution of a religion course as it was a continual reflection upon the course of the course, questioning and changing as need arose the process, procedures, and teacher himself. As Murphy put it, it was "a beginning from a teacher-centered and directed class to a student-centered approach, an approach that demanded a new look at the students themselves, the material used, and my role" (p.7). What did this new look reveal?

One can imagine Murphy's astonishment, mild at the very least, at the discovery that the students in his class were part-time pagans. True enough, Nebreda had spoken of Christian decline amid ghettoes and penthouses, but here was Murphy teaching away in a seminary for the Catholic priesthood. Nonetheless, he found it partially the case that students "do not want to live in our land where we are at home, but want to go to a new land that seems more fertile and productive" (p.116). So they were not where they should have been for the type of religious instruction which we were prepared to offer them. One strategy in response is to go ahead and give that to them anyway. Murphy took another tack. He dropped what he had been prepared to do, accepted the students as they were, and embarked with them on a risky "catechetical experience."

Part of the risk was entailed by the transition from a teacher-centered approach to a student-centered one. Quite an array had to pass in transition:

> What all this requires of a teacher is a new look at aims and structures, methods and techniques. Basically it calls for a reorientation of the meaning of faith for ourselves and our students, a restudy of what it means to be or to become a believer" (p.118).

There was no question of faith given at baptism—everyone in the room had been baptized. But Murphy came to learn in a new way that "faith is a human response, or better a *personal* response" (p.115). This lesson is not easy to learn. It is much easier to preach and altogether hard to practice. John Murphy achieved all three. How did he put it into practice?

In a scene which must stand as a beautiful blend of liturgy and catechesis, Father Murphy gathered his students to celebrate the eucharist and to receive the good news that they would have no final examination. Murphy had had to go to some lengths to achieve faithful practice of his views; he had betaken himself to departmental chairman, academic dean, and seminary rector for prior "clearance" of the announcement (p.104). Further he found it impossible to assign homework or to base the class on a textbook outline. "The lesson for me is to teach without the book, using materials for resource, but making the lesson come from them in connection with the general theme of the year" (p.106). Moreover, he experimented with new class arrangements, such as dividing into two groups to be taken first singly and then together on three successive days (p.21).

It hardly needs pointing out that these efforts entailed a great change in the teacher's role with consequences for his person. Thanks to his experience alone, Murphy came to formulate the teacher's role in terms more flowery but no less accurate than those flowing from theological pens. "We are called to be pilgrims with our students rather than pilgrim directors watching from afar" (p.117). Lest any believe that such a role change is a placid affair, attend to how Murphy experienced it. Throughout the entire year in question he lived in a kind of anguish mixed with fright. Throughout the length of the book he recurs to the personal changes which he voluntarily but by no means serenely suffered. "This transition from teacher-centered to student-centered opened a dimension whose full effects are still being felt in me" (p.8). He talks of giving up security and protection, of occasionally being like "a fearful midwife . . . unwilling to assist at the birth," of being frightened by student challenges to personal beliefs and by the riskiness of the whole venture (pp.8,118,119). These were admittedly hard to bear at times, but on reflection Murphy believes them to be the lot of any Christian who agrees "to take the risk of Pope John XXIII when he asked us to look to the new life around us" (p.125).

One might well estimate from a reading of Murphy's book that the risks he took were all in all somewhat limited. And that is true, on the author's own admission. With the next author we will come to face with far more pronounced daring. But even so, Murphy's undertaking in 1965 must be said to represent a remarkable step forward which a decade later some teachers and schools have yet to make. The important element is accepting the uneasiness created by whatever risks are involved, to agree to set in motion a process which will take us into the unknown, to become like unto the Jews who had left the fleshpots of Egypt but had not as yet reached the Promised Land flowing with milk and honey.

This theme was raised pages back while reproaching Gabriel Moran a bit for the ease and comfort of his visionary stance. John Murphy consented to traverse the desert in person. The image of a journey arose of itself to his mind to express the teacher's role as co-pilgrim, not a director watching from afar. "Pilgrimages demand a willingness to go forward and to search long and strange paths" (p.116). The merit of Murphy's undertaking may lie less in how far he penetrated than in how willing he was to sign on at the start, and then stay on.

Personal Teaching—J. T. Dillon*

In the experience of this teacher we come across a perspective on education which succeeds in being applied very nearly to the ultimate degree in practice.

*This section of the text, to the end of the chapter, was conceived by DJP; it has been translated by JTD.

The title alone, *Personal Teaching,* indicates that ventures of this type involve risking the person and, likely as not, foregoing the protection of institutional roles and structures. In this regard an earlier article by Dillon takes on several levels of significance.

> We may begin to see that taking such a "personal view" of religion teaching means reworking the whole system of religious education and rethinking our somewhat entrenched prejudices about teacher-student roles.[15]

This remark points to an endeavor in which Dillon was at the time already engaged. In addition, it occurs in the midst of his review of Babin's *Options* and, further, was stimulated by a thought originally placed in the preface by the translator—none other than John F. Murphy. Thus, unknown to each other, the two were colleagues in that communal search which Murphy had called for to renew religious instruction.

It is hardly surprising that a title like *Personal Teaching* should have appeared in a series called "Studies of the Person," nor that Carl Rogers should have undertaken to write the preface. "It is an exciting thing," says Rogers, "to see him as he works with his students in a close personal relationship which makes the classroom more of a place for living learning than an academic ritual and a fulfilling of subject-matter norms" (p.vii). Beyond recognizing a person-centered approach, Rogers reads the story of an endeavor "to learn what the teacher of tomorrow, and hopefully the school of tomorrow, may become" (p.viii). Finally, he recommends the book as "of enormous value and significance to every high school teacher and administrator" (p.vii). The support that Rogers lends to this venture is of particular significance for a major question at issue here. In what way is it possible to be truly and unreservedly "student-centered" and at the same time to "teach religion"? In what way, if any, did Dillon succeed in doing both?

The experiences which Dillon relates took place towards the end of the period we are concerned with (1967–1970). But the conceptions upon which he was to base these efforts had found earlier expression in a number of articles and a book called *Catechetics Reconsidered.*[16] Interesting to note, of the twenty or so introductions he wrote for this anthology the longest and most articulate one heads a chapter on freedom, and at this time this essay already constituted a manifesto. It begins:

> Everyone agrees that we should educate youth to freedom. Very few agree on how this is to be done. Arguments about authority and freedom are getting tiresome. It is time to put up or shut up. Teachers who believe Jesus came to make us free should start acting like it in school. . . . The possibility remains that some educators can widely despise manipulation while still widely practicing it. They can abandon outright methods of manipulation and adopt subtler ones (p.100).

Lest any misunderstanding come between him and the reader, Dillon makes his position even plainer.

It is not now, nor has it ever been, a question of giving students more freedom. Nobody can give freedom to anyone. Teachers can only recognize that students are free and that they have the right to use their freedom (p.102).

Again, all of this is easily enough said, and we have seen how certain theorists went about inviting teachers to act after this fashion. But there comes a moment when the choice must be, as Dillon says, to put up or shut up. For his part he chose to attempt a venture in practice.

In *Personal Teaching,* Dillon gives as his belief that the aims of religious education are "in no way different from the announced aim of education in general" (p.13). Thus he pursues the same overall approach in English and French classes as he does in "Religion." But for our purposes we shall concentrate only on his efforts in religious instruction. How does he conceive and practice it?

The conceptions which he recounts follow much the same form as we have seen from theorists like Moran and Nebreda. They entail shifting the center from teacher and doctrine to student and life, and Dillon does not hesitate to go the limit: "the student's freedom is paramount, and the task of the religious educator is to foster it" (p.13). The basis for all this is given as that man encounters God in the experiences of current life. So much for the ideal face of things. But Dillon is also conversant with how things really go on behind the scenes. He knows the school inside out. And what he knows about religion classes in high school does not exactly make his day.

In religion class in most high schools, "anything goes." The reason that anything goes is that everything has already gone. . . . It is hard to find someone on the faculty who really wants to teach senior religion. God knows! The good old days are gone. Religion has become a complex, changing, and unsure thing to live, let alone teach (p.14).

Against this background blend of real and ideal, Dillon set about working some fundamental changes. Among other developments he came to modify a number of institutional features in order to befit his task as he conceived it. These concerned classroom attendance, course requirements, discipline and subject-matter.

Attendance. Attendance in all of Dillon's classes was optional. Moreover, students could come and go as they wished. And what happened? Exactly what one might predict in such a situation. At the start, out of 35 on the rolls, 10 would show up. But then the number plummeted to three. The story of that morning when only a tiny trio of senior girls was discovered in the room must be read in full to appreciate the phrase "taking risks"[17] and the manner in which the teacher extricated himself from stunned discouragement. Equally predictable was the later, slow increase in numbers to a steady average of about a dozen, representing an admixture of different students in various groupings day by day. But then one day attendance abruptly shot up to 35 and fixed there. Why? School authorities had relented and come back to stand on principles which they had earlier agreed to put into question—for the time being, of course. Now everyone *had* to attend, and did, "and they were a grim lot" (p.44).

Requirements. In a series of innovations, Dillon refused to assign grades, to require assignments, and to give tests. He would give assignments but would not require them; students graded themselves as they wished. Again, predictably, grades were high and assignments low. "In my four senior religion classes, nobody ever did any homework" (p.28). All but a few went on to give themselves the highest possible final grade. "I say, 'So what?' " (p.22). The teacher's attitudes here were less a depreciation of academic matters than a prizing of individual students. "Only the student can judge whether or not it is valuable," says Dillon; "I respect his judgment even if I regret it" (pp.27–28). Such a position must not be thought to come by naturally and easily. Like Murphy, Dillon is forthright enough to see his reactions for what they are and to share them with us: "Meantime I regret the loss of prestige which I suffer because my course isn't as tough as the others" (p.128).

Discipline. Given such an approach, discipline evidently is far and away another matter than usual. Dillon practices nondirective attitudes to the hilt, and without fearing to lose class time doing nothing. The story of how one entire class period passed in this manner will make the hair of more than one religion teacher stand on end (p.30). But he explains this behavior. He esteems it more profitable in last analysis to lose five or ten precious minutes at the start of a given class than to deprive the youngsters of a chance to make personal decisions. Here we see in full flush the practice of Simon's approach to the valuing process. In Dillon's class there is no need for formal lessons on the subject; the ebb and flow of classroom life itself presents continuous opportunities to choose among several alternative behaviors, attitudes, responses and activities—this after due reflection and with the invitation to give the reasoning behind the choice (it goes without saying that the teacher led occasional sessions where he and students evaluated what they had been doing).

Subject-matter. Finally, the content of class lessons bears little relation to classic conceptions of curriculum. "I never knew what the class was going to do or be like" (p.47). Topics for discussion would inexplicably surge and die. Students seemed to prefer jumping from one topic to another without following any apparent interest or logic. Dillon finally came to perceive that his logic was not theirs, and that students were not so much fickle or disinterested as they were evincing a manner of viewing things far removed from manners accustomed of old. "I gave up making students stay on the topic as I conceived it when I finally realized that the logical sequence of topics bore little relation to the actual sequence as perceived by the students" (pp.48–49). But at times the discussion itself would wane and no topic at all would catch on.

This was an unexpected development. Dillon had often heard that "if you give 'em the chance to talk about what they really want to talk about, boy will you have the classes!"

> Well, I did give 'em the chance, and boy we didn't have the classes. Their lassitude was astounding. We even had a discussion once on their apathy, but of course I did all the talking (p.47).*

In this last regard two clarifications come to mind. First, the teacher did not pursue the experiment far enough. Second, students do not constitute a group merely for the fact that the school schedules them into the same class. Not constituting a group, they can not uncover a common interest or problem to resolve by group means. Interestingly enough, when Dillon questioned the class on this difficulty, the students themselves came up with the very points made.

And as to the success of the whole affair? First to the students for their reactions.

At the end of the year, and occasionally at points of crisis, Dillon would have students write out evaluations of their learning and doing. Well over a hundred student evaluations figure in the book, taking up three chapters in all. It is clearly impossible to cite or even summarize them here. However three recurrent themes can be noted. Students whose overall attendance had been scarce were nevertheless greatly influenced; quality here wins out over quantity. The self-discipline demanded of students was the greatest sore point, nearly all the comments on this issue being negative. (The respectful care taken in editing student papers has guaranteed surpassing authenticity to these texts.) Some students proffer as reason the fact that their years of prior schooling had in no way prepared them to take such responsibility for self, even at age eighteen. In one way or another students judged the class exceptional, "different" from all others, and some exclaimed that it was the "best" or "only" real religion class they had ever had.

To these reactions may be added some assessments of Dillon's mastery and mistakes, changes and conflicts.

No one should try such an approach unless it represents in truth one among several choices really open to him. That is to say, he must be capable of mastering as well other approaches to teaching. J.T. Dillon fits that bill. In years previous he had acquired a high reputation in strictly traditional approaches, receiving several awards as "most effective teacher of the year." Later, in modified approaches, he was given "master teacher" status. Then in personal-teaching approach he won published praise, including from Carl Rogers, whom some consider the dean of humanistic education and psychol-

---

*Here, as elsewhere, we observe our author to turn upon himself that mordant humor which otherwise applied puts off many a reader. And the latter case is really very unfortunate, for the irritation provoked distracts from the worth of the message.

ogy. By this time Dillon had been teaching for a grand total of eight years only. This case is made to those who dismiss his teaching efforts with contempt. If they would adopt an approach with conviction, so Sidney Simon would remind, the choice must be open and made freely after mature reflection. So too if they would reject one and not rationalize their way out of it. Before condemning Dillon's approach we ought to assure ourselves that we are capable of putting it into practice. That way we make proof that rejection is not based on fear of having to adopt it.

Such an approach is open to multiple mistakes and failures. The book swarms with pointers to this and that misstep, as Rogers notes with approval: "perhaps the story of his pain and his mistakes is just as important as the story of his success" (p.viii). But what about the poor students, one might interject. Is the whole point of religious instruction only for the spiritual improvement of the teacher? After all, students ought to get something out of it too, wouldn't you say?! Most assuredly so. But this objection is based on an implicit assumption that all is well with things as they are in the traditional system. Now, no assumption is more suspect than that one. In acting as he did, J.T. Dillon was not exchanging a system of proven worth for one fraught with hazards; he sought to pass from a system which on the contrary is a manifest failure, to venture upon one which might possibly be a success. As noted, he did not do so without stumbling along the way.

The greatest error of the whole venture was the wish to move too fast. "I moved too fast for the students, and I may have moved too far for me" (p.140). Note that this impatience applied not solely to system, structure, and authority but to the students themselves—who had never been exposed to such practices in the past, and who were being taught differently in other classes during the same day. We thus arrive at the paradox of a "student-centered" religious education which can wholly neglect to take the students where they are. For those who would follow up with their own try, let Dillon himself spell out the mistake:

> I was to sound the golden trumpet, the old order was to dissolve, and the new to arise. What a blunder. I had all the theory, but I forgot the practice. I was ready to move, but the students were not. Did I meet them where they were and start off from there? No. Did I listen to their needs and adjust my teaching to them? No. Did I extend to them the same opportunities which I had had to change slowly and gradually? No. What a record (p.140).

This is a frequent error in the postconciliar church. Change must not simply be introduced, but planned and executed according to a comprehensive theory of change which would provide for among other things intermediate steps, delays, regroupings, acclimatization, and so on. Another conclusion is that such ventures would be much more easy and successful if in addition to being joined to a theory of change they would be joined in by the entire institution in question, and not by a solitary cell such as one teacher in a lone classroom.

Needless to say, any teacher so imprudent must expect conflicts with authority. Dillon had his share. He had not worked out the relations between experimentation and the system within which it proceeds. His two certitudes were: "enlightened" teaching is possible in the present school structure; and, to change your teaching is easier and more possible than to change your school. "You can't fight The System. But you can teach in it" (p.144). His suggestion, then? Ignore it, leave it alone (p.143). Now, this is a little like solving a military problem with the battle cry, "every man for himself!" By the same token, however, he attests that his approach is based in personal experience and so might not befit anyone else's (p.144). And what but this can one expect from "Personal Teaching"?

And so maybe he is right. Then again, we probably ought to steer clear of any hard and fast positions in this domain. It may well be that the route Dillon carved out in those years pointed to a way out of the dead end we were in then, and deeper in now. Still, there are other ways out.

CHAPTER 5

ENTERPRISE AT REST

With this chapter we come full circle in our view of developments in religious education between 1955 and 1975. Our manner of structuring this history has argued the thesis that developments over the two decades have on the whole amounted to little or no progress in the enterprise.

We have seen other views of recent history to be inadequate on two scores: either they fail to account for the dynamic of DIA development over the years; or they neglect to take into account elements of the enterprise as practiced. On the whole they serve to illustrate one aspect of recent history, namely an emphasis on theory without practice. The converse was demonstrated by examining historical turns in practice to psychology and pedagogy. This search represents an emphasis on practice without theory. In the last chapter we constructed a scheme for certain selected developments which represented in our view an enlightened incorporation of theoretical and practical aspects. There we reviewed conceptions of catechesis, theology, and education which seemed to constitute a foundation for a renewed enterprise; and we considered two cases of practice pursued within this conceptual framework. These we termed ventures of promise. They were not taken up by the enterprise as a whole.

Thus our historical view points in the main to a series of disjointed efforts. The picture is of an enterprise proceeding nowhere, now borrowing practices without shifting its fundamental mode of education, now proposing theological conceptions without reworking institutional structures accordingly, now taking approaches which violate underlying purposes and assumptions, now assuming views which contradict the approaches—and so on and on, ever changing, ever frustrating, never progressing. The last chapter described an exception. In this chapter we reenter the mainstream of events.

At the time that the story last told was unfolding, other ventures were taking place as well. In one respect some of these were as hardy. But they were not as promising. We shall select two for consideration, one conceptual and one practical. The first represents an effort to construct a bridge between two worlds, without, however, having the underpinning required to sustain the span in design or execution. The other represents an effort to restructure practice without, however, giving thought to whether the new structure could be supported or indeed was ever called for in the first place. These two serve

74

not as targets but only as examples of persisting tendencies; they are presented to argue the vanity of semiventures which disjoin conception and practice.

CONCEPTUAL DISJUNCTION

The great majority of religious educators between 1965 and 1970 cannot be fitted into the exceptional scheme proposed in the last chapter. They may however be legitimately thought to have aimed at the same result but without managing the appropriate structural dispositions, without taking the risk of total renewal. They left intact two worlds, that of God and that of man, and then tried to build an equally solid bridge between them. The major obstacle to this task lay in the theological conception of these two worlds as distinct realities.

Most of these religious educators had received their own religious formation during a time when the reigning view of revelation served to harden the distinction between the worlds inhabited by God, who was on the one hand, and man, who was on the other. In proposing another version, Gabriel Moran urged religious educators to restudy theology and appropriate from recent thought a number of conceptions which would make it possible to adopt far more realistic approaches in practice. It was not enough to essay new approaches alone.

> People in the field of religious education who speak glibly of experience-centered education often present very little evidence that they have agonized over this question or indeed understood the question at all. If the question can be answered, it will require considerable rethinking of the nature of Christianity and the function of bible and doctrine in the Christian churches. It is not at all clear that this theological revolution has occurred in the minds of many people trying to change religious education.[1]

This is a call for considerable change and it went largely unheeded. A way of thinking about God, man, and their several relations is not easily exchanged for an entirely different one, especially when it is a product of one's own religious education and has informed one's practice over many years of Christian life and education. Without making this shift in thinking, many religious educators tired to reconcile the two worlds they were left with but had no theological basis which would render such a reconciliation possible.

A paradigm for those in this plight may be found in the work of Marcel Van Caster. He may be taken as representative of a body of desires, efforts, and difficulties between 1965 and 1970, perhaps to this day for some. In a labor of thought both admirable and fascinating, Van Caster has sought to situate himself in the midst of opposing views and to achieve a reconciliation, synthesis, or correspondence. With Van Caster we find ourselves faced with a view of two distinct realities between which it is the aim of catechesis to establish a bridge or liaison: to join God and man in different worlds. This effort he sets forth in a trilogy under the general title, "God speaks to man."*

Marcel Van Caster is quite clear as to what he does not wish to see in religious instruction, and on this basis he is without question a contemporary thinker. He rejects equally the tendencies to make the enterprise either overly intellectualized or moralized (*SC*, 11). He is as well fully appreciative of the importance of human experience and values in today's religious instruction. He recognizes values throughout, as when he states: "Man increasingly becomes a man both personally and socially through and in the progressive realization of values" (*VT*, 217); and as when proclaiming: "Catechesis must embrace this form of manifestation by adopting an approach based on values" (*SC*, 13). The third volume of his trilogy is entitled *Values Catechetics*, and another book of that same time is called *Experiential Catechetics*.** But these titles and quotations may not give an accurate rendering of his deeper thought; Van Caster does not at all accord to values and experience, however important, the place given these by theorists and practitioners seen in the last chapter herein. The book on experience, for example, is more or less the creation of an editor who sets Van Caster's view against that of the co-author, Jean LeDu, representative of the most pronounced position taken on the place of pure human experience in French religious education. The title of the book on values, moreover, is lifted from a subheading for one section of the second part of the trilogy. As noted, the original title of the whole is "God speaks to man." For Van Caster the primary hearing must be given to the word of God, not the word of man. From this position follows the first rule of religious education: "to say what God says as he says it" (*SC*, 168). Religious instruction is characterized by "immediate service to the word of God" (*SC*, 182); "the word of catechetics is at the service of God's word" (*TC*, 205).

Nothing could be clearer. We are in the presence of two distinct worlds untouched by the theological revolution which Moran claims is required for experience-centered education. How then does Van Caster do it? Here we touch upon the problem. And although Van Caster may not have revolved his theology, he has turned this problem over and over, presenting every bit of "evidence" through the years that he has truly agonized over this question, *placet* Moran.

The problem for Van Caster and the company of religious educators we take him to represent may be put as follows: If man and God inhabit two

---

The Structure of Catechetics (Herder & Herder, 1965), hereafter cited as *SC; Themes of Catechesis* (Herder & Herder, 1966), hereafter, *TC; Value Catechetics* (Newman, 1970), hereafter, *VC*. (The general title is given only in the French original, *Dieu nous parle*.

*Jean LeDu and Marcel Van Caster, *Experiential Catechetics* (Newman, 1969), hereafter, *EC* (all quotations refer to sections by Van Caster).

distinct worlds, how do you join them? If the word of God is to be given primary hearing, but if the experience of man dominates his own world, how do you get man to hear the voice of God from another world amid the din of this one? Van Caster tries several solutions, starting now with God, now with man, trying to connect up the two.

The most recurrent suggestion is to adopt the method of the beatitudes (e.g., *VC*,43). Each of these blessed sayings leads in effect from a human aspiration to a realization which surpasses it. "Blessed are those who hunger and thirst after justice, for theirs is the kingdom of heaven." Van Caster proposes to show three phases: first, that the message is in accord with human aspirations; second, that the message goes far beyond these aspirations; third, that the message departs from aspirations, which must be judged in need of being purified accordingly. On this strategy are built all of Van Caster's models for religious instruction. In this sense he takes the risk of starting with human experience, and he speaks of classic categories like preevangelization (*SC*,153–154). His problem from that point on is to find a way to get as smoothly and naturally as possible from the human to the divine.

A glance at the outline of his trilogy shows that Van Caster has tried several approaches to the problem, which speaks well for the earnestness of his search. In the first volume, the movement goes from God to man; in the third, it goes from man to God. *Structure* has three parts: (1) the word of God; (2) man; (3) communicating the word of God to man. Each chapter in *Themes*, similarly, starts off with the word of God, then considers "the human background," and lastly again, communicating the message. All the "themes" are strictly Christian. Then in the last volume, *Values*, we meet up with what might be called human themes—for example, freedom, love and sexuality. Here the order is reversed. Each chapter starts off with "data of man's existence." These anthropological reflections are followed by theological and then catechetical reflections. At bottom, Van Caster is never quite sure about starting with the human. Does it assure that the bridge to God is solid enough? Can it permit man to make his way across the gap separating him from God? Hence he is forever recommending two methods: the latter one, and a variation of the Munich method, going from divine revelation to human experience by means of successive appeals to the senses, the intellect, and the will (e.g., *SC*,170–171). A final recommendation is to use the scheme of his fellow countryman Canon Cardjin of Catholic Action. "Catechesis has a threefold task, corresponding to seeing, judging, and acting, the three phases in the development of experience," (*EC*, 244). These three he specifies as follows: say what it is about; show its value; stress the value of an encounter with God (*SC*,20).

In spite of these attempts, Van Caster perceives that he has not solved the problem. He accepts this limitation, all the while relying on the discrepancy between natural and supernatural (*TC*, 185). This desire to fill in the gap at the same time as respecting the breach between sacred and profane lends to Van Caster's style a rhetoric of casuistry.[2] A train of complicated and involuted thoughts passes through tunnels of ifs, ands, buts. Human experience is a good thing, certainly, but "in a certain sense" or "up to a given point"; religious instruction may rely upon the activities of the student "in certain perspectives," and may answer their hopes by "transcending" them or passing "beyond" consideration of what men and the world are in themselves; there are human experiences but also Christian experiences and these are different, "Christian" specifying that part of man which is not uniquely "human" (*TC*, 178,190,205). His final position seems expressed in this conclusion (*EC*, 246):

> The existence we actually enjoy is clarified first, and to some extent, by our own consideration of human values, but its Christian meaning is made clear only when the great events of saving history are proclaimed, for these reveal the basic meaning of human existence, and to understand them fully we need instruction.

The attention to human values comes down in final analysis, therefore, to constitute only a method.

The impression is left that the entire scheme has for aim and result only a better way to push the gospel. It is perhaps a reasonable effort, given the way Van Caster views the world. And one cannot help being struck with admiration over his desire to find a solution to a difficult problem and his anguish over not being able to come to a resolution. Some will see in this example the mark of true Christian spirituality; others may see the error of enclosing one's self in a given world of thought. Which is correct may be subject to discussion. But to compare Van Caster's way of viewing things with, say, Moran's is to wind up with two different world-views and hence two different versions of religious instruction.

Quite apart from all considerations of Van Caster's influence, how have things actually gone on in the world of practice? A great many teachers have come to, or remained with, positions similar to Van Caster's, caught up midway between desire and hesitation without perhaps his finesse. They might start their lesson off with a consideration of some human value— friendship or love, power or wealth, for example. Then there would come a moment when they would use the magic formula which was to hoist the proceedings from one world into another. According to local usage, the phrase could be "that's just like . . ." or "that brings to mind. . . ." Or the teacher might light upon a symbol in some student's prosaic remarks and give it more poetic rendering: "the sunshine which you so affect to absorb is not the sole light to illumine our darkened straits here below, etc." The teacher by this point has already noticed that the students, surprised at first by the novelty of starting off religion class by talking about their weekend experiences, have just tuned him out. When the talk leaves their experience to make it something else again, students leave off the talk; and nothing is more woeful to the teacher than to see students turn off, especially when the lesson had been going so nicely. Accordingly, whereas the teacher had put into his lesson plan, say, a twenty-minute discussion on human values to be followed by a consideration of "illuminating" Christian values, he would now begin to stall off for thirty, then forty, even fifty minutes of the hour. And the more he stalled the harder it got to think up a connection between the parousia, for example, and what by now had become a heated interchange between partisans of different makes of motorcycles. And yet some teachers stayed with it, anxious to speak of Jesus to their students until one day giving up and speaking like everyone else of beach parties and motorcycles and experiences and values, and no more of Jesus.

At this point it is conceivable that some good come of the whole affair if one could only know on what basis he is proceeding and if he can find a theology to justify this manner of acting. Without this conscious awareness and theological foundation the business is a catastrophe. This very sort of catastrophe explains the confusion of these latter years.

STRUCTURAL DISJUNCTION

Among the innovations of the period was the institution, around 1967, of parish "coordinator" or director of religious education. This new agent began to show up with surprising suddenness and frequency throughout the United States (and Canada). By 1970, a scant three years later, a survey could discover some fifteen hundred persons in the new role. "There were many more parish coordinators (directors) working than anyone had imagined."[3] While perhaps only minor in itself, this development has been called "the new frontier in parish religious education," and "a new ministry in the church"—"not just a new role, a new *kind* of role, a new kind of co-official in the church."[4] We may take this development to represent a number of strands in practice, permitting as many lessons to be pointed.

In examining the factors behind the creation of this new structure we come upon several themes of development and decline. In examining the features of the new structure we can reflect upon the mode of response to the frailty of traditional forms of religious instruction and to the opportunity presented for easing in entirely new and fruitful ones.

In the early 1960s a nation-wide research survey discovered a number of startling facts. Fully two-thirds of Catholic school-age children were not attending Catholic schools, while one-third neither attended Catholic school nor were receiving any sort of formal religious instruction, such as provided by the CCD. "Despite the tremendous amounts of money and work put into the Catholic educational system, it is not meeting the religious educational needs of the majority of Catholic children."[5]

At the same time we find that a considerable number of parish schools were being "phased out." Between 1966 and 1976, the number of parochial and diocesan schools declined by some three thousand, or one-fourth of the total. Enrollment in elementary and secondary schools dropped by 40 percent, a decline of fully 2 million students. [See Table 3].

During that same period, moreover, we find as well a pronounced decrease in vocations to the priestly and religious life. Considering only those who taught full-time in the Catholic schools, we observe the number of priests, brothers and sisters to drop by one-half [Table 3].

These dramatic decreases occurred within a curious context of circumstances. They followed—seemingly by minutes—an enormous upsurge in Catholic enrollments, a burgeoning of religious vocations, and a proliferation of school constructions. In 1963, for instance, enrollments stood at 5.8 million, as compared to half that in 1940, and a nation-wide survey had just published its conclusion that "there is no evidence of a decline in this expan-

Table 3.   CATHOLIC SCHOOLS & PERSONNEL, 1966 and 1976

Category	1966	1976	Difference 1966–1976	
			Number	Percent
SCHOOLS*				
Elementary	10,550	8,139	−2,411	22.9%
Secondary	1,506	969	−537	35.7
Total schools	12,056	9,108	−2,948	24.5
STUDENTS*				
Elementary	4,409,476	2,512,164	−1,897,312	43.0
Secondary	687,961	563,411	−124,550	18.1
Total students	5,097,437	3,075,575	−2,021,862	39.7
TEACHERS				
Priests**	12,373	6,374	−5,999	48.5
Brothers	5,724	3,604	−2,120	37.0
Sisters	103,832	52,957	−50,875	49.0
Total 'Religious'	121,929	62,935	−58,994	48.4
Total 'Lay'	80,768	108,502	+27,734	34.3
Total teachers	202,697	171,437	−31,260	15.4

Source: *The Official Catholic Directory. Anno Domini 1976.* P. J. Kenedy, 1976. General Summary, pp. 1–4 end-paper.
*parochial & diocesan only
**full-time only

sion.''[6] Yet scarcely had we turned our backs than all about the whole thing seemed to come tumbling down. As the dust began to settle, we could perceive seminaries and motherhouses of every kind, newly and hugely built, standing grandly empty in their diocesan and provincial prairies. On parish lots officials were dedicating a spate of new schools in the knowledge that now there was in effect no one (read: only lay-people) to staff them.

At the same time there could be observed in some quarters a movement to regularize the standing of religious educator. Professionals were appearing who called themselves specialists in the field, devoting their efforts to five religion classes per day instead of one, for example. Others were ''released'' to work full-time as directors, consultants, curriculum experts and the like in the offices, departments, and boards of religious education that now and again could be seen about chancery and motherhouse. These were thought to be innovations. As noted, one of the more prominent was the role of coordinator.

The institution of parish coordinator, as far as one could tell, unfortunately showed little capacity or promise for constituting an innovation in any true respect. Four features in particular left doubts.

First, a rapid tendency to create a bureaucracy of religious instruction. The person who assumed the post of coordinator had been engaged on the grounds of his and her professional training as a religious educator. In most cases this training was considerable and effective; moreover it was followed by a teaching experience of some length and distinction. Now what did these professional religious educators do in their new post? They spent a great part of the time in administrative pursuits, not educative ones. An amazing number of things now arose to stand unexpectedly in need of being coordinated.[7] Anxious to truly coordinate, the professional wished to keep abreast of everything, to keep and render account of everything, to inspect and collect, tabulate and duplicate data on whatever had been going on or should have but had not been the case.

Second, a rapid tendency to view figures as measures of success. The parish now had a new salary to pay out and the coordinator understandably felt solicitous before the assembled faithful. The temptation in consequence, and often enough in practice, was to justify this burden by pointing to the number of programs initiated, meetings held, youth reached. One's progress in the post, as in school, was conceived in quantitative terms; if not in these terms alone, then in these more easily, quickly, and demonstrably.

Third, a possible danger of divisiveness. In many parishes the projects introduced by the coordinator became after a time a hotly contested issue. In particular were parishes where parents would not abide the dubiously beneficial results they saw in their children. This was not the sort of religious training they had hoped for, were sending their children for, were providing in the home. . . ; and other parents to the contrary. Not that these plaints were always just or true—far from it; very often indeed they were in error. But the fact that they arose reveals the post of coordinator to have been ill-founded from the start.

Last, a possible danger of confirming the status quo. To avoid divisiveness and perhaps even clerical disapprobation, some coordinators could see only one solution: do what was being done before. Fewer feathers in the flock were ruffled over unobtrusive conformity than spectacular innovativeness. What might have become a chance to exercise imaginativeness in the creation of bold new ventures was restricted to a chore of overseeing and probably sustaining the moribund.

These four circumstances might be thought unduly sombered by an observer's pessimism. But they have been no more lightly depicted by a certain number of coordinators themselves.[8] If enlightened response is not brought to them the picture may darken considerably. The institution is still young. It may yet be moved to take better shape. Otherwise complications will set in as the institution settles in. These will be excessively hard to clear up and the church in America will wind up with a brand-new thicket of growth to entangle its progress.

The whole situation is given parallel and penetrating analysis by Joseph Neiman, who undertook a large-scale survey of coordinators in the U.S. and Canada. In his book, *Coordinators,* Neiman stresses that the creation of the post is in no way a cure-all for parish problems but rather an occasion for parish renewal at the moment when the issue of establishing some such post is broached. *"Other options are possible,"* he insists; they should all be discussed and, if more suitable to the problem at hand, adopted (p.21). "In undertaking this preparation process, the parish may decide that it can best meet its educational needs by an option other than hiring a professional coordinator" (p.27).

Neiman points out that the source of parish problems may not be its educational program or skills but "the very root assumptions about the parish and its educational work" (p.46). If these are not examined but a coordinator is hired forthwith, nothing much should be expected. "A coordinator is no educational messiah and the parish needs to learn this through the preparation process before they hire someone and grow 'disappointed' in what he or she accomplishes" (p.46).

There are thus conditions to fulfill before a coordinator is summoned. A group of parishioners must first be constituted. This group must then take stock of the needs experienced by parishioners as a whole. Having sensed the needs, the group must also find that a coordinator is suitable and desirable to help them meet these needs. "It cannot be emphasized enough that the parish (the broad base of people involved in the decision) must know clearly why it is hiring a professional and what it expects that person to do *with* them" (p.77). On these grounds the coordinator may then arrive to situate his effort within a process of educational change already in significant development. Indeed,

Neiman recommends as much as a full year of preparation before *beginning the search* for a particular coordinator (p.24).

In other words the coordinator ought to arrive on the scene *after* the people have completed a certain course of deliberation; his arrival in an unprepared parish cannot be hoped to set this course in motion. The first circumstance provides that parishioners assume a responsible adult stance with respect to questions of religious education. The second keeps them in a state of dependency, unable to discern their needs and regulate their affairs without calling upon the wisdom and maturity of professionals at the very outset. In the best of circumstances, perhaps, the professional will coordinate efforts and not initiate them. His contribution will be valuable to the community in the strict sense of being prized and publicly affirmed, as Sidney Simon would have it, after having been appraised and chosen freely from among several alternatives during a long course of deliberation.

It follows that the work of the coordinator ought to bear two additional features. It should respect the sentiments of the community and it should be ended after a given time.

By the first is meant that it can be truly educative and generative of change only if it takes the individual parishioners into account. Their expressions of needs, wishes, and fears ought to be listened to attentively and then reflected or "mirrored" as Neiman puts it (p.38). In this way the people may themselves come in the end to accomplish what they most need and want to achieve.

The coordinator's efforts should also end after a certain term, for reasons regarding both parties to the contract. No one should continue being engaged year in and year out in nothing but religious education; one may have to stay a priest for eternity, but not a catechist. In either case it can often prove disastrous from a psychological and professional point of view. The human being may get to the point where he can no longer function or figure himself outside the role. He can end by losing contact with himself, the outside world, and even his profession. When life becomes religious life solely, or life in the classroom, the world and its enormous problems and potential comes to be perceived through these particular lenses alone. And these will distort one's view of the world and of religious education as well. For the parish's sake too the work must come to a specified end. Otherwise people begin to establish a set of relations which settle into what Eric Berne described in *Games People Play*[9]. And with that they settle out of any professional educative relationship.

One betrays no visionary stance by observing that a rush of events transpired in the years between 1965 and 1970. But a certain perspective is required to discern which among these represent a development and which a decline.

Some new shapes for religious instruction appeared. These followed the general line described by the prophets in, or above, our midst: a change not only in method, but in spirit and structure as well. Such at least they took in rough outline, for their actual figure is still a little too ambiguous for drawing definitive conclusions. It belongs to us now to prevent these promising shapes from fading into the background of recidivist conception and practice. Part Three will present some means which might be taken so that these arrivals establish the foundation for a renewed church.

During this same period a number of old forms appeared to be dying out or just hanging on. In 1970, one notes, Christians were found enough to buy Baltimore Catechisms in the number of two-hundred-and-fifty thousand copies.[10] Someone must be misinforming people somewhere, but at least the message is clear and consistent. Consider, rather, those of religious educators who saw hope in a number of new approaches and then hopelessly confounded them. They seemed to lack the boldness to carry through with ideas as required, to change structures in practice as demanded by Gabriel Moran and as pursued by Murphy and Dillon, for examples. Perhaps they were restrained by a given theological training somewhat as Van Caster was. But at its worst religious instruction in the schools went up for grabs. It became a sort of wastebasket serving simply to be filled by what-have-you, anything to occupy space and time. The evidence is there. In school, parish, or CCD, any pretext serves to excuse dropping religion class—choir rehearsal, play practice, pep rally, candy drive, stuffing envelopes. Imagine dropping a math or physics class or even a study period for any of these. But religion class can go because everyone knows nothing goes on there anyway. The kids just sit around and talk and the teachers have a time of it just saving face.

These practices must die. We best be quick.

A World in the Making: Contemporary Implications

CHAPTER 6

TO CONSTRUE A WORLD

To make a new world takes more than a trice but only two big steps. Let us take them together.

The first is to apply our minds to an understanding of the world in process of change. To construct that world is the adventure of Part Two. Then we need to apply our minds to an undertaking condign to that world: we have also to construct a catechesis. That is the venture in Part Three. We are setting out to remake the world. Who but us can do that?

Some mighty helps are at hand. For one, we have the personal activity of intelligence, bringing to bear on experience our power of genius on the make.

For another, we have the public enterprise of scientific study, proffering all manner of disciplined notions and data and modes of inquiry. These have been hard-won for us by the long labor of uncounted scholars in diverse fields, and the fruits are there for the plucking: from history, anthropology, psychology, sociology and education; from physical, biological, and technical fields too.

For yet a third helpful companion we have the coherent views embodied in official church documents. Here we shall be recurring throughout to three remarkable texts that present themselves as guides to the remaking of religious instruction:

- the international, or General Catechetical Directory [hereafter cited as GCD];
- the American, or National Catechetical Directory [NCD]; and
- the pastoral message on education, To Teach as Jesus Did [TJD].[1]

These documents have excited much discussion, admiring and critical;[2] they have captured interest and raised hopes, not only among Catholic but also Protestant educators.[3]

These are among the helps we have for us: the power of our intelligence and experience, the knowledge from science, and the guidance from pastors. For the moment let us sensibly ask of the latter only the one question, where would they take us?

On the whole the official documents are wise and experienced guides. They know their ground and can be trusted over it. Yet there is also an unknown world to explore, and in face of that the guides cannot be thought venturous but hesitant and temporizing. They evoke at once edification and zeal and doubt. To note their failings is not to lay blame or reproach but merely to find fault and avoid it on our way.

87

The General Directory puts us from the start in face of the "Reality of the Problem" (GCD, 1–9).* Then it brings us back to fantasies of old, leaving us in a state even more muddled perhaps than before. What is striking is the balance of style in the text, whereby a firm and bold move into the future is pressed upon us with manifold cautions and counsels of prudence. Consider this formula:

> Of course we must find new solutions, yet in these changing times it is incumbent upon us to act with prudence.

Consider using the very same words to say:

> Of course we must act with prudence, yet in these changing times it is incumbent upon us to find new solutions.

The Roman accent marks the first of these formulations.

The American guides push somewhat further into the interior before faltering. They enter upon a "World in Transition" (TJD, 33–41) and run up against the "Impact of Change" (NCD, 13–19). Their reaction is foursquare: religious education must take these changes into account and itself change in consequence. No passing deference to change here, as some aesthetic to open with, but as a problem to grapple with; these texts roll up sleeves to get right down to it. It is at this point that something curious supervenes, likely enough for good reasons not at all clear. For having announced, with genuine insight, a given principle they contravene it in application; or, having deduced the appropriate conclusion they counter it with an affirmation that could only have arisen from a competing, unstated principle; and the like. Suppose we ask for directions and one bystander tells us,

> Head north.

while his companion counters,

> Head south!

That is one plight. Suppose now the one bystander to say,

> Go west, young man!

and, finger on map, he specifies:

> Head north,
> then south.

That is a second plight, made a third when the other bystander advises:

> Head south,
> then north!

---

*The numbers in citation refer to numbered paragraphs or sections; thus (GCD, 1–9) refers to the paragraphs numbered 1 through 9 in the Directory's text.

Lastly, suppose both of them to agree:

> Head north and south,
> then east and west.

All of these may be heard at once in the American texts, as pluralistic as the nation, yet *e pluribus* not *unum* but *contrariis*. To be sure, we are all subject to inconsistency and ambivalence, all the more when joined in a collaborative effort. By preference though, we would make plain the alternatives, identify them as such, and forebear plunking for both at once.

By no means are these passing doubts a review of the documents, and on no account do they characterize the whole of their content or, especially, their achievement. Consider them in another perspective. There must be few other documents in contemporary education that could take their measure. One wonders too whether any other corporate body could devise such an encompassing view. What system of education is not fraught with exclusive compartments—one controlling its philosophy, another the methodology, a third the curriculum—in such manner that a unifying conception is precluded? How impossible it must seem just to cooperate in such a world; how unthinkable to collaborate in constructing a new one! In contrast stands the overreaching conceptual unity of our enterprise, and in that light religious education appears unique in fortune and opportunity. Not the least of our blessings is the presupposition there for the taking, that we can not only move to redesign but—marvelous to recount!—actually proceed to execute in practice a whole, renewed enterprise. For that is indeed what we think to do. That is a premise that tempts. That is at once the promise and the glory of the Directory. Hence these guides are remarkable in every way, and we must mark what they point us toward. But we must also make headway, venturing beyond to the world we would have for our own. We follow in this way with confidence in our ability to read the signs of the times.

The signs of our times are all about us. The things that are called signs are not arcane: they are world-factual events that present themselves to our every eye. One is struck by some phenomena among others. One selects these out and accords to them the status of sign; these are then the events that signify for us, that are significant to us. These are the events that seem to mean something and to have something to say. To wit?

The activity of reading the signs is no more mysterious. It is an activity proper to intelligence at work in our every mind. To know the world is, after a fashion, to have construed it. Again after a fashion, it is to accord meaning to events. One first poses the question, what must they mean? and in giving the answer one then knows what they mean. Thus in our perplexity do we master and order the world.

By greatest of all possible contrasts there stands the scrutiny of heavens and entrails in hopes they will open of themselves and yield forth their secrets.

Yet there is a trick to reading the signs. The trick is not in espying the events nor in construing them, for everyone can do that. The trick is: what can you do with your reading, and can you get others to do it with you? Here we leave the privacy of our individual world as we have made it and sally forth into the public domain to seek a meeting of minds and a joining of hands. And that is no mean trick for any of us, far from it. It is the fragile achievement besought since the emergence of the human spirit: to make a world to live in together.

Happily no one is called to construct in ten chapters that civilized whole eluding humankind for some ten millenia passing. We have only to make a try at it, and it is only the little world of catechesis that we have to try to make. But the process is fairly the same and we are all continually engaged in it. This book reports one mere try: a try with a measure of reflection, perhaps, and coherence—not to the full, to be sure, yet neither fleeting and fragmentary; prompted by particularity of experience, yet calling to collective purpose; comely to its maker, yet fetching beyond to seduce entourage; withal, a try on the hunch that a better world can be made, and in the hope of having construed one useful for our noblest endeavor as religious educators.

Herewith, then, one reading of the signs of our times, rendered for the three parts of this book:

We have seen the procession over yesterdays and it has gone by us as a pavane. We have followed its starts and turns and watched it come to fitful rest in impasse.

Turn now to the world of today and see process all around, as a lyrical stirring. See things not as they are but as they are in being and becoming.

And dream on with us, of life together in a world we could make to become. See, a chorale is convening to celebrate life: we hear a crescendo; we feel a tremolo; we are caught up in a mighty surge to flourish over death!

For us the great sign of the day is change-in-process. The world of catechesis is made of humans-in-change and religion-in-change, of changing educational forms and changing instructional modes.

The sign in our fellow humans we see as a changing consciousness of time.

The sign in our religion we see as a changing conception of God.

The sign in our schools we see as a changing structure and milieu.

The sign in our instruction we see as a changing procedure and model.

To see these same signs and to construe a world of them we are all invited by a turn of the page to the next four chapters.

CHAPTER 7

THE CHANGING CONSCIOUSNESS OF MAN

Most people find it easy enough to grasp the notion that the world around them is subject to change. What they might find harder to conceive is that they themselves are apt to change with it. We tend to see ourselves as standing aside and watching change happen, witnesses on the remove to events beyond ourselves; far below swirl and rage the currents of life while on the embankment we stand safely high and dry.

Yet that view may bear little correspondence to things as they are. For the phenomenon of change can embrace and attain the nature of humanity as of reality. Human nature too is changing.

CHANGE AND HUMAN NATURE

We may ease ourselves into this startling line of thought by considering human designs upon society. Mere centuries ago people seemingly could not conceive that nature and society are susceptible of *being* changed, surely not by the hand of man. The American Bicentennial serves to remind how recently it was that society was thought beyond repair because wholly out of hand. A mere two hundred years later we make confident moves to change what is called the environment, a collection of matters once dubbed the natural order of things. Among these was the human condition, given and immutable.

Today we expect most phenomena to yield and all phenomena we think assailable. Americans, for instance, will have a go at anything—the old college try. It may not succeed, but the significance lies in the attempt. Note that when success eludes, we are wont to conclude to deficiency in our designs rather than to obduracy in the event. Nothing but taxes seems exempt: we will take on poverty, disease, and crime; weather, reproduction, and perhaps even death. Having come to accept as a commonplace the notion that nature can be transformed, we might now begin to entertain the view that human nature too is liable to change. How so?

Although the redesigning of society, as in revolution, represents at bottom a rejection of determinism, historical fate and all that, in one respect efforts to change the environment are based on the view that human beings are in some wise affected, if not modified and determined, by environmental influences. Moreover, on popular view the times are a-changin'. Society is undergoing rapid transformation before our very eyes. Perhaps, then, as humans act upon the environment in order to change it, the changing environment in turn acts upon humans—with the result that they too are changed. Thus sociologists state that "society is a human product," and in the next sentence they state that "man is a product of society."[1]

Conceived as a dialectic process, social change begins with the action of humans upon the external world. It eventuates in the action upon humans of the external world they had created—transformed now "from structures of the objective world into structures of the subjective consciousness."[2] Hence we can survey historical changes in human societies and at the same time observe, as one treatise title has it, *The Changing Nature of Man,* concluding that humans of long ago "lived a different sort of life, and that they were *essentially* different."[3] In contemporary society, then, the question of change refers not solely to social circumstances but also to social beings; not solely to human artifacts and accoutrements but also to human nature. As Pierre Babin* fairly chants:

WHAT IS CHANGING?
The organization of cities?
The architecture of houses?
The types of hobbies people have?
The assembly-line work in factories?
Yes, indeed.
But, above all,
Man is changing.
A new kind of man is being born (p.7).

We do more than contemplate and accept the changing scene before us; we contribute to effectuate that change. And as the nature of that scene is transformed, so too the beholder is in process of changing with it.

To complete this preliminary view we need only specify that which is regrettably not obvious: all of us are implicated in this change, young and old alike. Youth and change, it is true, are so nearly co-terminous that we have accustomed ourselves to seasonal alterations among the young people whom we teach. But what of us? It is the human kind that is changing, and we can hardly put ourselves beyond that pale. To exempt ourselves from the effect of change may be habitual but it is neither reasonable nor realistic, merely a claim based on a wish that it were so.

To be sure, official documents draw attention to changes among young people instead of among humans generally, such as would include us too. The

*Pierre Babin (ed.), *The Audio-Visual Man* (Pflaum, 1970), hereafter cited as *AV* (all quotations refer to chapters written by Babin).

Catechetical Directory, for example, devotes considerable concern to the "impact of change" upon youth (GCD,82; NCD,16). But there is scant admission that those who are to read and apply these texts might themselves be touched by the very changes to which they point. Let us concede in all honesty and reality that such an attitude is yet one more way to avoid facing the problems before us. The reality of the matter is that we are all—youth and adult, man and woman, teacher and student—implicated and affected by the consequences of present-day transformations and mutations. Everyone in the "eco-system" is involved. Perhaps we are wont to attend more to changes among youth because these forebode, and because they are sometimes flaunted, and because they may appear more suddenly, with flash and flair and dramatic jangle. Yet however we overlook change among adults, the process is taking place and it may hit harder, more substantially, more unexpectedly. It would seem that we as religious educators would want to make good our claim to understand youth by taking a closer look at the process of change as it occurs within ourselves as well as among our younger and older students.

In what follows, therefore, let us forego the approach whereupon youth remains an object of detached viewing by an adult observer, as an ethnologist recording the curiosities of some obscure tribe. (Perhaps we could even take up the question of present change with the presumption that it does *not* apply to our students. Naturally, that is an extreme; yet in taking it we might have a better chance of striking the middle.) To the whole of us, therefore, as idiom has it—what's happening?

Any number of scholarly and popular accounts have appeared of late that advance various perspectives and frameworks within which to situate change in process.[4] Here we shall make our own points as a basis for the programs of instruction in Part Three. First we will identify that one change which appears most significant. Around this central point a number of other changes will be organized more or less as following from or relating to it. Some general implications for religious instruction will also be identified so as to keep us in mind of our purpose throughout.

AWARENESS OF TIME

There are those who would maintain that the changes in our time are no more singular than those of past centuries. But we find to the contrary that only three or four times in all of history has the society of humans been known to undergo a process of change equivalent to that of our present day. The drama of our times derives from one crucial element characterizing all of present change and surpassing in importance any one change and perhaps even the notion of change itself.

The central fact is a change in consciousness. We are passing from a state wherein we were once conscious of duration to one wherein we are now conscious only of immediacy. Our focus is on the present; past and future are fading from awareness.

Focus on Present

An emergent conception of time has been noted by various observers. Pierre Babin for one sees us embarking on an epoch of "nowness and simultaneity" (AV, 19). Bruno Bettelheim speaks of "our new yardstick of time" based on the measure of mechanical speed rather than biological growth; and Walter Ong reminds us that for the first time in history events anywhere on the globe—or indeed, off of it—can receive immediate attention of people everywhere around the world: "Simultaneity today is more sweeping both in space and time."[5]

This focus on the present moment is reflected in the favor that the word "instant" enjoys in all sectors of human activity: we drink instant coffee, see instant replay, seek instant relief, demand instant results. It would seem that in our day more than any other, perfection of psychic equilibrium lies in accommodating to the here and now. The past encumbers with memories of regret, the future forebodes with visions of alarum. We are sustained in awareness of the present alone.

Yet the present cannot be experienced save in relation to past and future. Time has been lost to us and we are orphaned in the now. Little by little we are losing touch with the dimensions of past and future. In this respect the young may well be more stranded than those who have lived their formative years in a world still conscious of duration and stability. But at work in all of us to some degree is an erosion of past and future.

Fading of Past and Future

As for the past, the erosion is apparent enough. We are becoming less and less sensitive to the weight of tradition and the historical dimension of events. Precedent is no longer a referent for action, be it in morals or politics. This weakening of tradition and history has for effect that the experience which we have acquired is of little use, and not just for our cadets. No one dares require high schoolers to study history, but "current events." Worse, "the familiar study of Current Events may become a class in Immediate Events."[6] But we have studied history, and we have forgotten the lessons of the past. Not only the young, for we ourselves had probably never learned them in the first place.

Yet in another sense many of us do not realize the lessons of the present either. "Our thinking still binds us to the past—to the world as it existed in our childhood and youth," comments Margaret Mead.* Born and bred before the latest revolution—electronic, atomic, rock, what have you—we are like landed immigrants in the country of our birth, unable to use the wisdom we had acquired in that other land to help us know how to live in this new world; there sit our children listening with half-comprehension to our curious tales of a life long ago and far away (CC, 72–76). The question arises as to how a society can possibly be built under these conditions. Yet Mead gives as her belief that we are on the verge of developing a new kind of culture altogether, one in which children—and not parents and grandparents—will prefigure and represent what is to come (CC, 87–88).

As to erosion of the future, we suffer a weakening of interest in long-term planning for individual life, a continuing indecisiveness over career choices—now having to be made two and three times over—and above all we are made impatient: the Future is Now (CC, 97). If so, little wonder that the past no longer serves to guide present action in anticipation of future consequences. A blind spot for past and future may also explain the difficulty of finding suitable bases for one's life; such bases may well exist but eyes only on the present will fail to perceive them. Thus parents who guide their children along today's approved routes to new and better living are likely to discover with anger and bitterness on the morrow that the road so faithfully and confidently followed has left them quite simply in the middle of nowhere. What they had hoped for, for their children, no longer exists (CC, 91).

As past and future fall away we are left to stand on the moment we have now, as if all of life were lived in the moment.

LIFE IN THE MOMENT

What kind of life is this? Our notes will be gathered under convenient rubrics of individual, society, and life cycle.

Individual

In pointing to the birth of a new kind of man, Pierre Babin attributes to him "a new way of communicating, of living and understanding, a new mental framework, a new kind of activity and involvement" (AV, 8). These are much the same as we point to. In contrast to a person fully aware of time in all its dimensions, one conscious primarily of the moment alone will exhibit a new manner of grasping the world. He will cognize it differently; he will value different aspects; he will experience different needs.

*Margaret Mead, *Culture and Commitment: A Study of the Generational Gap* (Doubleday, 1970), hereafter, *CC.*

Anyone having taught school over the past twenty-five years or so can testify to what amounts to a transformation in the students' cognitive processes. Their mode of thinking was formed, as indeed ours was, in part by the media through which information came to them. Recent years have brought a slew of novel media. These not only accelerate change and multiply knowledge, they "of course change the structure of knowledge and of the psyche."[7] Veteran teachers are given to observe that students just don't read, write, memorize, and recite anymore; one wonders if they need to and even if they can. Students today are widely said to know less than their forebears. They are also said to know more. Perhaps it is that they know differently, being neither more nor less intelligent than youngsters in the past but rather construing the world in another way.

Reality may be apprehended in various ways, including by reason and intuition, analysis, and insight. That much we know from theory. And from experience we may have concluded that humankind had once for all entered upon the era of scientific thinking, casting aside such outdated modes as the artistic and poetic, the intuitive, mystic, and mythic.

Instead, behold these to have returned in force. Instant-conscious persons seem to be possessed of a wholistic, global, encompassing intelligence, featuring "the prevalence of a sensual and experiential grasp of reality over an intellectual and impersonal understanding of it" (*AV*, 22).

No development could have left the young at more variance with the school. Here we may see old patterns of learning conflict with the new. For example: students are to learn by sustained attention, but today's youngster learns by in-depth involvement; students come to understand the universe by examining symbols in textbooks and classrooms, whereas today's youngster "understands primarily by direct contact and not by abstract representation" (*AV*, 22). Moreover, as things are at present, an acute sense of duration is required in order to profit from schooling, for the enterprise is founded upon the promise of future benefit entailed in present activity. The young, then, are required to possess that which they precisely lack, the ability to perceive relation between what they do now in school and what will happen to them six or ten years hence. Insofar as school is a preparation for life it can make little sense to those for whom life is what they experience now, and only now. The overwhelming boredom and indifference that may be observed among a major proportion of the body scholastic may perhaps be laid to the utter disparity which students perceive, howsoever incorrectly, between what school has them do and what life is like and for.

In no wise exempt from these reactions, religious instruction too stands to receive the indifference and disfavor of the young if it is conceived, as so it traditionally is, as preparation for future Christian life, not to say eternity. But as James Michael Lee demonstrates from vantage points pedagogical, psychological, philosophical, and theological, religious instruction must have "nowness" as its basic axis: "To make the religion lesson a preparation for life rather than life itself is to sacrifice the present, and thereby render the lesson irrelevant in the perceptions of the learner."[8]

People who live in the moment also value the world differently, for example work and human relations.

Concern for work has been replaced by concern for happiness. In the form that it has long taken, work can only be undertaken if the worker has a pronounced sense of time. He will willingly labor five days a week to rest on the weekend, fifty weeks a year to vacation during two, and forty years of life to spend five or so retiring upon the modest sum he will by then have accumulated, thanks partly to his simultaneous anguishing over future, present and past. The economic system in large part—e.g., life insurance, funereal enterprises, stock market—is founded upon this view of things. But for those who conceive of the future only with difficulty, work, like school, is acceptable only if it is at the same time a source of personal satisfaction and fulfillment, more or less immediately. Otherwise it meets with repugnance. In a way that stance can favor artistic and creative endeavor, adding a sort of feminine counterpart to the masculine valuation of strife and progress that has created the accoutrements of industrial civilization and if unchecked will likely proceed to destroy them.[9]

Other values are in question too. Fidelity and commitment, for example, not only assure ties between humans but also link past, present, and future. Here we can abandon our pretence of perplexity over perfidious youth, for fidelity among none of us enjoys the prestige it once had: in social and political as in marital affairs. It is as if life can no longer be depicted as a sort of straight path stretching unerringly into the misty horizon; rather it seems a series of unconnected dots and dashes striking out here and there. The pot of gold we now suspect to lie hereabouts, not somewhere over the rainbow.

But if the moments and activities of which life is now made up do not conspire to traject a trustworthy path, we may be sure that they are each of them distinguished by a purity and intensity of experience unknown to generations past. For this generation lays far greater stress on authenticity of present experience than on fidelity to a grander design and purpose beyond self and present. Authenticity is a virtue of the moment, fidelity a virtue of duration; what we have lost in fidelity we might well recoup in authenticity.

As fidelity assures passage from past to present, commitment assures passage from present to future. We can expect commitment to be as endangered. "Today, the central problem is commitment" observes Mead: "to what past, present, or future can the idealistic young commit themselves?" (*CC*, ix). Indeed, for how is it possible to commit oneself to the future if this dimension of time is unseen and inconceivable? As a result of what it calls "the cult of immediacy," the Directory maintains that "many are unable or unwilling to commit themselves to enduring loyalties" or "to take responsibility for the results of one's actions" (NCD, 16). These are accurate observations. Unfortunately they refer to youth alone and are set in a negative, condemnatory context.

Let us entertain the proposition that in all these respects, touching upon today's new modes of thinking and valuing, our efforts in religious instruction ought to be based in a clear and calm understanding of contemporary human beings, whatever they are. We mean to apply in practice that principle ever ready to our lips—namely, to start with the learner where he/she is. Far from ignoring or condemning the young and the modern we ought first to appreciate them and then devise responsive and realistic programs of instruction, confident that something fine can be achieved with our fellows as they are.

People who live in the moment have special needs. Many of these center around community. Unable to count for support from history, from institution and tradition, from certainty and security, our contemporaries strongly experience the need to join with others and find at least for the moment a sense of community, togetherness, personal encounterings. In groups of all sorts they can find friendship and warmth, wit, imagination, and grace—"qualities of the soul."[10] Perhaps also they find excitement and renewed daring: only by uniting in human community can they move confidently into the future (CC, 97).

Insofar as individuals become persons as a result of social interaction and experience, a crucial aspect of community is dialogue. By contrast there stands institution. Whereas in an institution a problem may be imposed or given by one party, directed to be solved by another, according to the method prescribed by a third, and for results demanded by a fourth, in community problems are experienced and resolved by the members together cooperating in a process of problem-solving for their own present purposes.[11]

Each member may lend voice and give ear, two activities of exceeding importance for the individual as for the common weal. The human voice is "a manifestation of the person"; more than a symbol of objects or their comprehension, speech is "a calling of one person to another, of an interior to an interior."[12] Hence from several perspectives it is said that persons become in dialogue: one of its purposes according to Reuel Howe is "to bring persons in being. Man becomes man in personal encounter." The same from Gregory Baum: "Man comes to be through dialogue with others."[13]

If every religious educator could take such reflections to heart, he and she would better appreciate the importance of enabling people to express themselves freely and fully to one another—would we wish them to enter within themselves and there find person and Spirit.

Society

When a somewhat significant number of people begin to lose awareness of past and future to become ever more attentive to the moment at hand, the society they conspire to form evidently assumes a changing shape. It is not that society is merely changed in the sense of being different; it is that society is continuously changing. The normal state of social affairs can be characterized, in part, as unstable, indeterminate, and pluralistic.

Consider that for persons focused in the now the social fabric is woven of community patterns, not institutional ones. Institutions are set in an overarching framework of duration, indeed durability, and they occupy a particularized, delimited space; whereas community exists when and where assemble the people who compose and constitute it. Institutions are run by law and regulation, persisting over time and set above the parties at hand ("no man is above the law"); communities operate on emergent norms, formulated and followed by those who presently make up the group. Thus, community partakes of process, and the process evolves as the group and its membership evolve. By contrast, institutions tend to perdure, even resisting in a sense the impact of those who operate within its structures and strictures.

Consider too the relationship between perception of time and that of space. Peoples who lack a sense of duration, of before+during+after, prove to have equally little awareness of spatial limits and borders. Nomadic peoples, as an instance, live in an open world of space and time. They typically disregard whatever frontiers may have been erected by other groups; they typically possess no past or future, nor writing to preserve past deeds or anticipate future ones; their movements seem dictated by exigencies of the moment. Humans concentrated on the immediate may be likened to nomads wandering in an open world. For them the world is perceived and apportioned in altogether different manner from that of people conscious of duration and sensitive to tradition. We may expect to see in our time a decreasing awareness of frontiers and barriers separating the men of this earth, and a new awareness arise in its place, as even now humans strive to create a "world without borders."[14]

Among our younger contemporaries, this phenomenon is widespread enough as to give rise to some concern. Youthful ecumenism is often so encompassing that it neglects to discriminate those perduring or endangering traits that, to all appearances as we perceive them, do indeed separate men in reality. On that view, youthful flattening of certain barriers appears less the fruit of more lucid perception than of more pronounced myopia. Psychological nomadism perhaps likens the young in our society to the barbarian at the end of the Roman Empire—they are "the barbarian within," says Ong, reminding one of Parsons' quip that the birth of new generations represents "a recurrent barbarian invasion."[15]

Yet such a perception of the world may also serve to reduce the great divisions that can no longer be justified today. No wonder that students, cut off from the historical and traditional dimensions, can hardly conceive that Christians East and West could still be maintaining schismatic lines first drawn for some obscure reason in the 11th century! How odd must seem to them the splits that continue to occur today. This year has seen, for example, a group of local Lutheran churches to split off from the Missouri Synod on a "conservative-liberal" basis; Episcopalian bodies threaten to split over the "male-female" clergy issue. Evidently the "borderless mentality" is not shared by all, nor does it characterize the whole of contemporary developments. We know that an equally significant aspect of contemporary change is actually a heightening sense of separateness. The daily press could not make plainer the violence and divisiveness among Protestant and Catholic in Ulster, for example; Christian and Moslem in Lebanon, Arab and Israeli; black and white in South Africa and black and black in Angola; and so on and on and on. Are the peoples on this globe coming together, or are they drawing more distinctly apart? The dichotomy is probably falsely drawn, for we may perceive and emphasize either term. Similarly, we can emphasize the level where small communities form and people are more apt to ignore differences between individuals or the level where nation-states form and people are more apt to stress differences between peoples. In any event, social arrangements appear to be continually shifting and we may say that society is indeterminate.

Three striking developments that affect society as well as individuals are the increase in life expectancy, the acceleration of rate of change, and the proliferation of electronic media. These are all old hat now, but they conspire in impressive ways to render our social arrangements shaky: unstable, indeterminate, and pluralistic.

Not to put a fine edge on it, we note that the rhythm of social evolution ever so imperceptibly accelerated from beating in millenia to centuries, and then from centuries to decades. At the same time, at least during the Christian era in the West, we observe a secular increase in life expectancy. In the "days" of classical Greece and Rome, the average term of human life is thought to have been something on the order of twenty years. Two thousand years later, during the 18th century, it was thirty years. In 1900 life expectancy was fifty years. Today it is passing seventy, and will likely reach eighty before century's end.*

Time was when social change could not be observed and measured. In the modern age, the evolution of society could once be measured by that of schools of art—in centuries. In all of that time an individual, along with his parents *and* children, was born to live and die against one and the same societal background. Everything around them bespoke stability, continuity, lastingness. Today social change can be measured by that of technology, on the order of not one hundred but ten years. Given today's life expectancy, an individual can now be born into one society, grow up in another, mature in yet

*One can take one's pick of numbers; these are mostly from Herant A. Katchadourian, "Medical Perspectives on Adulthood," *Daedalus,* 1976, 105 (2), 29–56. Hereafter, "MP."

another, and die in still another, with others again in between, all perceptibly different. Everything around is now bespeaks frailty, passingness, momentariness. With devices like TV and computers,[16] events no sooner occur than they are transmitted; no sooner are they transmitted than perceived and thereupon superceded—so many more are to come, so many more are in occurrence. Would attention rest at any rate, one wonders, upon a televised image even if it were to linger on the screen for so much as half a minute? The scene before us is, and is expected to be, transitory, ephemeral, ever-changing.

Life Cycle

In such a society, composed of such individuals, and given the increasing life expectancy, we realize that our notions of childhood, adolescence, and adulthood must be taken on new, uncertain, and shifting meanings.

For some decades now anthropologists have been informing us that no such thing as our adolescence can be found in this or that culture, and historians that childhood cannot be found in this or that century.[17] Now we learn from doctors in own society that they have no generally accepted definition of puberty, none at all of adulthood, and no clear concept of "to grow up" ("MP," 30–35). They remind us once again that these periods of life are not so much "natural" as artificial divisions.

There is nothing fixed or immutable about life phases. They simply cannot be dealt with out of historical and cultural contexts (p.53).

To settle upon a conception of any one period of life, we must take into account not only the peculiarities of time and place, but also the biological substrata and psycho-social filigree of the growing human.

Given the complexities of human nature and the pluralistic and rapidly changing nature of the world, to agree on such definitions is a difficult task (p.50).

We are therefore not surprised to learn that "as a society changes, its age grading is also likely to change."[18] In what general way is this grading changing in our society today?

Adulthood is a useful phase to begin with, since adolescence and old age are probably situated with reference to the model of adult maturity. This is the model that to all appearances has fallen apart. Once upon a time our society may have delineated one or two fairly clear and dominant pictures of the adult state—was it not wisdom? balance? stability? did not adults finesse? had they not, finally, "arrived"? Today we cannot agree upon what an adult is nor when adulthood begins. (Ask around.)

Of one thing we may be sure, that adulthood is defined socially, not only in terms of physical maturation or intellectual skill. Of most significance is how we as a group define social maturation and, equally, how we recognize and accord it to an individual.[19] That is, an adult is an individual recognized to be one. This is the recognition now so uncertainly met with. Adult status is denied to those having manifestly adult traits, while adult traits are denied in those having manifestly adult status. From certain individuals aged around fifteen to twenty-five, for example, recognition of adultness may be withheld even though they manifestly possess skills and capacities of mind and body thought characteristic of adults—that is, of those who are in fact given adult recognition; on the other hand, as with individuals aged somewhere around sixty-five to seventy-five, it may be denied that they are in possession of these very same traits (e.g., job skill, sexual capacity, intellectual acuity), all the while that it is maintained that they do have adult status, senior status yet.

Perhaps no population is changing so markedly, and no notion so imperceptibly, as "the aged." No one can on unquestioned grounds specify when it is that an adult becomes one of the aged or aging, since "aging, after all, is a lifelong process which simply becomes more evident with the progress of adulthood" ("MP,"34). In this plight we have had recourse to industry and labor. These have obliged by setting the mark at year sixty-five and then setting the marked ones aside, whereupon we in turn regard them as rightly lapsed from productive endeavor as well as the job market, duly apart from human congress and utility, and, oddly, exempt from growth except to grow old. We are amused and sometimes we are taken aback by what we think of as exceptions to this regimen.

> We go on marveling at the number of active, alert, "youthful" people in their seventies without recognizing that the same chronological age span now perhaps represents a different state than it did in the past (or may in the future) ["MP",53].

No doubt a society dominated by present-oriented people has difficulty conceiving of this kind of change, not to say of how human life must be beyond the pale of sixty-five. Yet the economically-oriented and tax-paying contingent has begun to take note of these changes, since with the increase in life expectancy, not only are people living longer but also more of them are persisting, with the result that more require or may lay claim to subvention. Fully 10 million more persons over sixty-five are alive today than in 1950, accounting for more than 10 percent of the American population. Taking due note of this development, which it calls "an important warning," a recent editorial[20] declares its most obvious consequence to be financial; it cites the taxes and benefits that must now increasingly be paid out; and it wonders whether the mandatory retirement age ought not now be changed, "so that more of the elderly can continue to support themselves and reduce the burden on those younger than sixty-five?" With a nod to the need for bettering their life and for re-including them in our community, the editorial ends by urging us to change our attitudes so as to make growing old less of a stigma but above all less of a burden—on us: "and above all to use their abilities productively rather than make them an increasingly heavy burden on job holders." Thus may our notions of old age be in process of redefinition by the very enterprises that originally gave us the notion as we have it.

Within our own enterprise too, new note has been taken of the aged. The Catechetical Directory wonderfully directs our special efforts to them, conceding that we have not sufficiently recognized the importance of this pastoral aspect (GCD,95). They still have a claim on our efforts in much the same way as before: "They need education to help them understand and respond in faith to their experiences to the same degree as they did in earlier stages of life" (NCD,169). And what are we to do? We are to teach the aged "to have supernatural hope" in face of death, "which biologically is near at hand, and sociologically is to some extent already present" (GCD,95); we are to help them make a "creative response and resignation" to aging, to physical suffering, and to death (NCD,169). To be sure, these are of the utmost, yet can we think of no others? We probably are in possession of more knowledge about the aged, and more ideas about old age in a changing society, than about any other period past the teen-age.[21] If a catechesis of death is the limit of our thoughtfulness and ingenuity, we might inquire into the extent to which our conception of old age merely reflects that held by those whose concerns center upon the marketplace and the tax-rate. For which experiences and developments other than decay and demise could we provide the aging and aged with religious instruction?

Adolescence takes its sense and form by comparison with the prevailing social notion of adulthood. If adolescence is preparation, for what do adolescents prepare? As received notions of adult maturity become more diverse, even fragmentary, in a society marked by change, presentism, instability, and pluralism, there must appear in consequence multiple, incoherent models of adolescence. Already decades ago observers were concluding that adolescence as a developmental process was "obsolete," and we heard tell of "the vanishing adolescent":

> Homo sapiens is undergoing a fundamental model change. . . . A different kind of adult is being produced, representing a different conception of maturity. . . . The change can be described most simply as a weakening in the relationship between maturity on the one hand, and stability of identity on the other hand.[22]

To many of our ears, this pronouncement rings as oddly today as it did twenty years ago. Who cannot tell an adolescent on sight? Well, medical doctors for one. So far has their science advanced that it now knows, as we all do, that the transition to adulthood occurs over the second decade of life: one enters it a child, one exits an adult, "while in between he occupies biologically and physiologically ambiguous and fluid positions" ("MP,"34). We retort, out of knowledge hard-won years ago in courses on adolescent psychology, that the period itself is marked out by unmistakeable physical changes collectively termed puberty. Can we not therefore say that adolescence begins with the onset of puberty and that adulthood begins with its completion? Yes, we can;

the doctors cannot. They do not agree in defining puberty, nor in distinguishing it from adolescence ("MP,"34–35). Moreover they know better than we do the timing and function of pubertal physiology. One learns that the earliest pubertal protrusion in the female, breast development, normally starts between the ages of eight and thirteen, and normally ends between thirteen and eighteen (pp.38–39). This allows us a generous ten-year range within which we might be calling "adolescent" those whom others are calling an eight-year-old child or a young adult. And so on for other supposedly definitive traits. Should this matter require complication we are apprized that maturation of certain traits has been observed to occur regularly earlier and earlier: menarche, for instance, now occurs on the average four years earlier than in the nineteenth century, and two years earlier than at the start of the twentieth (p.42). This information throws a different light on such revelations from anthropology as that puberty is defined by various cultures as occurring anywhere from eight to twenty years of age. For us as for others, the lesson reads:

> So long as society defines it clearly, its members can adapt to it. What is difficult is when it is not clearly defined, as among ourselves.[23]

Out of this muddle arises a major part of personal, social, and educational "problems of adolescence."

In these changes and effects we meet with a complement to those observed at the farther reaches of the life-span, leaving us in perplexity as to a grounded notion of adolescence as of senescence. It is said that adolescence was invented around the time of the steam-engine, by Rousseau in 1762 to be precise.[24] We have noted how it has lately been declared an obsolete social invention. Little wonder, then, that in 1976 a clinical report could refuse to characterize its adolescent clientele: "In the past half century the period of adolescence was first discovered, then described as prolonged, and later as vanishing."[25] Perhaps our entire society has become adolescent, hovering in an unfinished, uncertain, and indeterminate state.

Our conception of childhood must similarly be affected. A society of children is possible only when the right to speak is denied them, when they must slowly acquire the means of acceding to secrets that adults hold at their remove. The word infant means "deprived of speech." In our day the spoken word has become ubiquitously salient—everyone has at least one transistor radio at hand or ear, even in ear-muff; it is hardly possible to prevent children from speaking or to deny them access to spoken knowledge as before they could be denied access to books and libraries wherein knowledge once reposed. Consider this vignette: During the Democratic Convention of 1976, the only matter of public suspense was the identity of the vice-presidential candidate, a name held *in pectore* by the party's choice. One single newspaper discovered this name and scooped all other media by headlining it a full day before it was officially announced, and even before it was privately announced to most of the bigwigs. The paper was *Children's Express*. The scoop reporter was a twelve-year-old boy. He had roved the enclaves where knowledgeable grown-ups conspired: "My main advantage is that adults don't think children listen or understand."[26] There is some truth therefore in plaints and sighs that children grow up too fast nowadays, no time for childhood anymore, etc. That may be so because society as a whole finds itself in something of a childhood state. People now need to consult and bespeak their mind in order to discover where their values lie and how they might live them.

This chapter ends with the notion that religious instruction must re-form in congruence with the shape of persons who are to receive it and the world which is to profit from it. The chapter began with the notion that humans and their world are in process of assuming a fundamentally different shape from that long held. Then, as we might recall:

The dynamic of change was proposed as an interactive, dialectical process wherein the consciousness of man interacts in reciprocal influence with the world such that both are at once producer and product of each other. Human nature too is changing.

The crux of change was given as an emergent consciousness of time: a fading awareness of duration and a sharpening focus upon immediacy. Consciousness is as it were circumscribed by the moment, cut off from the dimensionality of time. The present, as well as past and future, is lost to awareness, and the immediate is not experienced as an intermediate.

By relating the rest of change to this altered consciousness of time, we thought to understand something of human life today, life as it is lived in the moment.

- Individuals seem not only to have different ideas than before, they have *different modes of construing*. They meet and take hold of reality in a new manner. They see and think and know, they value and need and learn differently.

- Society formed by such individuals not only has a changed but *a continually changing contour*, moment-to-moment as it were. Points of reference and rest cannot be located in a kaleidoscopic field. Human association appears normally unstable, indeterminate, and pluralistic.

- The cycle of life is expanding, its nodal points shifting, its *periods slipping from definition*. Individuals who move about in a moment-to-moment society are of several disparate minds as to the model of mature living. By what signs shall an adult be known? By what means, then, and to what ends shall children be prepared in transition ("adolescence"); by what marks and for what purpose shall adults be terminated in function ("senescence")?

Together these give one view of some of our changing world. To be sure, certain changes were selected and others omitted; some were emphasized and others neglected. It is foregone that this perspective is not exhaustive of contemporary changes nor of the principles that might organize them after a fashion. Yet some such an attempt must be undertaken if we intend to design and execute in contemporary light an appropriate religious instruction. What broad catechetical lessons can be drawn from this perspective as offered?

From ruminating about the changing life cycle we can conclude to *a catechesis over the course of life*. That would entail, for example, designing special programs for each and all periods as much as we can make them out at the moment: not merely for children and adolescents but also for infants and oldsters; not merely one program for adulthood but several throughout the fifty-year span of developing life after adolescence.

From observing our pluralistic and unstable society, we conclude to religious instruction *via community*. That might involve, for example, rebuilding the local community of faith and then proceeding within along a variety of approaches for diverse needs and groupings.

From reviewing changes in individual modes of construing reality, we might conclude to *a catechesis of experience*. For example, we can favor dialogical, interrelational methods so that persons could discover and express an emergent sense of faith.

These are merely suggestive of implications for our enterprise. Overall we conclude to *a dual-structure model of religious instruction,* one that at each step makes equal and simultaneous provision for group and for individual, for development of community and person in Christian living. As the bishops have expressed it, each of our programs and all of our efforts should aim to form "persons-in-community" (TJD,13).

We may assume it possible to view human beings as they are now and then adapt our instruction to them. We may assume the reverse, preferring to view human beings as we would have them be and then insisting that they adapt themselves to our instruction. The first assumption has been chosen as more strategic.

The Christian message must be announced, as of old, in ways conducive to understanding and converting to Christian life, for the Christian life too, as of old, must be lived in the only time we have. It is this which shall transform the world for us, would we not first lie in wait that the world transform itself unto our purpose. But on what terms is the Christian message to be announced and lived in such a moment as ours? We next look to the ways in which the changing consciousness of man might issue in an emergent conception of God.

CHAPTER 8

AN EMERGING CONCEPTION OF GOD

It is one thing to speak of changes in human nature. Clearly it is another to speak of God also changing. We can come to accept that human nature might perhaps be liable to change. But how can God change? In all this kaleidoscopic world—or perhaps above and beyond it—there must remain at least one steady, fixed, and unwavering point: God. And with that, our faith in him.

This altogether reasonable and comforting view may surely be maintained. However, we shall not maintain it. Rather we invite another view, whereupon God, along with humans and their world, is thought in some wise in process of change. For it would seem that as we ourselves change, particularly in manner of construing reality, so also our manner of thinking about God and coming to know him. Insofar as that is the case, nothing could be more portentous for religious instruction.

How might the changing consciousness of man alter his conception of God? This question has been taken up in several impressive studies that we may all consult with profit.[1] Far from attempting a formal study or even a review, this chapter proposes to offer an impressionistic account in service of our thinking about religious instruction. What implications might follow from the viewpoint developed in the preceding chapter? Now in one sense any answer could describe the course of development followed by an individual respondent, his and her own religious experiences and the sense made of them within a particular group of associates in the faith. To render something more than a merely personal and subjective statement, then, we can adduce in illustration of the points to be made statements from official documents, contemporary theologians, and colleagues in the field of religious instruction.

CONCEIVING AND SPEAKING OF GOD

God made man in his image and likeness—whereupon man in turn, rejoined Voltaire, has made gods after his own image. Indeed, a character study of deities in mythology and religion down through the ages might well confirm the suspicion that most gods are patterned after their own worshipers.[2] We can expect that the forms of religion will partake of the social structures established by action of human beings and, like the latter, subject in turn to their reciprocal influence: religion, too, is in part a product of the social environment.[3]

At another level, religious forms are a product of religionists' perceptions of the world. As these change, so will the religion.

> In a very big upheaval what really happens is epistemological. Whenever man changes, he changes the way he knows reality and the way he responds to reality. And that's exactly what is happening now.[4]

And could it be otherwise? Our perception and understanding of reality is expressed through symbolic systems such as language. Everything that humans come to know about God is said in human language; everything that touches our perceptions of reality must, it would seem, in turn touch the representations and expressions that we make of God. And so, in brief, as humans experience a change in consciousness and begin to perceive reality differently than before, so they begin to conceive and to speak of God differently.

Representations

Part of our difficulty in grasping God anew may be that we think we ought not to. In several respects we may regard it as disloyal, even impolite, and surely faith-less. Yet if we can adopt a perspective permitting us to create and entertain new representations of God we will at the same time have placed ourselves in a position to overcome what is altogether the greatest obstacle before us to the renewal and effective practice of religious instruction.

That is not to say that such a perspective is easily adopted. But at very least we must grant, in recogniton of observable facts, that among a significant portion of our contemporaries God is thought of in different ways than in the past. It ought to be more easy for us to recognize than to adopt this changing viewpoint. Surely most of us, formed in another world, have a hard time of it to grasp such novel and upsetting notions. On the other hand, our students have a time of it trying to grasp our instruction in other notions. In both cases the difficulties are entirely understandable, even if the viewpoints are not. In neither case should anyone be too quick to attribute the differences in the way all of us represent God to ourselves and our associates to a lack of good faith.

Yet another part of our difficulty may derive from the aloof position which the church asserts for itself, and still another part from the attitudes that individual Christians hope to maintain in face of the world around.

The church in official documents can speak as if it were out of this world or suspended above it, beyond the reach of vicissitude. Of course the church is ready to accept the fact of change; willing to grant that change creates new situations for its attentive concern; and able to face even the contingency of adjusting its place in a new world. And as for the possibility that current changes might possibly touch and transform the church itself? On this matter one hears fewer pronouncements. To the contrary, the image given off is of some higher-up issuing from splendidly detached elevation a series of assessments, judgments, and corrections to the course of current events witnessed below. It puts one in mind of academic and theological clubs to which we occasionally belong, sitting in contented exchange of none but meet and seemly views of the fastnesses observed from our retreats.

Such a position is taken in anticipation of the wishes of individual Christians. We are wont to rely upon the faith precisely to create an island of stability, a safe refuge and anchorage for mooring our poor boats battered and beset by the perilous seas of life's endless waves of change. For some of us, the more the world changes the more we demand that the church remain exactly as it is to counterbalance the effect of change around us; to this end also we expect our schools and religious teaching to serve as corrective to ambient instability. More deeply and poignantly we fear to lose our faith if our image of God, Christ, and heaven were also to suffer alteration, however slight. We have not heard perhaps or understood within us God's message in the Old Testament, that throughout history and through the signs of the times which make it up, he cleanses ever so more finely the religious concepts of those who serve him. Have we grasped the *process* which the sons of Abraham had to forward as the years went on, refining and adjusting their image of the promised land, the kingdom, the temple, the covenant. . . ?

Unless we breach this last step we shall effect nothing in remaking religious instruction. For a decade now we have persisted otherwise, pouring new wine into old skins, patching old cloth with new. But only a new theology can make for a new religious instruction, as Gabriel Moran keeps insisting. He is right. This does not mean that we must now set about *teaching* a new theology but rather *conceiving* one within ourselves. A new view of God once grasped by and for our own minds will at once open to us new vistas and clear away old obstacles. Thus the renewal of practice awaits the renewal of thought. This renewal is visceral and theological: it must occur within our own innards, and it must touch our conception of God. In other words, if we are to understand the present plight of religious instruction, we must be willing to say to ourselves that it is not a matter of crisis only in religious instruction, but much more profoundly and widely a crisis in the church and even a crisis in the faith.

The word crisis can easily frighten many of us. But in one sense it ought not to precipitate fear. If we reflect on the course of other human affairs such as science and politics,[5] we can see that progress, as it is conceived, can only come about following a disequilibrium (in biblical terms, death) which then issues in a reordering of elements into structures of higher equilibrium (in biblical terms, resurrection to perfected life). The source of danger and fright is not the risks, certain enough, engendered by crises but rather the widespread sclerosis, pertrification, and fossilization found where crisis is not. Historically it has been the case that crises in religious consciousness appeared during those three or four moments when humanity underwent a form of mutation in its process of perceiving either time or space. (On a smaller scale we recall that it was when the wandering Hebrew peoples abandoned the nomadic state and established themselves as settlers in the land of promise that they passed through a serious religious crisis; in the ensuing period of change, prophecy took on a new role and organized priesthood emerged.) We can easily foresee, in light of the considerations in the preceding chapter, that the very same will apply to our own time. On that note, indeed, Gregory Baum opens his work *Man Becoming:**

> A Christian meets his crisis when the spiritual experience of his culture is no longer reconcilable with the religious outlook he has inherited and God seems to be more powerfully present in the former than the latter (p.vii).

As a result we find in the present hour an entire generation in process of redefining its faith. Such an activity was formerly an exclusive appurtenance of adolescence, that stage of life marked by modifications and adjustments in coming to new terms with the world. In this sense we have all become adolescents in faith, hesitant, confused, changeable, and uncertain.

Expressions

Among the very first implications, tied in the closest way to a reconception of God, is that we will have a new manner of speaking of him. In the measure that man experiences difficulty in discerning his personal identity in the midst of this world in flux, he will experience difficulty in speaking clearly of God. Man can enunciate precise discourse about God only to the extent that he can do so about his own being. As this self-discourse is a halting one at present, it is foreseeable that we are moving towards a period of relative aphasia of faith. Much in contrast to the past generation, we shall soon have nothing much to say about God anymore. And this constitutes, moreover, one aspect of present difficulties with religious instruction, become an impossible task not simply because the young will no longer listen but because we no longer have anything to say to them. On this observation alone we ought to find our enterprise far overweighted. We need to invent new structures that will lift us out of the role we must play onstage, whereby we are made to mouth the lines though we lack both script and speech.

The term aphasia specifies that in this relative impotence to say something precise about God what is in question is not the faith but only its expression. A

*Gregory Baum, *Man Becoming: God in Secular Experience* (Herder & Herder, 1970), hereafter cited as *MB*.

certain ineffability of faith is traditional in the church, constituting even a sort of "negative" theology compared to the articulated systems of theologians. The mystics are a good example of believers whose faith was unshakeable but inexpressible. They could say nothing about God beyond a literal "nada." Curiously enough, the church has canonized the mystics but fails to set their writings for serious study in the seminaries, whereas it does set for study the works of theologians who know very well how to talk about God—so effusively in some cases doubtlessly because they have never encountered him. Characteristic of these is the French Sulpician Tanquerey. His tomes were much in evidence and influence in American seminaries, and while his dogmatic theology comprised several hundreds of pages, his mystical theology cannot cover a hundred. No wonder then that church people are often viewed, as Harvey Cox* notes, as "fully equipped with quick and easy answers to questions no one is asking" (p.143). In place of long boring disquisitions he would recommend a certain verbal reticence, deferring perhaps the answer until someone indicates interest in it by asking the question.

But in another respect we recall that religious faith is comprised of more elements than verbal formulations of belief. Beyond "a series of propositions to which we subscribe," our faith represents "a relationship with God who both accompanies our personal growth and in fact triggers that growth."[6] That more or less psychological statement is echoed in the catechetical phrases of the Directory, which speaks of faith in terms of friendship and personal relationship with God (e.g., NCD,161). Religious instruction would stand to gain a lot in years to come by being more mystical than doctrinal. It could, for example, bring people to prayer rather than telling them things about God in the hope that somehow these would excite auditors to pray.

Not overlooked in these remarks is an opposing trend in development among advanced theologians, some of whom even predict a renewal of God-language in present times.[7] Yet this trend does not seem to reverse what has been said here. What these theologians mean, in fact, is only that we cannot rest content with saying nothing about God. The faith which does not seek expression will shortly find itself withering away. Nonetheless, no one intends to assert that we have discovered a rich new language for speaking of God. For such is the great drama of our generation that we must ever set ourselves to uttering words about God in order to bespeak our experience of him, yet all the while the words we employ prove too fluid, shifting, and evanescent ever to satisfy.

In this way we come to see how manifold and diverse will be our expressions of faith. To contemporary humans as we have described them, pluralism is a normal state of affairs. It is to be expected in any human association and it is not seen as destroying unity. The same applies to group-

*Harvey Cox, *On Not Leaving It to the Snake* (Macmillan, 1967), hereafter, *LS*.

ings of Christians in a variety of traditions and confessions. The bishops teach us so: "Within the fundamental unity of the faith, there is room for a plurality of cultural differences, forms of expressions, and theological views" (TJD,18). The Directory cautions us to point out that church unity "is not to be confused with uniformity," for "the church recognizes a healthy diversity among her members, corresponding to what is today called pluralism" (NCD,44). Theologians too, like Richard McBrien,* recognize plural expression of faith:

> Different churches have different ways of expressing themselves about one and the same mystery of faith. We cannot automatically conclude that Christians differ among themselves just because they don't use the same language to describe a commonly perceived reality (p.24).

Unfortunately this generous ecumenical spirit is not shared by all camps, or perhaps cannot be operative in all situations. One curious result of the ecumenical movement appears in what Baum* calls "committee ecumenism," the official gatherings of representatives from various Christian churches. Far from providing a forum for examining differences, the gatherings guarantee, as a point of protocol or etiquette, that none will be raised; far from providing impetus, they have co-opted the movement. "The official ecumenism has become so highly institutionalized today that it is hardly a movement any more" (p.143). This is an intriguing comment on the function of structures designed for a contrary purpose.

Perhaps a pluralistic viewpoint is more readily adopted by those who find they can stress the immanence of God over a theology of transcendence. Implied in an immanentist conception is a recognition that the signs of faith and revelation may differ, or be read differently, in divergent cultures and epochs, at different times and in various places. Immanence and transcendence represent two ways of conceiving and speaking of God. In brief, they characterize two answers to the question of God's presence. Let us raise this question and then see what answers we may formulate.

LOOKING FOR GOD

For all that we know, or rather for as we know, there may well be subtle relations between asking where God is and conceiving him to be somewhere; between looking for him and locating him. Is it we who do all of these, setting the answer and then posing the question? These and other perplexities crop up when we explore how it is that human beings construe the world and, in

*Richard P. McBrien, "Doctrine and Community: Problems and Solutions." *Living Light,* 1972, 9 (4), 21–35. Hereafter, "DC."
*Gregory Baum, *New Horizon: Theological Essays* (Paulist, 1972), hereafter, *NH.*

changing their manner of construing it, also somehow change their manner of encountering and knowing God. Thankfully without trying or having to resolve problematics of epistemology, psychology, and theology, we may yet pursue our modest inquiry into the conceptions that our contemporaries seem to find most befitting and those which appear most apt for our efforts to provide them with instruction in the faith.

In general it would appear that in our times God is no more to be found where our forebears found him, nor even where we ourselves might once have found him in younger days. Where then is he, and what will we find him to be like? We can develop our answer in terms of observed shifts in four domains of religious study: spirituality, theology, christology, and eschatology.

Spirituality

A most interesting approach to the question is to follow the history of Christian spirituality and to see in it the diverse forms of God's presence stressed by Christians down through the centuries of pious life. But even in a single Christian's life God has been found present now in this way and now in that. As here we are thinking of our own development, we cite forthwith ourselves in illustration.

It so happens that in their youth the authors were trained in what is called the French School of spirituality, dating from the seventeenth century. Can readers but indulge such archaism, we take for example the method of mental prayer. In this method we were trained to consider no less than six different ways to place ourselves in the presence of God to begin our meditations.

1. We could ponder God present everywhere by virtue of his omnipotence.
2. We could lift our eyes and hearts upwards to God present in heaven.
3. We could find God generally present in the worldwide church.
4. We could look directly ahead and discover God present in the tabernacle before us.
5. We could also look within and find God present in our soul.
6. We could look about (in mind's eye, never literally of course) and perceive God present among us as we all knelt down to pray.

For each of these methods we had a scriptural quotation to guide our search, as it were, upwards, forwards, within and round-about. But despite this variety of methods and presences, meditation never failed to take place in the chapel before the Blessed Sacrament. To stay in one's room was out of the question, much less to gather two or three confreres in an exchange of amity and piety, that Jesus might appear as promised in our little midst. The only serious, veritable Presence was the eucharistic one. Moreover, the eucharistic presence was not in the form of convivial communal celebration, as in the liturgy, but a silent, static, and solitary seclusion in the tabernacle.

Now we are all too fully aware, though not painfully so, of the historicity of the example, and we realize in recounting these oddities that their comprehension is beyond hope of reach by the young people of today, and a good number of older ones. And that is just the point. To put it safely, things have changed since the seventeenth century and our youth. The form of God's presence that captures, even excites, interest and responds to contemporary needs and minds is that within the communal gathering of brothers and sisters. And what reason to pay less heed to Jesus' promise of presence in that circumstance than to his promise of presence under accidents of bread and wine?

Theology

That God should now be present among us in this way of human community flows from our diminishing sense of borders, limits, and separations. A border-conscious mentality tends to divide and separate the worlds of divine and human. The one is called sacred and holy; the other, secular and profane. But what we are going to see in our day is far less emphasis on the transcendence of God and more on immanence. God will no more have a special place set apart for him in the above and beyond of the other-world; he will be with us together in one world.

> The God who is supposedly alive in a special world, separated from our own, from which he intervenes at certain times in the course of human history, does not exist at all (*MB*, 9).

Thus to all appearances the God who is other-and-elsewhere has really gone away.

This remarkable occurrence has been observed by numbers of theologians who moreover link it to what we have called the changing consciousness of man. In summarizing recent theological works by Baltazar, Dewart, Fontinell, and himself, Baum gives a nice rendering of a main point in this chapter.

> They are all convinced that the traditional doctrine of God is in need of being reinterpreted. The manner of thinking and speaking about God in traditional Christian piety, and even in most professional theology, is no longer in harmony with the contemporary experience of reality. What is wrong, for today, in the traditional manner is the objectification of God. Because of the change in the understanding of man and his world, it has become impossible to think of God as being over against and above human history (*NH*, 56).

Regrettably, this view of things is not at all widespread in the church. It may represent a growing consensus among theologians, but these cannot be equated with the church as a whole. In fact certain documents and official texts on religious instruction hardly brave the way in applying such a view, or so it seems in the reading. What reticence to vary by jot and tittle!

And a real shame that is, for our failure to adopt an immanentist viewpoint in preference to a transcendist is one reason we fail to reach the young people of today. Any teacher of religion who has managed to come through a half-hour's honest exchange with youngsters in New York, or in Detroit, Chicago, Denver, or Los Angeles can bear witness to the degree of truth in these observations. Conviction grows that we must incorporate into our thinking the substance and justice of some such view before making any change in our approach to religious instruction.

Our efforts often as not fly in the face of things as they are. Our teaching just does not take the present situation into account. Students really need to have patience, understanding, and commiseration to keep on listening to us even as little as they do. The things we say to them! They must think we come from another planet. Q.E.D.

Christology

The terminological poles of immanence/transcendence find a parallel in christology, emphasizing now the historical, now the mystical, Jesus. At one time the stress is on Jesus who lived, died, and arose in Israel at the start of our era, and whose life on earth constituted the Good News of God's concern for humankind. At another time stress is on the mystical Jesus, present in sacramental manner, whose continuing life in the church bears manifest that life has meaning and that death will never win out.

It was towards the second half of the nineteenth century that the scientific study of history arose to play a significant part in various systems of Western thought. Part of this methodology was to rely upon, and interpret, artifacts such as ancient texts and monuments, deducing and correlating and reconstructing the past therefrom. During that period interest in reconstructing the historical Jesus burgeoned, first in the studies of Harnack and Renan, then later within more expressly Christian circles. These developments left their mark on the religious instruction that we received in this century. Perhaps we may recall tracing the steps of Jesus in textbook maps of the Holy Land, arguing over discrepancies of time, place, and procedure of crucifixion, seeking to accord ancient records with the gospels and holy relics with science.

But now our generation has become not only oblivious of history, as always, but impervious to it. In more than the nineteenth-century sense, something like *The Quest of the Historical Jesus*[8] becomes quixotic and superfluous to boot. "The search for the historical Christ is in most senses a futile enterprise," concludes Denis Kenny: "Christ is made present to our age in the sociological phenomenon which is the church" (p.175).* We may therefore expect a greater stress to come on the mystical rather than the historical Jesus.

*Denis Kenny, *The Christian Future: A Strategy for Catholic Renewal* (Australia: University of Queensland, 1971), hereafter, *CF*.

It may strike us that, if religious conceptions have recently shifted from one emphasis to another, then religion teachers might tend to "identify" with the one and their students with the other. That circumstance, if not wholly imaginary, should give us plenty of cause for reflection. Virtue is not in question, for each person is merely conceiving after the manner he and she learned. That, as they say, is only natural. So when we see that our students appear indifferent or resistant to what we after all take to be essential to our faith, we might perhaps wisely hesitate before pronouncing it symptomatic in any way, shape, or form, of atheism, paganism, fecklessness, obduracy of heart, or heaven knows what other assorted maladies of youthful spirit and flesh. Given the changing world, could not their reaction be unavoidable, and healthy at that?

It may be that students appreciate certain aspects of Christianity other than those to which we happen to have been exposed early on, then learned and lived, and now quite naturally favor to teach. Yet the question could arise as to whether we, as educators, ought to favor such emphases in teaching and, further, whether they can be learned even if taught. The life experience of our students may well have sensitized them to different emphases or expressions of equally authentic aspects of faith that we might, if unprofessionally, risk refusing to set before them or mentioning only hesitantly, with faint voice and heart. Thus, as educators, we are moved to analyze the situation, detect differences and potential problems, and devise appropriate educative responses: in doing so we must not neglect to consider the conceptions that underlie our view of the faithful life and the expressions that we give to these in language, gesture, behavior, and other symbolic forms.

Eschatology

If God has already come down from heaven to remain present among us, then what in the world becomes of eschatology? What about the parousia, the last judgment, *dies irae, dies illa?*

These and other events of glory to come evidently take on a new sense for a mentality of the moment. Compared to minds that can embrace past and future, presently-oriented ones by stipulation find enormous difficulty, perhaps impossibility, in conceiving of end-events to take place in some far-distant and quite unimaginable future, wholly without reference to personally-owned and present-felt experience. Such a vision of Things to Come can generate neither motion nor motivation in contemporary psyches. It is enough to get them to do homework for tomorrow.

Here again Christian tradition provides another polarity of emphases, the already-here and the yet-to-be. In translation, we have heard of obtaining grace as a sort of first installment of future glory; we have been promised beatific vision but also that the pure of heart verily see God right now, as have some of the grander mystics in ecstatic transport; now we prepare for the kingdom of heaven, now we build God's kingdom on earth. Here too the emphasis has differed over the centuries.

In very early days the young church stressed the imminence of the Lord's coming, so much so that some Christians evidently quit work and literally waited and watched for it in the skies. The generation just prior to us were transcendists in the main, relegating God to heaven for the time being and afterwards to eternity. In our day we are seeing a return of the concept of God's kingdom on earth. This has befitted in a thrilling way such movements as the struggle for brotherhood and justice among American races. It also seems to fit well with the American sense, or lack of it, of time. Freedom now! Americans have often been observed, not kindly one should add, to lack that pronounced and respectful sense of duration and tradition which is said, also unkindly, to weigh or drag upon the atavistic Europeans—those left behind, after all, in the rush to build the new world. Thus epic American traits and history favor the ideal of establishing the kingdom-on-earth-right-on! According to H. Richard Niebuhr, this has been the most persistent and pervasive theme in the history of American theology (cited in *LS*, 138).

As to what in the world has become of eschatology, the answer is rather literally "in this world" and not in another. "Christ's message about heaven and hell," says Baum as clearly as can be, "is not information about another world"; revelation is not "a set of truths about a world we have not traveled" (*MB*, 99). For this present generation we shall have to translate terms of transcendence and final ends into expressions of presently-ongoing revelation. This much we must do if we wish salvation at hand for them.

REVEALING OF GOD

Beyond new concepts and terms, we need to recognize new signs of God's presence in this world of change. Among new signs, or new readings, are the church, the world, person, and liturgy.

Church

"The chief of these signs is the church herself" (GCD,35). In the world of here and now, the great sign revealing of God is the church, sacrament of Jesus' continuing life amongst us.

> The central Christian fact of today is not God or Christ, but the church. . . . Christ is made present to our age in the sociological phenomenon which is the church. Christ is today what the church is today (*CF*, 175).

What the church in turn is today, we may be sure, is not what it was yesterday—as we conceive it. Contemporary human beings are attuned to life in human community of the present rather than to institutional life that persists fore and aft current members' span of days. The church as sacrament of Jesus is thus not understood after the fashion of institutional church of hierarchy and curia, but as servant church of community, supporting our existence and enhancing our freedom. Above all by diffusing love for and among human kind it constitutes a sign and source of the presence of Jesus among us.

Thus it is that externals and appearances take on new meaning. "The visible *style* of the church's life will become a much more significant element in the communication of the gospel" (ls,28). To the present generation, this style must reveal a loving and helping communal church. That is the kind of church that spells good news, and it may be the only kind of church that most people today can conceive of and belong to. The greater part of humankind seems to have become allergic to institution and legalism, artifice, and conformity. They simply cannot perceive that the church of Christ and companions could be "a spiritual consumer organization" as it once loomed, retailing truths, recipes, and ceremonies that guaranteed God's favor won for heavenly eternity in consideration of payment in currency of obedience, docility, fidelity (*CF*,217). The church will embrace all of us in loving communion or church it will not be.

Needless to say, a transformation of attitudes and structures is called for if we are to find the church a loving communion. For instance, older attitudes about church unity may constitute a problem for those whose mentality encompasses pluralism and rejects artificial barriers to human association. Catechists are directed to explain that the unity and catholicity of the church is not to be confused with uniformity (NCD,44). How are we to proceed in explanation of that? Theories and models made available to us by ecclesiology over the past century are demonstrably insufficient, as Avery Dulles has shown,[9] to explain church unity to contemporary minds. The ringing phrase, once so ready to lips in palmier days, "extra ecclesiam non est salus," can simply not be comprehended by present auditors, even if delivered in vernacular. Consider further how our fellows might receive such bizzareries and niceties as the *exclusivist* doctrine, whereby the church is really constituted of the one substantial (Roman), and the rest, pseudo-churches; the *dualist* doctrine, whereby in a sphere invisible the church enjoys unity but suffers division in the visible world; or the *eschatologist,* whereby the true church exists only potentially, in hope and promise whereas the actual church existing historically is a mere approximation of the one yet coming to be. As for reform of structures, every writer has advanced a number of proposals.[10] To some in fact we are now in the middle of a "big change," even a "revolution" that may well prove to turn out in the long run "more far-reaching than the one which shook the church during the sixteenth century" (*LS*,141).

If attitudinal and structural reform are not accomplished, we may expect present-day persons not to adhere to the church. They will believe themselves to constitute the church there where they happen to be. In consideration of this possibility we can pose to ourselves the question, whether the preferred role for religious instruction ought not to be before any other to work for change in the conceptual and institutional frameworks sustaining the church.

World

The world as well reveals God's presence in this moment. Contemporary minds cut off from historical dimensionality cannot conceive of a revelation restricted to some one privileged point or party past. They stand in need of a conception whereby revelation is continuously, universally, and presently in process, within their own personal experience as well as that of others.

It so happens that just such a conception lies to hand, and in fact has always been available from the earliest biblical and perduring Christian traditions. In terms recalling Old Testament theophanies, the Directory proclaims: "All creation can speak of God" (NCD,30). After retailing God's disclosure in olden times, the Directory moves to reassure us in a passage of grace and beauty, "God Still Reveals Himself" (32–39).

> Nevertheless, God has not fallen silent. God still reveals himself through the creatures he has made, through the events of daily life, the crises of history, and the struggles of people (32).

It is useful for us to recall these ancient and official lineages of terms that we have often used herein to delineate the "modern" emergent concept of revelation so apt for our times; we realize anew that contemporary theologians such as Moran "have thus recovered," as Maria Harris reminds, "the ancient theological tradition according to which the entire universe is Revelatory."[11]

Perhaps then we can henceforth be less squeamish in our approach to personal and present experiencing of the world and humankind as promising for catechetical endeavor. It is not pagan. By the same token, to spurn the world may not be Christian.

Person

Continuing in this same spirit, we can reemphasize person as revealing of God. "The fullness of revelation, then, is a person, Jesus Christ" (NCD,31). From that person to those about us, the discovery of God's presence within persons is a familiar notion even to those of us who might not be up-to-the-last-second contemporary types. We need only recall our persistent lessons of charity and respectfulness towards others, our hopes for community and fellowship. Perhaps we could edge a bit further into this conception and come to perceive some of its essence behind notions of encounter, relationship, and dialogue.

It is not a perverse step from church as communion, revelation as experience and person, to the thought that within interpersonal activity something of

God's presence might be conceivable. To be sure there is and has been faddishness enough in certain emphases upon encounter and dialogue, yet we might take care not to dismiss the essence with the whim. James Michael Lee is one exemplar of such discriminating care in this respect. Possibly on no other printed page in Christendom can there be read a more hard-nosed and cold-hearted scrutiny of "dialogue" as a theory of teaching religion than that sewn into one of his volumes; in eight pages of dispassionate dissection he cuts aways the claims of dialogical theory, lances its spleen of inflated rhetoric and releases to the careless winds its aura of overhanging "eerie spookiness"—whereupon he turns to pronounce dialogue now in fit condition for effective religion teaching.[12] Yet as he comes to describe in another volume religion class at its apogee, he sets within his carefully constructed learning laboratory a structural facilitation of "an engagement between the learner and God-as-he-is-in-another-person," conditions under which the students "can engage in God's revelational activity," often in "the open lived relationship with other persons in the learning situation"—and so forth.[13]

From other perspectives we have noted that a person's word and speech is an essential factor in expression of self, communion with fellows, analysis of experience, and emergence from torpor to life. It is also, possibly, one vehicle of revelation. "Believing that God's word is present in human history, the Christian discerns this word as the special summons available in human dialogue by which men come to be" (*MB,*46). Reuel Howe puts it simply in his *Miracle of Dialogue:* "Implicit in dialogue between man and man is a meeting between God and man."[14] Almost all of this we already know. The point is to highlight it once more so that we can go on to use it in our instructional designs. Enough to mention here that dialogue would entail our respectful participation in the person's exploration and expression of religious experience, aiding our fellows to approximate it in successive formulations. "They should be asked how they understand the Christian message and how they can explain it in their own words" (GCD,75). This is not a catechism of the individual but an invitation to interpersonal inquiry and discovery of God's presence within and between group members.

Liturgy

The discovery of God's presence in our group midst is greeted with delight and celebration. Liturgy evidently is one sign and summit of revelation, and our times behoove a new view and practice of liturgy. It is impossible to continue thinking of it as before, and for many of our contemporaries it is impossible to grasp how we could have thought of it as we once did and yet still do.

But have we not already reformed the liturgy? Or so it would only appear. Catholic reforms, as an instance, seem to have eventuated in certain practices that conflict not only with contemporary mentality but also with the very theological conceptions which purport to underlie them. In the eucharistic liturgy, that great celebration of life, love, and community, the president now faces the worshipers, layfolk read the scriptural lessons, and all exchange offerings, handshakes, and other gestures of appeasement and goodwill. Yet no one escapes the awkwardness with which all of these are executed, nor the subtle sense that the entire proceeding is something of an embarrassment.

> Many Catholics still do not derive the full spiritual benefit from the celebration of the eucharist because they do not really understand the reasons for changing it in the first place. They stand and sit, turn pages and sing, shake hands, receive communion, and go home ("DC," 27).

Why is it, one wonders, that the person who presides over all of this is called a celebrant? Unmistakeably he is not at all celebrating, and neither is anyone else; nor would participant or passerby likely judge otherwise. He is presiding over ceremony. Yet he (she?) ought rightly to be precisely a celebrant, for ceremony must give way to celebration in our liturgies.

We normally celebrate only those events that affect us personally and palpably. Now, Christ is present in our community, giving cause enough for celebration. Yet the presence of Christ must be brought to felt experience and the celebration of it must be felt to bind members still closer to one another. That surely must imply a revision of concepts regarding sacraments and ministry. How can we understand, for instance, the justice of dividing Christians so distinctly into cleric and laic, or apportioning the ministry uniquely to those of male gender?

The reform given to the liturgy constitutes the most notable failure of the postconciliar era. And the reason is simple: it was not brought about, nor was it accompanied by, nor is it presently sustained in, a conversion of mind to the theological basis that launched it. As a result the changed liturgy incongruously became a problem, not a celebration. People found it "routinized, stylized, and dull" just like the *un*reformed liturgy; they could hardly keep it going, much less enliven it, "without any real understanding of the values beneath the change" ("DC," 27). It would seem that the conceptual and practical tasks still remain: the first, "to elaborate a theology of worship based on the concept of God the insider" (*MB,* 253); the second, to despoil liturgy of its peculiar character and to devise appropriate means for "putting the liturgy in its place"—that is, after love of neighbor in terms of primacy and following upon this love in terms of priority in time.[15]

The fact that some such tasks remain unaccomplished measurably complicates the religious educator's task. Teachers can still often enough be found who do an excellent job of introducing youngsters to the new church; moreover, many youngsters are well brought up in the new church within their own family experiences. And these same youngsters then go on to the parish church on Sunday to a liturgy which contradicts the religious instruction so nicely received. The law as we all know it runs "lex orandi lex credendi." All things considered, the liturgy will always prove to have stronger influence than religious instruction does for forming the Christian spirit. Were the reverse true, successful religious instruction would curiously enough end by emptying, as we see on occasion, many churches of well-formed Christians. Are these Christians celebrating in secret? One would fain learn how: penetrate their mysteries, as with old centuries long past, and bring them to light for all of us to revel in the glory of the Lord.

This chapter has raised quite a number of topics in trying to tie our anthropological viewpoint of the preceding chapter to a theological viewpoint and several catechetical implications. Our central proposition has been that our conception of God is in process of changing.

First, we proposed that *our manner of conceiving of God is changing*. We thought that every change touching the awareness humans have of themselves and their world will in turn affect the representations they make to themselves of God. On the grounds that humans are undergoing a truly profound transformation in their manner of construing the world, it followed to our sense that their manner of conceiving God's place in it is also changing.

Second, we proposed that *our manner of speaking of God is changing*. We thought that conceptions are expressed in symbolic systems such as language, and that as conceptions were changing, our language and signs of God must also be changing accordingly. Two hypotheses were advanced.

-*Relative aphasia of faith* meant that soon we shall have nothing much to say about God, certainly far less than the previous generation; we will probably prefer nonverbal modes of activity and experience regarding him.

-*Pluralistic expression of faith* meant that soon we shall come to view as normal and perfectly appropriate that Christians with differing perceptions, experiences, and situations will couch their expressions thereof in differing terms, the which will moreover again vary as the world continues to change and language then essays to express new conceptions.

Third, we took up the question of where to find God these days and what manner of God we will find him to be. On the general hypothesis that he is no longer present where we once could find him, and is no longer the same as we once knew him, four particular answers were suggested. Each was developed by means of a polarity of terms.

- In Christian spirituality, *God is present in human community* rather than within the tabernacle or temple of one's soul, etc.

- In theological terms, *God's presence is immanent* rather than transcendent; he will be found in this world, with us.

- In christological terms, *Jesus God is present in mystical form* rather than historical, continuing his life through the church and giving to our life a special meaning and triumph over death.

- In eschatalogical terms, *God's presence is an event of the present moment,* not an achievement of the future; the kingdom has come, we are not to await it as yet to be.

Fourth, we read anew the signs revealing of God in our day.

-*The church signifies God to us by its style of loving communion,* serving life and liberty, supporting and informing existential experience.

-*The world signifies God to us by its present, everyday events* just as it did in ancient times; this world too is revealing of God, here and now as well as there and then.

-*Persons signify God to us in encounter and dialogue,* as we freely respond to his call and come together with others, discovering him in our midst and seeking to express our experience and understanding of him with our fellows.

-*Liturgy signifies God to us by communal experience and celebration* of his presence and the meaning that gives to our life together; liturgical ceremony will give way to family-community delight.

Together these points constitute one reading in hope rather than observation of *faits accomplis.* Yet it is this reading of the signs that shall serve as guideposts along the way to renewing religious instruction as proposed in Part Three. What points has this reading made for religious instruction?

To condemn, for one, the faintheartedness which leads us to accept the process and effect of change in the world without accepting these regarding God and church.

To stress, for another, that it is up to us to implement these changes in a forthright manner, now.

To show that no changes in religious instruction can be envisaged without a willingness to make appropriate changes in the system surrounding and supporting the enterprise, as for instance school and parish.

To denounce those who only flirt with the idea of change, bandy it about among students after the democratic and up-to-date fashion, and thereafter with altogether hypocritical and pagan lassitude flinch from its consequences within self and classroom.

To emphasize that religious instruction can serve a prophetic role for the renewal of the entire church community.

To enunciate the notion of value for religious instruction today, namely that it constitute an instrument for change in the church, not for comfort and conformity.

As Gabriel Moran never tires of saying, we will just have to restudy our theology, all of it, slowly, carefully, seriously. There is no easy way around, and none other effective. Yet this study is still not enough, for we must also study means of structuring institutions and methods of instructing students that are conducive to our theological conceptions. Let us have at these. Then we shall have done and may being anew in practice.

CHAPTER 9

ALTERNATIVES TO SCHOOL

Remember the counter-school movement? For a time it looked very much alive in this country and to some it looked very much dangerous. "Free schools" were sprouting up all around while proponents spouted about the imminent collapse of traditional schooling. Prophetic figures arose to point their fingers at the system, and following the line of pointed finger we were to see a corpse. "The system is going to pieces," some would say; "tomorrow will see the end of it." Worse, Ivan Illich went about telling us, "The schools are finished, it's all over—only you don't know it."[1]

However intolerable or fearsome these critics at one time, today they are not much in evidence. Things have quieted down: the free-school movement appears to have waned; attacks upon the school seem to have diminished; Illich has taken on the medical establishment now. We may conclude that things have more or less returned to where they once were, the school having regained its former importance and prestige in the eyes of students, parents, and society generally. From the truth as we here construe it, however, nothing could be farther than. The school in all its appurtenances continues to play its manifold parts because no worthwhile replacement for it has been articulated. Meantime the school system continues to all appearances as if having suffered a breakdown somewhere along the way and, profoundly shaken, having now to make do without the prestige once granted it generously as a matter of course.

Far from claiming to know or to study the whole of this endless matter of schooling, we propose merely to reopen the question of alternatives so as to inquire into its implications for Christian schools, for religious education, and for our particular task of religious instruction. The matter has not at all been settled insofar as we are concerned: it may have settled down for public education only to settle down upon the private sector. A review in quiet of the old issues made now with ourselves in mind, promises to evoke a number of suggestive pointers for removing certain problems that are fully athwart our path to enlighted practice.

CRISES AND CRITICS

What might be some signs of continuing crisis in the system of institutional schooling? No especial insight is required. We need only open our eyes or the daily paper to see that malfunctions and miscontents abound.

During a single week of nearly any month we may read of system-wide teacher strikes, or busing conflicts; student assaults, riots, vandalism; assorted shootings, muggings, rapings, firings, failings and other such scholastic activities. But quite apart from these special events, we find armed and uniformed policemen stationed in academe, in normal times and in normal schools—not to mention in nationally renowned ones such as Evanston Township High School with its dozen guards patrolling the halls.[2] Headlines inform us that the U.S. Senate has a committee struggling with the problem of school violence and vandalism; that state legislatures are actually cutting, not merely not increasing, appropriations for the schools; that here and there some counter-culture school is proving a grand success; and that the free-school movement would appear to have gotten under way again: "Perhaps the most volatile fuel for the alternative movement is disdain for U.S. Public Education."[3] In an inventory of leading ideas during 1976 we find this caricature of informed conversation ("the exchange of received opinions") on the subject:

> SCHOOLS: worthless. Nobody knows how to read or write. One of the reasons for everything that is the matter with the country. No standards.[4]

Doubt as to the efficaciousness of formal schooling is still with us.

As to private schools, we could first read in 1963 a book entitled, *Are Parochial Schools the Answer?* and then, in the 1970s: *Can Catholic Schools Survive?*, *S.O.S. for Catholic Schools,* and *When Parochial Schools Close.*[5] And while we were reading, the schools were closing: between 1966 and 1976 the number of Catholic schools declined by a quarter, enrollment by 40 percent, and religious teachers by half.[6] By contrast to this dramatic decline the concurrent increase in the "free schools" appears mercurial, for in the meantime their September openings began to double and triple: 20 free schools were founded in 1968, 60 in 1969; 150 more opened in 1970 and another 200-plus in 1971.[7] Catholic bishops issue official documents that proclaim "The Crisis of Catholic Schools" (TJD,112–118); Protestant educators publish manifestoes denouncing church schools and pronouncing upon "the end of an era" in formal church education.[8]

In these circumstances one may expect questions to arise about the essence and purpose of the Christian school. These questions are asked only when there is no longer any of that essence left or purpose fulfilled. When the Christian schools were on the periphery of the system and on the target of religious education, they had their essence and purpose assured and they did not have to mount a study to find either.[9] Now, however, having so faithfully imitated the institutional model of formal schooling we find not only our own replicas but the very paradigm in critical condition.

What must have gone so awfully wrong as to bring us to such plight? By examining some of the factors in the present crisis of institutional schooling we may be able to draw a certain number of consequences and implications for own enterprise of distinctly religious education.

Scholarly texts in education have examined the notion of schooling as a privileged means of access to societal rewards and the corollary search for alternatives in education.[10] These issues bring to mind the names of various critics of institutional schooling: Ivan Illich and Paul Goodman, for example; Paulo Freire, Everett Reimer, Herbert Kohl, and John Holt.[11] We will sketch a few of their major criticisms and suggestions, the while noting some questions that these raise for our own purposes and procedures.

INSTITUTIONAL FAILURES

These are primarily three. They entail the purposes of the school, the lessons it teaches, and the organizational features it exhibits.

Multiple Functions

The institution of school has taken on a number of functions that were not to its purpose at the start. School has become a multipurpose social organ, charged with accomplishing all the tasks which other social bodies—family, church, state, business—are no longer willing or able to accomplish. It would seem as if once a task is perceived to be of some utility for society it is thereupon assumed to be the province of the school. That is a social policy nowadays, as a recent editorial makes clear.

> The schools attended by children and adolescents are by no means concerned only with teaching knowledge and skills. By law and even more by social demand, schools are expected to provide meals, health care, counseling, discipline [if any], and so on almost endlessly. Many communities look to their high schools for spectator sports.[12]

Scholars have distinguished three principal functions confided to the school: transmission of culture and ethics; training for practical tasks; training in the use of intellectual tools developed by the civilization.[13] Altogether one could easily list five different functions.

1. *Custody.* With the collapse of the old-style family and the increasing problems of the social environment, this "baby-sitting" function grows in importance. Widespread unemployment today might well explain in part why it is that antischool sentiment is diminishing in some quarters: after all, better to be in school than out of work.

2. *Socialization.* This function has become more necessary as the family has passed from the extended to the nuclear state to become more and more isolated from the rest of the society.

3. *Professionalization.* Schools are to prepare the young to assume positions which will render them useful to society.

4. *Instruction.* This function provides the young with mastery over the tools which society has developed.

5. *Education*. This is the function of instilling mores.

Now when an organization is seen to be given too many functions, the risk is great of seeing it discharge none of them satisfactorily. For example: teachers are so exhausted by their hours of classroom instruction that they can no longer provide, with the same kind of assurance as twenty years ago, the service of monitoring and prefecting; security guards, teacher-aides, and volunteers are replacing them in this role. Similarly, the socializing function of the school is now less assured; whereas twenty years ago students might easily stay around after school to enjoy the various sports, clubs, and extracurricular activities, today they hasten to get away from the school and its deadening affairs to return to lively streets and neighborhoods. Again, the function of professional preparation is less well served given that the possession of a diploma no longer guarantees a job; teachers in any case are trained only for the functions of instruction and, somewhat, of education. Hence it is important to redefine both the tasks which society must accomplish regarding its youth and the social organs which might accomplish these. In so doing, care must be taken to avoid piling all these tasks upon the school. Relieved of these burdens the school will be able better to accomplish the tasks for which it was originally instituted, namely those involving instruction.

The questions which this first point raises for religious education are clear enough, as is our failure to ask them.

> Our failure to ask the basic questions first causes us to overlook the limited function of a "school" in the total ministry of the church and so to distort the entire meaning of school.[14]

We might formulate two questions as follows:

> *Q.1 - Have we too confounded tasks and institutions? Have we asked of formal religious education programs to fulfill functions better served by family, liturgy, community? To the extent that this is so, how might we identify functions appropriate to each institution, and then go about planning to fulfill those allotted to us in particular?*

> *Q.2 - To what extent might private as well as public schools be changing significance in the eyes of parents? Where Christian schools, as is sometimes held, are thought to be better than neighboring public ones, do parents tend to send their children to Christian schools not so much for religious instruction as for the academic and disciplinary environment? Insofar as this is the case, might not some spectacular changes be called for regarding the way religious instruction is presently nestled in the school?*

Further implications arise from considering the efficacy of our own schools in teaching or forming religious and value-oriented behaviors. In this regard we can put to one side all our good intentions and preferred opinions in favor of inquiring after the evidence. One piece of evidence was offered in the midsixties by a sociological research survey on the education of Catholic Americans.[15] From their data the authors concluded as follows:

> We can go so far as to say that, for all practical purposes, the religious impact of Catholic education is limited to those who come from highly religious families (p.85).

> Catholic education is virtually wasted on three-fourths of those in Catholic schools because of the absence of a sufficiently religious family milieu (p.112).

No doubt the school does indeed modify values and behaviors, as research has repeatedly shown (e.g., "the hidden curriculum"); the question remains, does it effectively teach those values and behaviors that we wish religious education to teach? The answer appears to be, not under present conditions. To be sure, that does not foreclose the possibility of rearranging school structures and procedures so that they might effectively achieve these purposes; and that is precisely to the point. To be sure, another possibility is to design nonschool educative programs to teach religious values and behaviors; that too is to the point.

In brief, if it is to our purpose to teach certain religious values and behaviors; if we have essayed to teach these via schools patterned after the public system; and if, further, we discover that these are in fact not being learned; then we may conclude to a restructuring of our schools to befit our purposes, or, equally, to a nonschool design for the same ends. Both of these strategies are represented in the next chapter, as implications of our present examination of the school. We might say in passing that whatever the strategy, old school or new, public or private, in-school or out, our instructional efforts will still be limited in efficacy according to the prior religious experience and present reinforcement by the family, by the peer group, and by other educational influences on the individual's patterns of believing and behaving. If no man is an island, neither is any school nor any instruction.

Hidden Curriculum

A second theme of the critics suggests that schools succeed very little in teaching the lessons they propose, while they succeed very well indeed in teaching a number of lessons they do not at all intend.

The school's lack of success in teaching its official curriculum may be laid in part to the methods it uses. If every class were to follow the best-verified principles of teaching and learning, results would likely be better. Only in dreams, however, can one see myrads of teachers, rapidly and adequately trained, sufficiently motivated and circumstantially well-placed to apply these methods as required for success. Upon rude awakening to reality, one is reminded that to the seeing eye the mediocrity of academic achievement needs no demonstration. Alarms go out yearly as reading scores fall lower and lower, seemingly apace with the student's yearly "progress" up through the system. On the other hand, the school teaches a number of other lessons successfully, and seemingly without either trying to or being aware of it. These comprise what is called "the hidden curriculum."

Numbers of scholarly investigators as well as of social commentators have drawn attention to the unsuspected or implicit effects that school has upon children. For example, in his suggestive analysis *On What is Learned in School*,[16] Robert Dreeben does not limit himself to what is taught nor to what is "teachable pedagogically" but includes the social norms and behaviors that appear to be acquired as a function of school structures and experiences. These lessons may be cited as "the good hidden curriculum" in that they facilitate the child's accession to and functioning in public life. But more often than not analysis tends to stress the bad hidden curriculum. For example, in a rather well-known series of books on adolescents, Edgar Friedenberg maintains, on the basis of his studies, that the school teaches conformity to social norms which exclude all deviation and creativity as means of making one's way in life, and further that school procedures impugn the dignity of youth, personal freedom "and other atavisms."[17]

Another well-known book by one of our critics also stresses the evils taught by school. In *Deschooling Society,* Ivan Illich describes the hidden curriculum as comprising these lessons:

1. *Academism:* "There is, first, the shared belief that behavior which has been acquired in the sight of a pedagogue is of special value to the pupil and of special benefit to society" (p.67).
2. *Formalism:* "The pupil is thereby 'schooled' to confuse teaching with learning, grade advancement with education, a diploma with competence, and fluency with the ability to say something new" (p.1).
3. *Clientism:* "Once we have learned to need school, all our activities tend to take the shape of client relationships to other specialized institutions" (p.39).
4. *Consumerism:* "School initiates, too, the Myth of Unending Consumption" (p.38).
5. *Empiricism:* "Once people have the idea schooled into them that values can be produced and measured, they tend to accept all kinds of ranking" (p.40).
6. *Elitism:* "Obligatory schooling inevitably polarizes a society; it also grades the nations of the world according to an international caste system" (p.9).

The list goes on. Illich scores the contemporary position of school as idolatrous. He calls school the "sacred cow" of modern times. He compares school practices to religious rites, school functions to those historically fulfilled by the great churches: School is the New World Religion (pp.37,46).

The existence and effect of the hidden curriculum come as no surprise for, on reflection, one would suppose it to have been part of the very establishment of schooling in the first place. However novel the notion may be in the awareness of religious educators, it has long been familiar to anthropologists and sociologists accustomed to distinguishing between manifest and latent functions of cultural institutions.[18] Analyses of such hidden curricula may be found not only in arcane research reports, but also in introductory textbooks in sociology, for example.[19]

Likely as not the notion is neglected rather than unknown to us. Thus Illich and his company invite us to keep in mind at all times that the medium may be stronger than the message. They encourage us to ask ourselves if the manner in which we operate our schools might not defeat the very purposes we set for them and mock the lessons we bespeak in words. John Westerhoff asks such questions about the structure of church and school buildings, what he calls "the architecture of socialization." He suggests that we may often have failed in our educational efforts because we have neglected to keep in mind "the hidden dimension" of structures and activities.[20] Didier Piveleau's reflections as to what we do teach, and what we ought to teach, by our structures and relationships within the school have already been made available to American readers in an article on structure as sign of salvation.[21]

Organizational Constraints

Issues such as these become only more pressing when we reflect that religious instruction over the years has increasingly been placed in the context of a school system—on the assumption that schooling provides a paradigm for religious instruction, and the school system a model for religious education (cf. chaps. 1 and 3). To some, school is The System. It has taken on centralized organization, bureaucratic administration, compartmental division, and compulsory participation. These features are viewed under different angles by various critics as constraints of one kind or another.

Illich, for example, situates the school system within a vaster societal structure which itself must be completely re-formed if school is to be reformed. Holt pays particular attention to mandatory attendance and the damage it wreaks upon children's spontaneity, creativity, liberty, and dignity. Christopher Jencks criticizes centralization as one factor that kills initiative and the possibility of change. It creates a system "whose first axiom is that *everyone*, on every level, is incompetent and irresponsible"; as a result, "everyone gets along by going along with the man over him."[22] Whereas Jencks speaks of curing "organizational sclerosis," David Rogers points to "bureaucratic pathology" as the feature that makes it "almost impossible to innovate in the institution" or even to operate with it: "Nobody can make the system work if the bureaucratic structure is not radically altered."[23]

Here too religious educators can profit by the analyses made by colleagues in education generally, if we would only ponder the implications. "Education is more than a school system," writes one religious educator, Francis Rotsaert:

> Schools and, in particular, school systems, are not and never have been *essential* to the essence of Christianity or Catholicism. Education, yes—schools, no (p.332).[24]

With that he poses the question: "If there were no Catholic school system, could we then not even reach some of our children?" (p.335). Enlarging upon this query, we might reflect that even with the huge system we have now, we are not "reaching" even half of the children, not to speak of adults. Other fruitful questions may be:

> *Q1 - On what basis do we justify making religious instruction a requirement for the individual student?*

> *Q2 - To what extent is our instruction as to personal dignity and freedom restricted to verbal techniques only? What other techniques might be devised in terms of structure, procedure, activities of the school?*

> *Q3 - In what ways and to what degree does our manner of holding school contradict the matter of our religious teaching? What insight, if any, might this issue give into the observed indifference or resistance of students to religion classes, lessons, and requirements?*

In discussing structural constraints and verbal artifices in formal education we can hardly avoid mention of Paulo Freire, a sort of socio-political, even revolutionary, educator. The theme around which Freire builds his *Pedagogy of the Oppressed*[25] appears to be that human beings must become masters of their own thought and language. The traditional, or "banking-concept" form of education constitutes in his view a form of personal as well as political and social constraint. It imposes a viewpoint through imposing language, screening the "clients" off from the world as it actually is and therefore as it might actually be made to become. As one peasant told him: "The peasant is a dependent. He can't say what he wants" (p.51). Freire would rework the Cartesian formula to run something like: "If I can speak I can think; therefore I can become."

> The important thing, from the point of view of libertarian education, is for men to come to feel like masters of their thinking by discussing the thinking and views of the world explicitly or implicitly manifest in their own suggestions and those of their comrades (p.118).

Thus Freire's pedagogy includes stress on personal freedom, self-awareness, and expression. It is through language that humans acquire a sense of self and it is through social discussion that they can ultimately transform the world.

Every human individual must be able to say "the true word" of and for himself:

> ... Saying that word is not the privilege of some few men, but the right of every

man. Consequently, no one can say a true word alone—nor does he say it *for* another, in a prescriptive act which robs others of their words (p.76).

Therefore Freire puts dialogue at the center of the processes of becoming human, transforming the world, and educating the person. "Without dialogue there is no communication, and without communication there can be no true education" (p.81). Only if free and equal can individuals enter into a dialogue; if otherwise, teacher and student merely have pleasant exchanges at best. To teach another, one must listen respectfully and assist the other to express self in successive formulations approximating his and her emergent view of the world. Dialogue is founded, among other things, "upon love, humility, and faith"; where these are absent, "dialogue is a farce which inevitably degenerates into paternalistic manipulation" (p.79).

These themes we shall encounter again and again in Part Three as we have in this and the previous part. Few lines of thought on contemporary education are as powerful as Freire's and as pertinent and provocative for religious education. Some questions come immediately to mind, as follows:

Q1 - What traditional, typical, or widespread features of religious instruction as it is practiced might actually frustrate or retard self-directed and responsible development of Christians?

Q2 - To what degree are our small Christian communities, in church, home, and school able to articulate their own language and subculture?

Q3 - Does our view of the role of religious educator involve helping others to describe and witness to their own religious experience in their own terms? Whose language is most often heard in religion class? whose expressions and formulations?

Q4 - Do we, and ought we to, engage in "dialogue" with students? Are all free and equal? Is "instruction" incompatible with "dialogue"?

Finally one general effect of the dysfunctions reviewed is that school no longer enjoys the esteem it once had. Certainly school looks different to young people today than it did to us in our own youth. In a former day we could have a certain confidence in school; it provided us with pleasant interests and friends, and it promised us success in later life. Nowadays school offers tedium and often violence, separation from friends, and preparation for nothing. It was at one time a good idea to put religious instruction into the school if for no other reason than that some of the high value placed on school might rub off on religious instruction. The question to ask now is, are things still the same today? Or, on the contrary, is religious instruction now appearing in the same bad light as the school is? Are we now sharing in its disfavor just as we once shared in its prestige?

If the answer to these last is in the affirmative, we have a case for pulling religious instruction out of school context. But it would not be enough simply to take it out of school and put it elsewhere, say in the home, if it were still to smack of school and look like just another case of study, instruction, learning, and so forth. Growing numbers of young people are finding satisfaction and fulfillment in activities which not only take place far removed from school but have a form characterized by not the remotest connection with things like learning and study. Efforts to form Christians might therefore well have to follow a form of structure and activity more in accord with those forms through which the youth of today seek their growth and fulfillment. Some suggestions in response to this question receive full development in Part Three.

EDUCATIONAL ALTERNATIVES

In consideration of school malfunctions, critics were led to call for alternatives. This call was badly met and misconstrued when it was first launched some years ago, whether by reason of its sensational formulation or malicious misinterpretation. That fury and shouting now having abated we may go so far as to open their books and read what it was that they were saying.

Let us be clear from the outset that Illich for one has never called for closing down the schools.[26] The title of his book, *Deschooling Society,* is such a striking phrase that for many observers (one will not say readers) Illich is the man who wants to deschool society; that is, they think that Illich wants to shut down the schools. One then hears objections of this type:

All right, let him do it. Let him shut down the schools. And then what is he going to do with all those kids wandering around the streets looking for trouble?

Having delivered himself of this much, the objector then turns away with a guffaw, as if with this one crushing blow he had finished off the scatterbrain who hadn't in the least known what he was talking about.

Yet should we trouble ourselves with the facts we realize not only that such a close-down position is frivolous, impossible to entertain granted a modicum of intelligence and concern—we discover, further, that Illich has never maintained it and moreover takes pains to state that he does not maintain it. To deschool society is neither to board nor blow up all the schools tomorrow, but rather to disestablish the school system.

All that Illich and company have asked for is to dismantle the conception whereby the school system is looked upon as the sole purveyor of learning. They have called for the abolishment of the monopoly that the school, like Tudor soap-makers, has been granted. They have requested that alternatives to that system be recognized. They have suggested that no substantial improvement can come about without substantive institutional change, within both the scholastic and societal support-systems.

Given the role of money in human affairs, to recognize alternatives to institutional schooling would imply a cut in monies for the school system and/or an allotment or reallocation of monies to other forms and styles of education (as well, in addition, also). Illich for one is quite clear on this point. "Only by channeling dollars away from the institutions which now treat health, education, and welfare can the further impoverishment resulting from their disabling side effects be stopped" (p.4). Friedenberg and Goodman, among many others, have proposed measures similar to the G.I. Bill to enable the beneficiary to seek learning how, where, and when desired. Reimer, as also Illich, makes a number of proposals for "learning webs" or networks and exchanges as a substitute for compulsory curricula and attendance, or in Goodman's famous title, *Compulsory Mis-education*. Current literature on education lists all manner of alternatives to public schooling.[27]

Difficult as it undoubtedly is to set such proposals into widespread operation in society, some of them seem practicable enough for religious instruction in Christian communities. The practicalities of the matter also apply to churchly endeavors. Ominous thought though it be, money will have to be taken, and personnel and buildings with it, away from the school to support other educational efforts if these are claimed condign to catechetical purpose. At very least the notional aspect of alternatives can be entertained, at no great expense, for Christian schools and religious education.

Alternative education is not a question of entirely abandoning all structured effort for religious education, any more than it is a question of closing down all our schools overnight. The question is rather one of not demanding that religious education or schools do what they are not capable of doing. It is a question of reviving and devising other forms of education likely to be of some fruit in the church. It is this that the movement for alternatives ought to suggest for us. It is this that ought to lead us to examine such views very closely. Indeed, we ought thereby to be led to an examination of just what there is about formal religious education in a school that cannot in fact be matched by other forms and locales, so that we might focus attention on these very aspects, enhance them and extract from them all that we can legitimately demand.[28]

Those who do examine the deschooling position with open mind might well find themselves neither antischool nor antialternatives but ready to concede the potential of each. Perhaps they will share Rotsaert's experience of becoming a "straddler":

> Do I advocate the closing down of all Catholic schools? . . . Not at all. I am, as stated in the title, a "straddler." . . . By a "straddler" I mean one who, though presently occupied in a position intimately connected with the Catholic school system, nevertheless does not hold to the concept that it is the only position which can be held. There will and should be other choices.[29]

Support for "other choices" comes also from official church documents, Protestant and Catholic. For example, the World Council of Churches, meeting in Bergen in 1970, issued as one of its conclusions the following statement:

We therefore support radical development of alternatives to elitist schooling.[30]

In its pastoral message on education, the Conference of American Catholic Bishops is careful not to prescribe any one form for the Catholic school (TJD,123) but to remain open to new forms and structures for all of Catholic education in years ahead (100). The bishops explicitly and passionately denounce as intolerable any coercive theory or practice, however rationalized, "which results in the elimination of viable educational alternatives" (149). They call the schools to reorganization:

The search for new forms of schooling should therefore continue. Some may bear little resemblance to schooling as we have known it: the parish education center; the family education center; the school without walls, . . . The point is that one must be open to the possibility that the school of the future, including the Catholic school, will in many ways be very different from the school of the past (124).

Leading educators have enunciated similar views, as for example these "new directions" proposed for Catholic schools (the first item is "continue mindlessly"):

2. high school concentration;
3. early childhood "mothering" education;
4. critical period religious education;
5. adult religious education;
6. moral and value education;
7. urban education concentration;
8. education for human development.[31]

Protestant educators decry the emphasis on religious education as schooling;[32] lament that schools are made to constitute the chief and sometimes sole encounter that youth would have with the faith and the church[33]; propose new conceptions and new structures;[34] call for an alternative future, even eliminating all school-based religious education.[35] In considering catechesis in particular we find official statements of the church in support of such individual views.

The Catechetical Directory, for one, makes plain throughout that catechesis has for agent, for locus, and for focus the Christian community—not simply and not primarily the Christian school (e.g., GCD,21). "There is one religious education but many models"; it gives as application: "In short, we need in our nation a variety of educational models to meet the demands of a pluralistic society" (NCD,184).

The reflections in this chapter have aimed to appreciate anew the significance of criticisms made a few years ago by thinkers such as Illich.[36] As viewed here, the alternative-education movement is more revolutionary than even first appeared, for in its earlier excessive, romantic, and outrageous forms it could easily be dismissed as not worthy of serious consideration. Yet as outlined here the positions appear to hold merit and moreover to mark a point of no return. The mindless growth and reliance upon the school system cannot continue. We must refine our thinking about education, distinguish its various functions, and allot these to appropriate social institutions—only one among which shall be the school. In addition we must begin to show great imagination in designing novel educative structures responsive to the challenges of our times.

Whether or no we take such burdens upon ourselves we can recognize that this wide-ranging effort of criticism and inventiveness directed toward public education and its schools entails similar activity for religious education and Christian schools. Pointed, if leading, questions have been raised to our attention and will receive partial answers in the form of programs advanced in Part Three.

Another part of the answer may be found in the following chapter wherein we take leave of the school in order to concentrate upon religious instruction proper, whether within or without school context. Here too we find alternative approaches. One of these has been devised within the school context but explicitly applies to nonschool contexts as well. James Michael Lee states of his approach:

> The analysis of the process of teaching religion which I shall make in this volume will hold valid for religious instruction in all sites and settings—in schools, in the home, in nonschool agencies, in peer-group clubs, and so forth.[37]

The other approach has been devised explicitly in a nonschool context, in opposition to the emphasis upon the school. But as John Westerhoff explicitly states, his approach can apply within the school as well:

> Thus we have a model for Christian education which does not require a school, although it does not rule one out.[38]

What precisely are these approaches to religious instruction, or catechesis? In answer we turn the page and begin chapter 10.

CHAPTER 10

APPROACHES TO INSTRUCTION

In tracing the path taken by religious instruction from 1955 onwards, we have seen it to lead up a number of blind alleys finally to come to something of an impasse in the years 1965–1968. Worthy efforts to advance the enterprise simply ran up against a stone wall, and there seemed no way around. But among the company of religious educators at this time were a few whose sensitive skill in practice or insightful articulation of theory ought to have won for them the character of pioneer or prophet, for they did in effect show a way out of the fastness into which religious instruction had by then erringly penetrated. Yet enlightened practice ran afoul of benighted structures seemingly incapable of transformation, while perceptive theories petered out for lack of hearing or, worse, turned up in distorted and most unseemly guise of supporting ventures contrary to all original intents and purposes. In face of frustration and isolation those who had grasped the vision, many of them, abandoned the field altogether; for the remainder there was left the alternative of bemoaning the vanity of their effort or of joining the majority who would do their part to see to it that religious instruction eventually occupied its place in the front ranks of the educational rear guard.

Against this historical background the past three chapters offered an analysis of environmental influences implicating the enterprise of religious instruction and accounting by the way for the impasse it had come to. That analysis purports to have shown that the changes taking place in the model of institutional schooling, the mode of human consciousness, and the manner of religious conception conspire to validate the foresight of those "prophets" in religious instruction during 1965–1968. The time has now come to take up their example with realism, forthrightness, and courage, to provide ourselves with the means required to translate notable ideas into workable practice. What means have we at hand?

Two approaches present themselves as choice ways out of the old world and into a new and better one; as such they represent a fitting articulation to the move into Part Three, while in relation to past developments they describe choice routes covering essentially one and the same ground and issuing in one and the same progress: Up and Out & Ahead. The approaches may be characterized as "structuring" and "nurturing."* The first conceives of religious

*To select these two is avowedly to omit numbers of others. Among these are viewpoints current in Canada and England. While these are esteemed not to apply to

138

instruction as a scientific procedure, the other as a social process; the first lays stress on behavioral modification, the other on intentional socialization. In both approaches the best of our knowledge is put to use with the aim of providing practices to foster individual and community development.

We will examine these approaches mainly through the work of one author representative of each: James Michael Lee for the structuring approach, and John H. Westerhoff III for the nurturing. After some preliminaries to orient ourselves, we will examine constituents in each conception and next draw therefrom a paradigm of religious instruction; we then assess their contribution to our enterprise, and lastly offer a critique in hopes of putting ourselves in better position to apply the approach. At chapter's end we allude to a conception that could conjoin the approaches and carry them over with us to the programs of practice suggested in Part Three.

STRUCTURING RELIGIOUS BEHAVIOR

James Michael Lee's ambitious trilogy on religious instruction has for sub-title "a social science approach."* While a number of other authors may be cited in this tradition,[1] Lee would seem on all accounts its most articulate and fervent representative; hence the usefulness of examining his work in some detail.** Competent analyses have been offered by several observers.[2] We shall approach Lee's thought from a different viewpoint and with a different purpose.

Orientation

It would seem important at the outset to clear away a number of misunderstandings that might arise for one who takes up these volumes.

First, it might well be that Lee's books were written years ahead of the times. When they first appeared, religious instruction was still an activity which took

---

the American scene and are passed over just on that account, they are nonetheless of interest and merit, as noted in the Appendix.

*Published by Religious Education Press at Notre Dame, the volumes are: *The Shape of Religious Instruction* (1971), hereafter cited as *S; The Flow of Religious Instruction* (1973), hereafter, *F; The Content of Religious Instruction,* in preparation.

**This review is restricted to the two published volumes in the trilogy cited. Lee has also contributed uncounted articles and chapters to numerous publications, and has published a dozen books. Some books are: *Principles and Methods of Secondary Education* (McGraw-Hill, 1963); *Seminary Education in a Time of Change* (ed. with Louis J. Putz, Fides, 1965); *Guidance and Counseling in Schools: Foundations and Processes* (with Nathaniel J. Pallone, McGraw-Hill, 1966); *Catholic Education in the Western World* (ed., Notre Dame, 1967); *The Purpose of Catholic Schooling* (Pflaum, 1968); *Toward a Future for Religious Education* (ed. with Patrick C. Rooney, Pflaum, 1970); *The Religious Education We Need* (ed., Religious Education Press, 1977).

place largely in the context of a school. Consequently some readers may have regarded them as a sort of manual of methods for teaching religion classes in school settings. Not a few who assumed this view were taken aback by what they found. Lee himself, however, takes pains to assert that his views are not restricted to the school situation:

> Religious instruction is *fully* religious instruction whether it takes place in a formal or informal setting, whether it takes place in a school-setting, a home, a church, a restaurant or a youth club. . . . *Consequently the analysis of the process of teaching religion which I shall make in this volume will hold valid for religious instruction in all sites and settings*—in schools, in the home, in nonschool agencies, in peer-group clubs, and so forth (*F*,6,9).

As the steps to be taken in the future must be far more diversified than those we have known to now, we will have to pass beyond the school setting, without however abandoning it altogether; on this view, a rereading of Lee's work shows it to have a sense and relevance quite different than it had a few years ago. His books are more suited to the future than to the past.

Secondly, the very appearance of these books—the technical style, numerous footnotes, and numerous subheadings—seemingly marks them as texts for graduate study in the university. One might erroneously conclude either that the nonspecialist cannot hope to profit from them or that anyone might consult the books much as one would any reference work, that is, by turning to a section of interest without much regard for the flow or argument in preceding chapters. Both of these attitudes, however, would only dissipate the sense and significance which the author has worked into these books. They deserve to be read chapter by chapter, much like a novel, so that the carefully worked argument which runs throughout these pages might gradually appear and be appreciated. The nonspecialist who can overcome the initial shock left by the scholarly apparatus of the books will find himself, if he persists beyond the first pages, carried along with ease in the flow of the author's reasoning.

A last possible misunderstanding may be laid to that dualism which seems constantly to encumber human thought. Thus one is led to suppose that since Lee is opposed to such-and-such an aspect of religious instruction, he must therefore be in favor of its opposite. Then comes the surprise of discovering that he is nothing of the sort, and a new difficulty arises in trying to follow a line of thought which does not easily fit into familiar categories. For example, Lee repeatedly insists that religious instruction not be viewed as a branch of practical theology—a view which in fact he holds "responsible for a substantial diminution of the potential effectiveness of religious instruction over the centuries" (*S*,217). One might therefore think, as has often been the case, that Lee will side with those who seek to base religious instruction on methods and techniques of teaching. But behold the author reject this view as well, scoring "cookbook formulas and Mr. Fix-It prescriptions" as equally destructive an approach (*F*, p.2). The reader is thus left with the unaccustomed task of discovering, by careful study of these pages, that third viewpoint which is the author's. The reader may also be left with the discouraging impression of being faced with a field of thought at once vast, tangled, and unfamiliar. On these accounts, it may prove both helpful and important to set forth as clearly as possible Lee's view of the structure of religious instruction.

Conception

Before passing on to a synopsis of Lee's trilogy we ought to bear firmly and clearly in mind where he sets off from, how he approaches religious instruction, and finally what he means by key terms in his argument.

Lee's starting point is a belief which unfortunately enough is fully supported by everyday experience with the practice of religious instruction:

> I firmly believe that one major cause for the relative inefficacy of much of contemporary religious instruction lies in the fact that most religion teachers hold one theory of religious instruction while at the same time they utilize pedagogical practices drawn from another highly-conflicting theory (F, 27).

The author's efforts are then directed to establishing a theory which will have two features: it will be broad enough to embrace all aspects of religious instruction; and it will be pointed enough to give rise to specific practices. For the source of such an encompassing and operational theory, Lee turns to the world of social science.

The subtitle "a social science approach" gives us Lee's approach to religious instruction: "The central point of this book is that religious instruction is a mode of social science rather than a form of theology" (S, 2). On this view the theory of religious instruction he will articulate promises to have both breadth and specificity: a social science approach is not limited to teaching, nor indeed to education, for "fundamentally this approach is a world view, a way in which a person meets, interprets, and integrates, reality" (S, 3); further it posits specified practices: "The central task of religious instruction becomes the conscious and deliberative facilitation of specified behavioral goals" (S, 2).

The word "facilitation" here represents one of Lee's key concepts and expresses a sense particular to him. Facilitation is not meant to express aspects of motivation, for example, nor of transfer of knowledge from mind of teacher to mind of student.

> By facilitation I mean the process by which the significant variables in the learning situation are consciously and deliberatively structured so that desired learning outcomes tend to be induced (S, 48).

What, further, is meant by "learning" and "structuring a learning situation"? "Simply defined, learning is a change or modification in behavior" (S, 55). This change in behavior is produced by changes in the stimuli which elicit behavioral responses. To structure a learning situation is thus to manipulate stimuli in the situation, whether by adding, subtracting, rearranging or otherwise modifying them so that appropriate behavior appears in response. Learning comes about—behavior is modified or changed—in consequence of having appropriately structured the learning situation.

> *It is this structuring of the learning situation to most effectively facilitate the modification of behavior along religious lines which constitutes the very heart of the religious instruction process (S,75).*

From these specifications one concludes that "to teach" is to so arrange the stimulus-situation that the desired response occurs.

On this view, teaching bears a sharply delimited, perhaps unfamiliar, referent. We must be alert to this sense every time that we encounter the word in Lee's analysis. If we bear in mind what he refers to by facilitation and learning, we can read a phrase like "to teach religion is to facilitate religious learning" (F,43) without thinking of anything remotely like "talking to" or "transmitting knowledge," or "getting a point across"—nor yet of "proclaiming the good news." Rather, to teach is to engage in a detailed, specific, and scientific procedure distinguished by utterly clear knowledge of what it is that we are about, whether or not we are doing it, and wherein our efforts have succeeded or failed. We should be able to predict what will come of teaching,[3] and we must be able at the end to answer the question, To what observable degree did the students learn?

If the distinctive element of teaching lies in that action which so disposes circumstance that the student's behavior is changed as desired in result, we find that "the distinctive characteristic of religious instruction is that it is the purposeful and deliberative modification of learner behavior along religious lines" (F,196). What does this look like in practice?

Paradigm

Taking any number of explicitations that Lee provides so generously, we can sort out three components to a model of religious instruction.

I. Structure Environment

The first step would be to structure the environment, at two levels.

A. *Learning Environment*

Shaping the learning environment is the task of the total religious instruction enterprise. The environment is "complex and variegated," comprising institutional variables, physical and curricular variables, materials, and "the human environment'' (*S*, 74–75). These all impinge simultaneously upon the learner; all must be shaped as ''the first precondition to effective learning'' (p. 75).

B. *Instructional Situation*

Arranging the instructional situation is the task of the religion teacher. While necessary, it is not sufficient to place the learner into a shaped learning environment: ''Everything depends on how the teacher structures the elements and combinations of elements in that shaped environment to produce the learning outcome'' (*S*, 75).

II. Give Instruction

The formal definition of teaching contains fifteen discrete elements (*F*, 206) but the act of instruction reduces to five steps [*F*, 230–232].

A. *Specify Objective*

The teacher defines his/her purpose and states instructional objectives for the day in operational terms: what is it that the learner is to come out with that he/she shall, specifically, do?

B. *Design Lesson*

The teacher then arranges things in planned or programmatic form so as to most probably achieve the objective as stated: what is it that the learner must do in order to be able to learn (i.e., to do what is specified as shall be done once the lesson is over)? what is it that I must do in order that the learner be able to do that?

C. *Test Lesson*

The lesson is tried out in a small form or scale and adjustments are made accordingly.

D. *Launch Lesson*

The perfected plan is now set into full-scale operation.

E. *Assess Results*

The teacher steps back and observes and measures, precisely, the extent to which objectives that were sought have now been attained: did the learners learn (i.e., do they now do as desired)? how do I know? The teacher compares the specified objective to present performance and then makes an inference as to "learning," namely a change in behavior between the start of the lesson and its finish; one notes the extent to which the change can be attributed *to the lesson*, and not to some other factor.

III. Facilitate Christian Living

The entire procedure bears on behaviors and aims at Christian living.

A. *Behaviors*

Which behaviors are to be modified or changed?—"the learner's entire behavioral pattern," inner and overt behaviors, cognitive and affective, product and process, everyday lifestyle. "In short, the basic role of religious instruction is to facilitate that total behavioral modification which can be termed 'enhanced Christian living'" (*S*, 56–57).

B. *Laboratory*

The religion class "at its most fulsome" is a "learning laboratory for Christian living" (*S*, 81–88, 216). Lessons, as it were, are learned *and* lived there and then. Learners not only think about things but experience them at first hand; charity is learned by practicing charitable behavior rather than hearing or reading about it. Within the perimeters of the learning situation itself are fused believing and living, cognitive outcomes and lifestyle patterns; within it learners deepen the bond of fellowship and form a functioning Christian minicommunity; within it they engage in God's revelational activity and live Christian engagement.

Lee's original point of departure was the observation that religion teaching is an ineffective, muddled affair because theology and pedagogy are hopelessly confounded. He then set out to assign to social science a normative role in the procedure of instruction, and to theological science a normative role in the purpose of instruction. Yet these are finally conjoined, in the paradigm as outlined. "Christian living is at once the means toward and the goal of religious instruction and indeed of all religious education" (*S*, 10).

Contribution

Lee urges upon us the need for "a reconstruction of the entire field from basic theory right down to the most particularized pedagogical step"

(*F*, 295–296). He has taken upon himself just such a task in his trilogy, and we must allow even as the third volume awaits completion that James Michael Lee has already achieved it.

We characterize Lee's contribution as *an articulation of the field of religious instruction*. The articulation is of three major sorts. One regards the expressiveness of thought. Another regards the relationships among conceptual elements. A third regards the applications of empirical findings. All three operate between our own enterprise and that of other fields of study and endeavor; all three conspire to form a coherent view within the enterprise. Some examples for each sort of articulation will establish that the body of Lee's work rather than our generosity of spirit leads to this view of his contribution.

This trilogy by James Michael Lee may constitute the best scholarly overview available today on the field of religious instruction in America. Indeed, in scope as well as detail, it resembles encyclopedic enterprises such as the *Handbooks* of *Research on Teaching* and *Research on Religious Development*.[4] However, these handbooks are collections of chapters each written by a different authority and overall lacking a sustained and developed argument; whereas Lee alone has written the whole and throughout sustains one perspective and argues one thesis. Moreover he succeeds in doing so with astonishing erudition and no less striking clarity in a field not hitherto distinguished on either account. One reviewer was led to offer the opinion that Lee includes "a bit too much."[5] But the usefulness of these volumes derives equally from the clearness of presentation as from the vastness of information. Numbers of topics so frequently the object of confusion in the field are treated accurately and lucidly, as for example the differences between instruction and guidance, or the relations between teaching and nurturing (*S*, 8,86). In brief, this aspect of Lee's articulation consists in his having assembled more information about more topics with more precision and clarity of thought than can easily be found in any other work devoted to religious instruction.

The other sorts of articulation bear on the relations that Lee establishes among diverse trains of thought, and practice, within the field and without.

With respect first to theoretical views, Lee succeeds in arriving, by altogether different route, at the greater number of conclusions to which various other thinkers have come. This would seem to constitute by the by a valuable confirmation of these particular points.

Ecumenism. Lee is convinced that religious education "must be an ecumenical affair in the fullest sense of the word (*S*, 4). His books endeavor "to be ecumenical in approach and concern" (*F*, 3), embracing viewpoints from various Christian traditions, and seeking to embrace as well the full range of human experience. By being thus "authentically and broadly ecumenical" religious instruction can prove "faithful to its Christ, prophetic to its church, and true to its people" (*F*, 3).

Revelation. "God's self-revelation occurs in one's own personal experience"; it is "ongoing, present, flesh-and-blood experiencing" (*S*, 16,18). It is this view—so clearly that of contemporary theology—that Lee thinks "makes it more possible for contemporary theologians to accept the social-science approach to religious instruction than it was for the theologians of bygone days" (*S*, 230–231).

Nowness. Religious instruction "is rooted in the now"; it is "itself life, and not a preparation for life" (*S*, 19). Lee's insistence on this point links him to observers of contemporary world developments. He analyzes the need for "nowness as a basic axis for religious instruction" from pedagogical, psychological, philosophical, and theological vantage points (*S*, 19–23).

Person and Experience. "Present personal experience," for Lee, is "at the heart" of religious instruction, while its "focus" in his belief, "ought to be on personal fulfillment" (*S*, 17,36). Learning occurs more effectively through direct contact and active firsthand experience than through symbols and verbalizations; consequently, religion teaching must be "rooted in and saturated with" experience "as direct, as immediate, and as rich as possible" (*F*, 74).

Community. "Over and above being a society, the religion class is—or at least should be—a community" (*S*, 85–86). In the course of his beautiful and encompassing passage on "a learning laboratory for Christian living" Lee himself takes note that his view "is in congruence with the nurture-model of Christian instruction" (*S*, 86).

Propheticism. Lee sees religious instruction to have a distinctly prophetic (or reconstructionist) role to play in the church. Christians must also act *upon* the religious society that acts upon them.

> In other words, the focus of religious instruction as facilitating the socializing of the individual into the church society is incomplete without its complementary aspect of facilitating in that very individual the vision and the ability to widen the frontiers of that church society (*S*, 27).

We are therefore "to push from within the society to ever newer dimensionalities," even at times "to depart and go beyond the parameters set by the church society" (p.27).

Such a body of views, which might seem on the one hand somewhat unexpected coming from a social scientist, and on the other hand so surprisingly convergent with views of contemporary theological writers, becomes under the pen of this author the issue of a striking marriage of heretofore unfamiliar and perhaps uneasy partners. Joining such various strains of thought and disciplines of study must remain for the appreciative reader one of the most impressive achievements of Lee's work—"something that few other American Catholics would be equipped to do."[6]

It should be understood that we are noting only selected examples. Yet in addition to these theoretical coups, Lee has articulated a number of original applications of social-science research to the practice of religious instruction. Again, some selected examples may be noted.

Learning. From research on learning Lee has assembled a large body—a mass—of studies[7] under ten "key findings" and shows the significance of each for the teaching of religion (*F,* ch.6). This transfer constitutes a unique piece of work that promises to be of great value in our field. One is left completely at a loss to understand why these principles are not in widespread use already, whether as suggestive bases for new practice or as points of reference for validating and evaluating more subjective views and practices.

Interaction analysis. From research on classroom processes, Lee describes several instruments for analysing interaction, showing how usefully these might be applied to our everyday practice (*F,*251–268). One would be hard put to state in modest terms the influence that even a brief training in the use of these instruments would have on the teacher's awareness of what is actually going on in his learning group—including his own behavior. So often we might overlook the facts of the matter in favor of our phantasies, assuming that goodwill for change automatically implements change in our practices. But these instruments might well inform us otherwise, and so aid our very goodwill to realize the fruitful changes we best intend.

Taxonomical analysis. From efforts to construct taxonomies in education, Lee proposes as categories of teaching: approach, style, strategy, method, technique, and step (*F,*32–35). These appear adequate to give some conceptual order to the field and to permit clearer communication among ourselves. One might perhaps have preferred a taxonomy of goals or objectives. Perhaps these are not within our ability to specify at present, although Lee stresses the "urgent need" and "principal priority" of developing taxonomies of religious behaviors (*F,*22–24) and objectives for the religious domain (*S,*68–69).

Typological analysis. Lee identifies eight theoretical approaches to religious instruction (*F,*ch.7). This ordering will be of the greatest service to study and thought in the field, by reason both of the number of authors, Protestant and Catholic alike, he includes as well as for the aptness of his observations on theoretical adequacy and empirical support.

Teacher training. From research on teacher education, Lee has derived some elements of a program for training teachers of religion (*F,*ch.10). Such a program deserves to be pondered, tried, adjusted as needed, and set in operation. A theory of religious instruction would appear of little enough value if it is not translated into an appropriate and standardized teacher-training program. It is through the preparation of teachers that a theory can become operational and effective.

In summary of the overall strength of Lee's work, we may characterize it as an articulation of the field of religious instruction. Lee is articulate in the precision and clarity with which he presents an enormous amount of information covering numerous aspects of the field itself. In addition he is articulate in the relations he establishes among various theoretical positions within the field and between it and other fields. And he is articulate in the applications he makes to religious instruction of findings from social-science research.

Critique

Can there be limitations to such encompassing achievement? Lee himself, articulate as ever, has anticipated three objections and then moved to confute them in advance. We might review these before passing on to other difficulties that might be raised.

The first objection that Lee deals with is that he would seemingly make of religious instruction a sort of conditioning process after the manner of Pavlov or Skinner, amounting to a sort of brainwashing for a good cause. To this Lee replies by advancing a distinction between "behaviorism" and "behavioralism." He would reject the former and adopt the latter.

The essential difference—"a vast difference" in his view—appears to be as follows. Lee construes behaviorism to be a psychological, and philosophical, position that takes a "monistic, atomistic, and mechanistic" viewpoint (as well as materialistic betimes) on human nature. His own position, behavioralism, is construed as a broader, apparently milder, position concerned with the purposive study and facilitation of "behavior" explicitly recognized (*F*, 288–289). Although both positions deal with explicit "behavior," recognize it as consequent of antecedent behavior, and employ "behavior modification," Lee insists that these alone do not rank a position as synonymous with or equivalent to Watsonian behaviorism or Pavlovian conditioning (no mention of Skinnerian conditioning) (*S*, 63). In explicating this somewhat obscure point, Lee asserts that his approach would alter behavior (1) "in a beneficial manner" and (2) "according to the Christian stance toward life." On his view, these suffice to distinguish his approach from others that also happen to use behavior modification procedures: "totalitarian and enslaving manipulative activities such as brainwashing" that alter behavior "in the interest of the manipulator rather than of the learner" (p.63). By contrast, "religious instruction cannot violate any Christian principles in its work of behavioral modification" (*S*, 207–208).

If the foregoing fairly represents Lee's response, as best we can make out, we can see at a glance that it fails to meet the objection. What in fact has Lee done here? Despite elaborations, he would appear to have distinguished not two positions but two vocabularies. He then discriminates two sets of intentions and attaches to them the two sets of terms. We are given to understand that the intention behind the use of behavior modification procedures may be philosophically good (Christian, beneficial) or evil (totalitarian, enslaving). When we think of Lee's approach, we are to name it "behavioralism" and speak of the procedures in terms as facilitation, instruction, teacher, and learner. We are to think of another approach named "behaviorism" and speak of the same procedures now in terms as manipulation, brainwashing, manipulator, and slave. It is a small enough courtesy, standardly granted, to follow an author in his use of terms as he chooses. But no one is about to think that two things now exist because two names have been devised. As to the two intentions, Lee has merely given testimony to his intent when he uses the procedures: beneficial and Christian. He therefore appeals to our good faith in his good will. This is a courtesy that cannot be accorded since the objection arises in the first place out of doubt and suspicion. Malevolence as well as benevolence may motivate behavior modification procedures, and Lee knows that and he even says that.[8] The point is that differences between the allegedly distinct positions reside only in the appellations and intentions regarding one and the same body of theory and practice on behavior.

Lee's reply here is uncharacteristically opaque. That is odd since fundamental questions are at issue. Without prejudice, one wonders if Lee might perhaps be afraid of name-calling: why cannot he say, "Yes, I urge the very same procedures as are used by the evil ones, based upon the very same view of human behavior, but for a noble purpose; I am a behaviorist for Christ"—or some such? Another possibility is that we have simply not grasped his viewpoint or reply in this case. A third possible explanation is that both critique and replique are ill-founded. Certainly we realize that failure to satisfy an objection does not thereby confirm it. Perhaps the question as formulated does not arise. There are surely some crucial issues implied; perhaps the objector has yet to hit upon those which could undoubtedly call forth a trenchant confutation from our author.

Two remaining objections that Lee deals with are based in theology. These are rather much in the manner of suspicions that Lee has given way to the errors of naturalism and pelagianism. To each he replies with more or less the same argument.

As to the charge of naturalism, Lee is careful to devote an entire chapter on the theology of grace (S, ch.9), in an effort to clear himself of any malingering view which would minimize the workings of the Spirit. Here he affirms that the social-science approach not only makes for more effective religious instruction "but also is more in keeping with the style of divine action in the world" (p.258). The general approach is that to concern oneself with the human is at the same time to concern oneself with the supernatural: "Man is a supernatural being by his very nature" (p.275). That would place Lee in the camp of the immanentists, as he is fully aware.

> Reaching the God transcendent through the God immanent is ultimately the most meaningful road which the learner can take in his eternal quest to experience as much of the infinite breadth and depth of the divine as he is capable (p.281).

In refuting the charge of Pelagianism, Lee contends that such an error could only have arisen in a culture which incorrectly poses the problem of the supernatural. By formulating it anew, seeing God in the very soul of man, one dissipates the danger.

> In my own view, nature, teaching, learning, and man are not separated in any way over against God; rather, nature is nature and can only be nature because of the presence, power, and being of God in all nature. Wherever teaching and learning take place, God is intimately and existentially present in every zone of the process (*F*, 292–293).

These replies are satisfactory, especially as they partake of the train of thought highlighted in previous chapters herein on God and man. In any event objections of another sort altogether may be raised, perhaps being more in the manner of personal difficulties.

Here and there while reading these books one can experience a peculiar kind of impression that this is just all too much. A sort of hapless or sheepish feeling starts to take hold. It is something akin to what one feels when, say, confronted by a colleague's peerless understanding of some unspeakably recondite matter, one reflects upon the confusion of one's past life and privately wonders about the obtuseness which must have characterized one's own efforts to that point not to have thus also apprehended the abstruse lo these many years—or, say, when having just been charged from on high with some task, one instantly realizes the utter disproportion between seeming monumentality of the demands and demonstrable poverty of one's own supplies of strength, vigor, and resourcefulness. To take a case in point, Lee's "teaching theory" appears to embrace all the virtues of all other theories—as he himself avers: "The teaching theory, then, incorporates virtually all the favorable elements of the other 'theories' in addition to those inherent in this theory itself" (*F*, 205). But the impression gleaned, if not planted, is that Lee has captured the universe of good while spurning any and all possible evil. One would like to be able to spot just one small imperfection somewhere—a mis-stitch, a slight rent in the garment; a tilt, a fissure, a peeling in the edifice—anything at all that might bespeak fallibility and thus render a little more like the rest of us, namely human.

This pervading impression of surpassing correctness is enhanced by the finality with which judgment is pronounced upon divergent schools of thought so unfortunate as to appear in these volumes. James Michael Lee is not to be trifled with. He will call a spade a goddam shovel. Witnessing the awful lot which befalls those who construe the world otherwise than he does, one fears for self lest Lee hap upon and clear away in front.[9]

Three further difficulties remain. One is Lee's description of teaching as pure function: "Teaching is pure function—nothing more and nothing less" (*F*, 225). This pronouncement might be hard to take if one has spent a number of years in speaking of religious instruction in terms such as encounter, witness, dialogue.... As a matter of fact, if one reads carefully enough he can see that Lee's conception of the teacher is much less stark than appears (e.g., *F*, 164), even though Lee's purpose might require him to be aloofly academic and unequivocal. A second bother is Lee's assertion that social science, and hence also his approach to religious instruction, are "value-free" (*S*, 142,207). Now, no human thing is value-free. It is not true that value resides only in the person who employs the method. No form is pure of itself; every form expresses a message. Lee would be taking a big step forward if he made explicit to his readers the values which inform the social-science approach. The third point is less considerable, and regards the highly professional character which on Lee's insistence religious instruction ought to assume. This is to take a rather too simple view of things. Certainly on the level at which he works—university preparation of degree students, program coordinators, and so forth—this sort of professionalization is highly to be desired. But on another level such high caliber is not necessary. This is the level where are found all those who by reason of their baptism wish to witness to their faith. By Lee's own account such witness is an authentic teaching act. We would have the fear that by setting the sights too high we might severely restrict the greater number from reaching the mark. Perhaps in spite of his lucid distinctions between guidance and instruction Lee has not fully appreciated the immense need our generation has of guidance. People everywhere need to be awakened, to be moved, to be enflamed to action. And for this task every Christian can and ought to be an agent effecting change. Our interest might therefore turn now in these pages towards another way of conceiving the task of religious instruction, namely nurturing.

But a final word on Lee's conception. He states that it takes from six to nine months or so for the Roman Catholic mind to open itself to this different way of thinking (*S*, 3). But the richness of the return fully matches whatever effort is put into studying his view. It is altogether to be wished that many of us will study his work, become imbued with its spirit, and go on to apply this social-science approach to religious instruction.

NURTURING RELIGIOUS BEHAVIOR

Viewed as it were side by side, the structuring and nurturing approaches seem to constitute entirely different worlds of thought and practice. Whether the differences place them in unresolvable opposition, however, remains to be seen. Yet the two conceptions do differ in a number of evident respects. We might orient ourselves to the nurturing approach by a series of comparisons with the structuring approach.

Orientation

The structuring approach, as we have seen, has a certain academic flavor, springing from university and laboratory studies which proceed via hypothesis, experiment, and validation. The nurturing approach finds its basis rather in such pursuits as history and ethnological field studies.[10] It has a "communitarian" connotation much as can be seen for instance in the practice of kibbutz education, in set-ups like the "psychiatric community" and "therapeutic milieu," as in the work of Bruno Bettelheim.[11] These various sources represent elements in the concerns of those taking a nurturing approach, insofar as they go beyond generally recognized means of establishing care for the young, to arrive at models based in a conception laying far more pronounced stress on a caring achieved through and within community.

Vocabulary and aim differ as well. Though differences in wording may at times obscure what appears to be fundamental similarity of reference, the words used by writers in the two approaches are markedly dissimilar. Thus the structuring view speaks of teaching and the nurturing of discipleship; the one emphasizes planning the curriculum, the other analyzing the hidden curriculum. As to aims, one might put it that the structuring approach seeks to perfect the old while the nurturing approach hopes to make the new. According to nurturing theorists, the structuring approach enriches what is already around us, sharpens up the rougher tools already at hand, certifies and validates practices already adopted on other, less examined, grounds. Again on the other view, the structuring approach cannot work a genuine transformation; it may equally be used to service reactionary, as revolutionary, concepts. By contrast the nurturing theorists see themselves as bringing a fresh breath of air into a world shut up as it were in a stale closet. We shall later inquire into the extent to which this self-perception appears accurate, or at least unquestionable.

If nurturing theorists conceive themselves to ambition a genuine transformation in the minds of human beings, it is on account of the special relationship that these theorists see themselves to have with the world around. For the structuring approach the environment is something to be structured; one pictures an all-powerful Education Engineer arranging stimuli and situations at will. The nurturing approach is more disposed to view the environment as having come to us already structured; one pictures an Education Radiologist examining the structure for subdermal or subliminal influences and implications. Whence the stress repeatedly laid on new conditions and developments, as in Wayne Rood's *On Nurturing Christians:*[12] changes in institutions, in relations between old and young, and so forth.

A final, broad element of distinction may be drawn by examining how theorists in the two traditions conceive of socialization and education. Taking him as representative of nurturing theorists, we find that John Westerhoff*

---

*John H. Westerhoff III and Gwen Kennedy Neville, *Generation to Generation: Conversations on Religious Education and Culture* (Pilgrim, 1974), hereafter cited as *GG* (references are to chapters authored by Westerhoff). Other works by Westerhoff, not cited elsewhere in the text, include: *Learning to be Free* (United Church Press, 1973); *Will Our Children Have Faith?* (Seabury, 1976); and *Values for Tomorrow's Children* (Pilgrim, 1970).

makes of schooling a specific element of socialization; Lee makes of socialization a major focus of instruction.[13] Nurturing is often spoken of in the same vein as socialization, although strictly speaking we must regard socialization to have a more global referent. In current usage, however, nurturing is rather clearly set off from the more school-like aspects of education, and takes on aspects of terms like enculturation. For example, Westerhoff distinguishes among socialization, education, and schooling. "Schooling is a specific form of education," while "education is a distinct aspect of socialization"; the latter includes "explicit efforts (schooling and education)" and also "formal and informal implicit means."[14] Westerhoff recommends that we turn attention from religious education to religious socialization (*GG*, 42).

One clear difference between the two approaches becomes manifest over the issue of schooling. In the nurturing approach, school and school-like things are decidedly rejected—a strategy which the structuring approach in its turn just as decidedly rejects. Westerhoff decries the "concentration on religious education as schooling," as referring almost exclusively to such things as classes, curricula, programs (*GG*, 41, 42). These have unfortunately far too often been made to serve as the chief or only encounter that youth may have with Christian faith.[15] One begins to get the impression that nurturing theorists have an attitude towards school amounting to distaste. Follow for example the development of Wayne Rood's attitudes, from his book entitled *The Art of Teaching Christianity,* to *Understanding Christian Education,* to, finally, *On Nurturing Christians.*[16] In the first two books his views on methods, materials, and dimensions of religious instruction are somewhat traditional. In the last-mentioned book he delivers one of the most passionate denunciations of the school yet to appear in print. So far he goes to say that, in the new perspective which he advances, the teacher can disappear altogether:

> It is now possible to speak of "disappearing teachership." The teacher joins the learners in the attempt to turn life into a pilgrimage (p. 160).

We have come here to a point far removed from those teaching-learning situations so much a part of the structuring approach.

Here we may pause in anticipation of a serious difficulty lurking in pages ahead. What are the consequences of distinguishing between socialization and education? On the one hand, it serves to set the two theoretical positions apart, and to direct practical energies towards one set of aims, procedures, and effects as opposed to another. But on the other hand the distinction may give rise to a particular problem with our thought and practice. As J.W. Getzels[17] has pointed out, we may risk transforming a conceptual dichotomy in effect into two separate realities. The effect upon scholarly inquiry Getzels put as follows:

> The consequence until recently has been a failure to consider on the one hand the process of education in the family ("the family as educator") and on the other the

process of socialization in the school (''the school as socializer''), to say nothing about the relation between the two (p.219).

Perhaps we might take this reminder to apply as warning for our own enterprise. To be sure we must fairly represent the two positions as their representatives actually take and express them. Yet we must also be alert to what it is that is being distinguished by structuring and nurturing theorists and to be wary of transforming their different emphases into separate realities upon which two distinct instructional programs must be built. The programs to be suggested in Part Three may be regarded as essaying to incorporate the emphases of both approaches without having to assume one or the other underlying conception. There may be an encompassing way to conceive of religious instruction. It is this possibility that we try to keep in mind as we review the contrasting elements of each approach. No part of this task is easy, but the problem becomes more manageable if we maintain awareness of that possibility and its alternative.

This preliminary comparison of the two approaches is enough to mark them off as really quite distinct from one another.[18] They spring from different sources and envisage different aims; they conceive of the world, speak of it, relate to it, and work in it, differently. Can they be said to live in different worlds, to the point where twain ne'er shall meet? Certainly one can uncover here and there an element or two of agreement, similarity, fraternity—reached often as not, one is lead to suppose, by accident. Perhaps a meeting on more significant ground might be proposed. But any such invitation will have to await the examination now upon us of the ground on which the nurturing approach takes its stance and calls its own.

Conception

Students of socialization* define it as *"the process by which someone learns the ways of a given society or social group so that he can function within it"* (p.4). On this view socialization can clearly be differentiated from schooling, whereby a number of things are learned which do not purpose to help the individual function better in his and her group. A dictionary of education[19] lists for us a number of interesting processes in socialization: establishing a feeling of group unity; bringing the individual to understand, accept, and actively cooperate with the ways of the group; placing emphasis on the social rather than individual aspects of institutions and activities; and changing these latter so as to benefit society as a whole, rather than individuals or small groups.

What is ''religious socialization''? Having recognized the diversity of us-

*Frederick Elkin and Gerald Handel, *The Child and Society: The Process of Socialization* (2nd ed., Random House, 1972), hereafter, *CS*.

ages and the difficulty of defining the term with precision, Westerhoff proposes to give it this sense:

> *Religious socialization is a process consisting of lifelong formal and informal mechanisms, through which persons sustain and transmit their faith (world view, value system) and life style.* This is accomplished through participation in the life of a tradition-bearing community with its rites, rituals, myths, symbols, expressions of beliefs, attitudes and values, organizational patterns, and activities (*GG*, 41).

The spirit of the nurturing approach can be grasped by specifying a number of elements in this definition and in other statements from proponents setting forth their general conception.[20] Four constituents may be distinguished.

1. *"Matrix."* A first element forms a sort of image or symbol, a play on "matrix." Nurturing theory is appropriately impregnated with it, for its proponents view education and society partly in terms of mothering. This symbol is reasonable enough, since the number-one model of socialization is widely held to be the relationship between child and mother.

> The mother-child relationship is where socialization begins. . . . This is the infant's first relationship with another person. It is therefore his first significant encounter with what it means to be human (*CS*, 38).

But the matrix of nurturing also embraces a micro-society.

> All perceptions and behaviors are learned in a social context, through interaction of persons with family, kin, peers, and significant others, and through participation in a community or ethnic group—that is, a group bearing a more or less distinctive culture (*GG*, 39).

Just as the womb of woman is needed to make and mother the human body, so the womb of society is need to make and mother the social being. That might well serve to characterize the nurturing approach.

2. *Community.* The first precondition for adequate socialization of the child is *"an ongoing society,* the world into which he is to be socialized" (*CS*, 9). The point of the process is to elicit a response to that world: "The most basic result sought is a *motivated commitment to sustain responsive participation in society"* (p. 29). To nurturing theorists this society is of a special sort. It is not a transitory grouping established merely to achieve a given task. (A task-defined group is surely within the province of religious instruction but is emphasized rather by the structuring approach.) Nurturing theorists emphasize a natural rather than designed society, value-based rather than task-oriented. The society is established not purposively for teaching and learning but to permit and to protect a given style of living and thinking. It is a faith-community.

> If we are to be the children of God, we need a community to convert us and a community to nurture us, that we may nurture our children in the faith. We simply cannot be Christian or bring up Christian children by ourselves (*GG*, 155–156).

Members of this community are led to teach and transmit their values because these are close to their heart, in the gut and life's blood; they constitute members' world view, even their very life. Hence to partisans of this approach, teaching cannot be a matter of "pure function" nor can the learning situation be a "shaped" event contrived for the purpose of instruction. Rather, learning occurs within a natural, value-based community existing independently of the teaching act: it exists not because it is to nurture but nurtures because it is what it is, already constituted in existence for another purpose. Such a formulation is not explicit in writings of nurturing theorists, but the emphasis appears to come down to that. Moreover, the emphasis on community as vehicle for Christian socialization appears essential to the Christian concept, "growing up in Christ," as a recent analysis of Christian adulthood concluded:[21]

> The primary experiences through which the Christian grows are social experiences. One encounters Christ and the opportunity to serve him in others; the maturity of the individual is realized only in loving unity with others. The power of growth is thus finally a function of community, and, at the same time, maturity finds expression in identification with other men (p.88).

3. *Particularity*. The society that mediates socialization is particular rather than general: "A child is socialized into a particular subculture, not into a culture as a whole" (*CS*, 67). Induction of the individual into Christian society was once mediated through the small groupings that were the parishes; these have today become in many cases vast institutions largely unsuitable for personal, individual nurturing. In consequence the nurturing approach tends to lay stress upon the work of smaller groups, finding itself more at home in the local than the universal church. "Without local communities of faith, the Christian faith can never be acquired, sustained, or communicated" (*GG*, 156). This emphasis amounts to a strategy of religious instruction, not simply a side-point. It opposes the widespread view that changes in society will follow upon changes in individuals. "I find that position difficult to defend," responds Westerhoff: "People change when they unite with a community which lives and supports a style of life different from their previous style of life" (*GG*, 151).

We might note here that such a view leads naturally to concern with adults as well as with children, the two equally implicated in the community and indeed socialized through it. Thus, for example, Westerhoff views the educational process as affecting "the individual and the life cycle"; under this title come chapters not only on the faith of children but also one called "Reshaping Adults" (*GG*, ch.9). In this respect the nurturing emphasis evidently responds to the urgings of Gabriel Moran for focus on religious education community, and on adults as well as children. Induction into a particular society has certain consequences for the larger society of which it is a component. A process that on the one hand brings an individual to function appropriately within a smaller group on the other hand also "in some measure *limits his ability to function in the larger society"* (*CS*, 69). Precisely in remedy, the school system was established to articulate the child's passage from particular to general society; one popular American view of public schooling is as a "melting-pot" for diverse subcultures. In one sense, therefore, the school has for aim to *de*socialize the young out of their little societies.[22] This direction would appear to reverse the nurturing process. On that account the school might not be expected to win high esteem from nurturing theorists. Perhaps more accurately, they would dispute the claim that schooling is coextensive with education, and would deny or at least minimize certain specific functions that the school has increasingly assumed, or been directed to perform, as its own.

4. *Wholism.* A final feature of nurturing theory is what might be called its global or wholistic conception of the process of nurturing-education. Socialization theorists distinguish degrees of formality in the organization of the socializing agency, and degrees of specification in the learner's role.[23] The case of the student in school may typify formal organization with specific learner role; the child in family might represent an informal grouping wherein the learner's role is somewhat less specifically prescribed. The second would befit the nurturing view of religious instruction. In Westerhoff's *Colloquy on Christian Education,* one contributor recommends mixed groupings, including those of adults and children together, and procedures akin to the open classroom; another would confront educational rigidity by a "noncurriculum"; a third asserts that the most significant part of education "cannot be programmed."[24] Any stress on one part of education that leads to taking that part for the whole is, as construed by nurturing theorists, such an error as to excite them to provocative response, often couched in abrupt and uncompromising terms. "Education is a mystery" heads Roger Shinn's contribution to the *Colloquy,* wherein he speaks of travesty and corruption.

> I must repeat that these three aspects of Christian education, although distinguishable, are not separable. I can imagine no travesties of Christian education more corrupting than a total concentration on intellectualization, activism, or interiorization. Yet such travesties do take place (p.23).

Thus over and again we encounter the theme that education is a global, all-encompassing enterprise that above all must not be restricted to schooling nor entrusted to schools alone. Now on that insistence the nurturing view evidently affords contrast with the structuring view. Lee's terms, as we have seen, emphasize specific, operationalized, systematic, purposive, conscious, and deliberative acts—what Westerhoff calls intentionality of effort. "Deliberate systematic and sustained efforts" define, for him, religious education; religious socialization comprises "both the intentional and the unintentional" (*GG*, 41). Thus nurturing theory is far from denying intentionality.

Nurturing theorists surely intend to effectuate results, but just as surely they do not intend them to be effectuated as the structuring theorist would. Results would appear to constitute something in the way of by-products of "the formal and informal implicit means by which a people acquire and sustain their understandings and way of life" (*GG,*38). Educators are alerted to the hidden curriculum that "always unconsciously underlies all their intentional efforts" (p.41) but of which many remain unaware in their absorption with school-like affairs and their focus on religious education as schooling. As one result, "a tremendous gap has evolved between what we teach and what we are, what we preach and what we live" (p.42). It is on this account that Westerhoff recommends turning attention to religious socialization.

> Not because I believe that education is unimportant, but because I believe we need to bring the hidden dimensions of socialization into view and include them in our educational activity. With a new consciousness of how persons acquire their understanding and way of life, we can turn freshly to plan for education—that is, make the whole life of the church part of our "deliberate systematic and sustained efforts." I've named this wholistic educational process "intentional religious socialization" (*GG,*42).

At this point two reflections come to mind. The first is to note what happens when theorists of nurturing set themselves to formulating the laws of learning upon which to base their recommendations for proceeding in an informal, global, and nonintentional world of education. Despite their starting off at such conceptual variance from the structuring approach, they nonetheless wind up basing their practice on one and the same set of formal principles of learning. Those which Joseph Williamson enumerates in Westerhof's *Colloquy*[25] are hardly distinguishable from those identified by James Michael Lee. One wonders too at the labor involved in such formal specifications. A very interesting contrast is provided by an Amish community in Indiana to which some university colleagues betook themselves in order to examine the system of religious instruction. In course of conversation it occurred to the visitors to ask, "Do you have an ungraded school? Do you use an open-classroom approach? What about modular scheduling?" To these scholarly questions the Amish hosts responded with wide-eyed confusion, having not the slightest idea of what these people were talking about. Upon delivering themselves of explanation, the academics received with some surprise in turn that the good Amish were already in process of doing all in question, only without realizing it: their children were regardless of age all placed in the same class, to come and go as they might wish, and to engage in activities which varied measure for measure with their particular needs at hand. One is moved to reflect that our laborious investigations bring us often as not only to the rediscovery of practices which our departure from good sense had caused us to forget in the first place.

Thus far in our exposition of the nurturing approach, we have attempted to orient ourselves to its general viewpoint by comparing it with the structuring approach; we have noted its definitional statements and reviewed four constituent elements in its conception: "matrix," community, particularity, and wholism. We have found that on this view education, like that of the community which provides it, is encompassing rather than narrow in scope, general rather than specific in aim, lifelong rather than preparatory, informal, natural, and implicit rather than deliberative, designed, and systematic. Nurturing is, as it were, an education without the school, a schooling without the system. It is a lesson without curriculum but the curriculum of life. It is the accomplishment of the person in a manner of living.

Our last inquiry shall be, what are the agents or agencies of this process? Westerhoff makes mention of these four.

1. *Family*. "The first and most important socializing agency is the family" (*GG*,45). It is within the family that the child acquires subtle attitudes and frames of reference, as a result of the way he and she is treated, learning values, sentiments, statuses, and role expectations (pp.45–46).

2. *Peer group*. "Of almost equal importance for socialization, particularly in American culture, is the peer group" (p.46). Here the child's social horizons are expanded and new values, attitudes, roles, and understandings developed.

3. *Faith community*. "While socialization in the family and peer group is important for religious faith and life, an intentional community of faith remains the essential key to religious socialization." (p.46). Without it, "the Christian faith can never be acquired, sustained, or communicated (p.156). It is "a family of families" (p.47).

4. *Environment*. "The most extensive socializing force imaginable is the overall environment in which people live" (p.44). The environment includes the space and ecology in which people live but also an interesting specific called "the architecture of socialization," for example the interior and exterior structures of church buildings. The church building, the way it is set in the community and used by it, constitutes a "schoolhouse" offering to impressionables "a boundless hidden curriculum" (p.144).

Socialization begins with attachment to person, in the first instance involving a child's relation with the mother, then interaction with "significant others." Early on these affect the child first by their actions and then by their words, and how they say them (*CS*,31,47,49). Of great importance to note is the fact that it is through interacting with the mother above all that the child acquires the language that will be his manner of structuring the world thereafter during the entire term of life. Folk wisdom has made no mistake in naming this first language "the mother tongue." We are brought back to the image of "matrix" underlying the nurturing model. As the matrix of human womb is needed to give birth to the fleshly being, and as the matrix of community is needed to form the social being, just so is the matrix of language needed to give rise to that emerging being of mind, spirit, and intelligence who will go on therewith to construe, grasp, and master the world.

It is the family that mediates for the child the culture available in the larger society; it is the family that accords the child location with the society (*CS*,101,103). The paradox of this approach's concentration upon adults is therefore only apparent, understood as it is that children almost automatically experience the effects of adult education. Some of these effects, as has been seen, are implicit, hidden functions of socializing agencies. Function here is distinguished from purpose, as effect is from goal. "It is important to bear in mind that socialization agencies have functions that are not necessarily among their purposes" (*CS*,97). It is to these functions that nurturing theorists draw attention. On this distinction one might perhaps characterize the approach as functional, and the structuring approach as purposeful.

The nurturing approach appears to entail above all the emotional and motivational aspects of educating a human individual. If these are accomplished successfully in childhood, the youth and adult will have little need of constant recall to the values of the society, but will stand rather in need of acquiring those objective and empirical modes of knowing for which a structuring approach is better suited. On the other hand, if these first tasks are imperfectly accomplished, it will prove necessary at that later time to return to the earlier task and again work on motivational, affective, and attitudinal learnings, for which a nurturing approach is again required.[26] Put in other terms, people must then be considered, at least for the time and task, children. Thus with some piquancy we can recognize the same picture being drawn on the canvas of socialization theory as was long ago drawn intuitively by religious educators who spoke, howsoever curiously, of preevangelization and the like. Nurturing theorists specify that the child, having first been nurtured, will then experience of himself the requirement for more structured learning, the which he would have rejected without that prior socialization in affect and attitude.[27] These sorts of considerations we will meet with time and again as we proceed to wonder about the nature and aims and structure of religious education programs over the course of life (cf.Part Three).

What, then, of the school? Surely nurturing theorists are not about to discount the school as a socializing agency. Westerhoff, for example, mentions it among factors that cannot be ignored in understanding socialization (*GG*,48). Neither, reciprocally, does the school discount nurturing as a factor in education. We should generously concede that the move to "humanize" education and schooling comes not only from social critics, psychological theorists, and religious thinkers; it has come from school personnel as well. Most interestingly, even those bogies, the administrators, join in this sentiment: their official yearbook commits them for the 70s *To Nurture Humaneness*.[28]

Yet perhaps tenants of the nurturing view do not share the belief in the school's efficacy (indeed, its right) to form the young in value-oriented behavior—of the type desired by nurturing theorists, that is. When these take to criticizing the school, they are not concerned with a failure to impart knowledge or technical skills—indeed, they as well as any other would have the schools succeed in this respect; rather they appear concerned with the school's socializing function and global influence in spheres of value, emotion, and attitude apart from academics: and here they are wont to espy frequent failure relative to wide and misguided ambitioning. When these same critics then take to praising the school they do so by reason of its functional success in providing for the young yet another matrix to articulate active participation in that other, larger society. The school is seen as another "learning space for a learning community."[29]

At least part of this viewpoint is energetically shared by sociologists and supported by various researches. "The effectiveness of the school as a socializing agency depends to a major degree upon the kind of family its children come from" (*CS*, 113). In the absence of sufficiently religious family milieu, "there is no reason to expect that the school will modify values and value-oriented behavior."[30] Some social scientists maintain that expectations to the contrary show a naive and exaggerated regard for formal schooling.[31]

In their concern with school, nurturing theorists have drawn attention to one unexpected function, no doubt overlooked in planning. One of the primary effects of schooling, it so turns out, is to serve an important function of socialization thanks not to the school's deliberative instruction but through the community of peers that the school helps to call and maintain into being, time, and space. Researchers have been able to demonstrate this particular effect of schooling as it appears within the informal society or culture of students.[32]

Paradigm

For Westerhoff, the aim of religious education includes community as well as individual growth; its agent is the total parish community; its methodology is the actual everyday life of the community of faith (*GG*, 33,87,88). But how is one to go about it? From hints and indications in various chapters,* we can piece together one possible model. Its three components can be teased out of this phrase: "not only new educational programs for children but new efforts at the resocialization of adults through institutional change" (*GG*, 159).

I. Rebuild Community

The first step would be to reform structures within the faith-community. One strategy is to form a number of groupings at three levels. At each level

*From *Colloquy on Christian Education* (hereafter *CC*): ch. 9, "A Socialization Model"; ch. 10, "Celebrations". From *Generation to Generation* (*GG*): ch. 2, "What is Religious Socialization?"; ch. 4, "Religious Education for the Maypole Dancers"; ch. 6, "The Faith of Children"; ch. 9, "Reshaping Adults."

the groups develop through two stages, or they do two things: they develop an understanding of life; and they decide on ways to live out that understanding (*GG,* 119–120).

A. *Develop Consciousness*

Each group, at its own level, engages in an explicit examination of the ideal and actual place of Christianity in its respective contexts. A way of life is made conscious and is given commitment.

1. *Home group.* Parents and adults meet in homes to ponder the heritage of Christianity in their own lives as individuals and families.

2. *Parish group.* In boards, committees, and other organizations already existing in the parish, individuals gather to examine the ways in which people encounter Christianity in the parish—its buildings, rites, leadership, etc.

3. *Faith-community.* Through much the same groupings, now as members of a faith-community, people turn to examine their corporate life as it affects and is affected by the society of their local area and in the nation as a whole.

B. *Establish Structures*

Having made plain among themselves an understanding of life and having committed themselves to live it, members of all groups then turn to the issue of establishing structures that will sustain their way of life. They plan what is needed, they decide upon it, and they go do it. The home group makes adjustments and provisions in the context of the family; the parish group revises and provides in the context of the congregation; the faith-community disposes and acts in the context of the society.

II. Resocialize Adults

The next stage fairly follows of itself as adults are reshaped via the supportive, reformed structures. The education that takes place by and within the community of faith is accomplished by providing three sets of opportunities.

A. *Ritual*

"Religious education requires meaningful celebrations of faith" (*GG,* 83). Individuals become more aware and more committed to their way of understanding and living Christianity by participating in ritual action, movement, song, dance, and storytelling. These represent "a coming together of learning and worship" (*CC,* 96). New ones are devised for all significant times, events, and persons: for example, for those who decide to have children, and for those who decide not to; for those contemplating marriage, and those divorced; for inductees, and for draft-dodgers.

B. *Experience*

Experience in a social context, consistent with a people's faith and life-style, "is a key to both the formation and expression of our faith" (*GG*, 85). The community provides for two dimensions of shared experience.

1. *"Felt" experience.* This is the often-neglected "experiential religion" or shared feelings.

2. *"Examined" experience.* This is making-sense of experience, or shared thinking, understanding, and believing. In intellectual reflection and expression, group members frame a way of looking at their experience and together develop an integrated set of answers to questions arising therefrom.

C. *Action*

Here the emphasis is "on things done as well as believed and felt" (p.86). Together group members make conscious and overt plans to translate faith into action. "For every belief that we profess, an opportunity must be sought to make it real in identifiable and interpreted action" (p.87). The group not only makes the decision and then executes the action, it has to learn how to act and it must have practice in acting. "The faith community needs to be seen as a laboratory and training ground" (p.87).

III. Nurture Children in Christian Living

Religious education turns to children only after having attended to reforming the community and reshaping the adults. That is the phenomenological order of things on a socialization view—the flow of effects whatever one does—and hence the order of attention in educational effort. Taking attentive care that structures are first established to sustain a way of life, then providing explicit means whereby adults will be resocialized, religious education will have engaged the community in reforming individual and corporate life according to its explicitized understanding and commitment, and may then turn its attentive effort to bringing children into this way of living. The effort is of two sorts, proceeding simultaneously.

A. *Intentional Religious Socialization*

These are, as before, provisions in the home and parish.

B. *Specific Supportive Education*

These are "teaching-learning efforts as distinct from intentional socialization efforts" (p.120).

Westerhoff's original point of departure was the observation that religious educators have failed to provide adequate education for adult and young parishioners because of a concentration upon schooling, and a semithoughtless regard for the actual influence of nonschool and nonexplicit factors. He then set out to direct attention wholly to these latter and thereafter to include the former in a wholistic educational enterprise. In the paradigm as outlined, formal and informal socialization is latterly joined by education as specific teaching-learning. "Thus we have a model for Christian education which does not require a school, although it does not rule one out" (*CC*, 90).

Contribution

Before attempting to characterize Westerhoff's contribution in particular, we can consider some implications of the nurturing approach in general.

It would seem in the first place that formal instruction is no longer initiated by act of the educator, either necessarily or uniquely. The young person may also initiate it. Once nurtured and socialized, once at home with his/her values and motives, the youngster may come to request or seek instruction of an intentional, deliberative, systematic teaching-learning type. Wayne Rood, *On Nurturing Christians,* speaks of the learning process as beginning with an offer.

> The offer may be either to give or to receive. Either the student or the teacher may initiate teaching, and it may arise almost imperceptibly from the stream of life (p.63).

The offer of instruction reveals a "teachable moment" and on the nurturing view life can be conceived of as a series of such moments. They are of two alternating kinds, functional and purposeful. During the first, community and group and family welcome the newcomer, mother him/her, put him at ease with them and help him to discover feelings, thoughts, desires, values. During the other sort, the individual seeks and welcomes a more structured learning upon having perceived self anew, or having experienced new developments in life such as marriage, parenthood, widowhood. From the nurturing viewpoint, structured learnings such as these are inadequate if not preceded by suitable development of the former sort.

Viewed in this light, the stages of life such as described by Erik Erikson[33] take on new significance as a succession of births into new modes, roles, and functions. One need only make place in this scheme for appropriate life-events at each period. But one must make place in the scheme for events that take place irrespective of actuarial predictions: terminal illness in the twenties, parenthood in the sixties, widowhood precipitate upon wedding and honeymoon; and the like. In these cases too the nurturing approach reminds us to base religious instruction at all times on a conception of teachable moments that call now for structure, now for nurture, but never for formal instruction in the absence of a grounded experience in nurturing.

A final implication follows from the view of community as recipient of the newcomer. This in effect inverts the teacher-student ratio so customary in school. Here again we see how facile is the slide from education to school, and how arduous the ascent. Schooling typically proceeds with one teacher and thirty pupils. From this circumstance there proceeds less a socialization of pupils than an infantilization of the teacher. Nurturing does not seem subject to such turn-about, as it proceeds with one learner among some thirty "teachers": gradually expanding from mother-child to family-child to relatives-child to larger and more varied communities. It may be this aspect which in the end best characterizes, in structural terms, the nurturing approach.

Thus the nurturing approach as a whole tends to call our attention and effort to wider contexts. Westerhoff for one makes some of these explicit. We might characterize his contribution as *an extension of awareness and endeavor* in religious education. As some examples we can cite these.

1. *From particularistic to wholistic approach.* "I began by affirming the need to direct our attention first to religious socialization and then to a widened concern for a more wholistic approach to religious education, or as I've named it, 'intentional religious socialization' " (*GG*,48).

2. *From school to community locus.* "Obviously the work of catechetics can no longer be understood as primarily the responsibility of a school. Now it must become the responsibility and work of the whole Christian community" (p.30).

3. *From child to adult focus.* "I recommend we center our attention on adults" (p.118).

4. *From individual to community objective.* "I suggest we shift our attention from seeking to help individuals acquire new knowledge, abilities, and motivations to aiding in the formation of supportive communities with knowledge, abilities, and motivations" (p.151).

5. *From personal to structural renewal.* "I would hope to make the renewal and reformation of the church, its organization and structures, a primary concern of religious education" (p.120). "New social structures can enable us to change our behavior" (p.152).

6. *From parochial to ecumenical concern.* Westerhoff recommends that education become ecumenical in three senses: first, that Protestants and

Catholics work together as educators; second, that education concern the world in all its aspects; third, that education foster an understanding of diverse human faiths, not solely of Christian confessions (*CC*, 250–251).

Critique

An intriguing note of passing criticism is that in being true to each of their own selves, our two writers seem open to complementary reproaches. Quite in keeping with the procedural specificity of the structuring approach James Michael Lee is specific, though perhaps overwhelmingly so; whereas John Westerhoff, in keeping with the encompass of the nurturing approach, tends to be implicit and allusive, though perhaps elusively so. Yet of more substance than style are the objections that come to mind. Again most appropriately, Westerhoff has not been unaware of these.

One first wonders whether this way of conceiving the educational enterprise might not turn out to prove, when all is said and done, more subtly manipulative than any other. Could there be a risk of veiled indoctrination and brainwashing proceeding apace under cover of all that community warmth and welcome—and pressure? In reply, proponents can point to the fact that even in the first months of life the baby gives off, among others, signals of discomfort and stress to which most mothers would be quick to accommodate. In this way "the infant modulates, tempers, regulates, and refines the caretaker's activities."[34] On this view manipulation would not be automatic but contingent upon a mother's unconscionable maneuvers for power or insensitiveness to the needs and desires of her little one.

Moreover, it may be that the objection rests upon a view of education and family that overlooks interactional aspects and, more pointedly, appears to assume that the infant is, by nature, a passive being. That assumption has interesting "theological" implications.[35] One cannot settle arguments by appealing to assumptions. Yet it is of note that current thought has shifted to the assumption of an active, positive nature of the child: "a new tendency to see socialization as an interaction process which involves the child as an active partner, rather than as a process of unilateral manipulation of the child."[36] So far as we know now, studies flowing from this more recent conception do not support the objector's fear of manipulation of the child. In fact, reviews of current research contain sections headed "the education of parents by children" and statements that the infant "socializes others more than he is socialized."[37]

As to religious instruction, the nurturing approach has available to it the same means of self-correction against contingent deviancy as have other approaches. John Westerhoff points out that religious socialization attains adults as well as children, entails changes in the community as well as in the person, and that any lesson not evidently lived has little likelihood of being learned. It calls for "Reshaping Adults" and hence the church (*GG,* pp. 149–162).

> We cannot nurture (socialize) persons into an understanding and way of life we do not hold and exemplify. . . . The cost of that discipleship is obviously great, for it requires not only educational programs for children but new efforts at the reso- cialization of adults through institutional change. And that means a new reformation in the church (*GG,* 159).

This necessity for self-reformation thus constitutes an appreciable restraint against the dangers of excessive manipulation of the rising generation.

Further questions raise the specter of atavistic conservatism. Does the nurturing approach fit the society we see around us, or the one we would fain see arise? Does it on the other hand aim to keep things as they are, or, worse, as they once were? One wonders if this manner of envisaging the world amounts to a blissful hope of harkening the past and haltering the future. And as for the present. . . . There is some weight to these objections, for the nurturing conception bases itself essentially upon the family, which enjoys diminishing influence if not increasing danger of disappearing altogether, and it presupposes the existence of a receptive society, while all about us we see societies coming apart at the seams, fraying consensus and frantic change bringing their very stability into question.

How might nurturing find a place in our society of tiny nuclear families, unwed, divorced, deceased, and estranged parents? Only on condition that the infant's entourage be conceived in terms of "family clusters" somewhat in the manner of the great extended families out of the patriarchal past.[38] Unfortunately the necessity for such postulated changes in no wise affects the difficulty of executing them. It is hard enough to change one's conception of family and harder still to change one's family practices, let alone effectuating a structural reorganization of interfamily relations. Some families find it an undertaking merely to unite grandparents and children. Nurturing theorists, family men as they must be, are willing to share our fears

> We are aware that we need to look seriously at our families, their structures and child-rearing practices. This is a painful process. . . . I'm not sure how many of us will ever be able, on our own, to make any major changes in family structures or child-rearing (*GG,* 129).

We can ask that if the church truly wishes to be serious when it speaks of the influence of the family, it then range itself among the forwardmost in favor of new ways to structure the interfamily experience.

And as to the danger of fossilization? Objectors find it in the aim which the nurturing approach is said to have at heart, that of merely transmitting the world view of those already engaged in the societal matrix. It may be said with some measure of surety that those cultural groups studied by ethnologists which base their education on a nurturing approach are somewhat static societies yet to dazzle the observer patiently awaiting some sign of movement or rhythm of evolution in their affairs. The danger is real. Gwen Neville addresses an entire chapter to it without arriving at a resolution beyond exhorting "a dynamic equilibrium" between continuity and change, persistence and flexibility; John Westerhoff thinks the danger of petrification is greater than imagined and marshals to remedy it with a plea for propheticism (*GG*, 163– 168). Yet the church has a sacramental remedy at hand. To save the church from comatosity, we must restore to honored use the sacrament of confirmation [cf. ch.14].

PARENTING: STRUCTURE + NURTURE

No one can fail to appreciate the evident differences between the two approaches to religious instruction characterized here as structuring and nurturing. Yet here and there a certain resemblance and relation can also be detected. John Westerhoff and his fellows in the nurturing tradition lay stress on the group, on community, on lessons learned in early life and from hidden curricula. But James Michael Lee not only does not overlook these dimensions of education, he devotes special care to their analysis. Lee in turn stresses the definition of goals, specification of concepts, reinforcement of behaviors, and evaluation of learning. And references to these very same may be found in the writings of Westerhoff and company. Nevertheless when all is said and done the impression remains that between the two approaches there exists an irreducible difference in emphasis and viewpoint.

The question may be not to reduce the differences but to relate the approaches. The decision may be not to choose one over or against the other but to use the two—precisely and specifically for their differences.

Conceive the structuring approach as a model of education having for symbol the father. He sets and administers laws, principles, goals, norms; he evaluates, adjudges, and accords merit, reward, punishment.

Conceive now the nurturing approach as a model of education having for its symbol the mother. She is welcoming, reassuring, comforting; she nourishes and fosters growth.

As father and mother are singly and jointly useful and necessary to the child, so also may be the two approaches as conceived. Moreover, the child even as adult finds himself during the course of life recurring to his parents, if not in the flesh then in the figure. So too in the course of life's term, and not merely in school years, may the person now benefit from the one approach, now from the other. Thus, at one time and another for one need and another, we provide one approach and another.

This analogy can be pursued with ease. Can it be pursued with profit? The decision is the reader's to make and follow in accord with his sense of its usefulness to his particular conceptual and practical pursuits. For our purposes here it is enough to propose the analogy and now to draw from it a final term.

If we have read the two positions aright, they seem to pair off perfectly in the couple of teaching and learning. The structuring approach accents obligation to the task of teaching; the nurturing approach accents sensitivity to the process of learning. Let us keep these two thus in mind as we move on to Part Three, there to advance a view of religious instruction for the human being as he or she emerges into life, grows, and flourishes in its course. For this view we shall need the two terms as drawn—a stern fatherly obligation to the task of teaching the child (structuring religious behavior), and an exquisite motherly sensitivity to the learning processes unfolding within him or her (nurturing religious behavior). Both are the stuff humans are made of. Can we bear the two in mind and then bring them to bear in practice, we shall stand a chance of perfecting far more than a conceptual union.

PART THREE

Convening to Life: Provisions for Persons-in-Community

CHAPTER 11

CALL TO ACTION

If words could but do as they say, our titles would have brought us out of the past into a world in the making, and now we would be coming to life. These next chapters advance proposals for the resurgence of religious instruction.

To undertake the union of theory and practice is of the very essence for each one of us engaged in religious education. That is the proposal, at bottom the only one we can offer. It is to cease acting without thought and equally to cease theorizing without action. We cannot pursue endless changes in practice without tying them to a theory that we have adopted on due reflection and for due evaluation of practice; at the same time we cannot engage in endless pursuit of the best of all conceivable theories without seeking to apply in practice what we have already found out to this point. The driving force of progress lies in this swing from theory as informing practice to the return from practice as improving theory.

What does this come down to? We have it ever so clearly in mind that short-term solutions are not the very best. To be quite candid, we might well dream of a church which would be so familial, with a liturgy so expressive and a clergy so prophetic, that in practice religious instruction could be reduced to a minimum as by and large useless. But this moment has not arrived. We are therefore to undertake short-term action in response to present circumstances. We are to aim for results within the possibilities of the moment, always bearing in mind a concern to approximate the ideal just described.

And so the remarks in these next chapters will be limited in scope. The suggestions are made in strict accord with the situation we are faced with. What guidelines might be set out as together we venture on change?

TIME TO ACT

The days of our prophets have come to an end. We are done with making and listening to talk about reforming religious instruction. It is time to act. Prophetic talk must now give way to pluralistic action.

The vision of reform has been given clear enough shape by our prophets. Their voice was needed to call for a new day against the old. That voice may not always have been heeded. But we know what it says. We have the books and articles, the suggestions and recommendations. As we look over the large company of gifted and insightful thinkers whom the Spirit has been pleased to raise in our midst over the course of latter years, we may esteem ourselves not just fortunate but downright spoiled. We even have digests of their views to consult if need be.[1] But now is rather the hour for individual action. We are each one of us called to do something where we stand. Our individual accomplishments can only be on a small scale of course, but at least they will be concrete realizations here and now of grand notions we have entertained in theory.

To act otherwise would be to continue out of joint with the times as well as the theories. It would be to depend for saving grace upon some other time and place and personage, whereas it is we who are to achieve salvation by acting where and when we find ourselves individually situated. Not to take concrete risks now, each of us, would mean we are still living-barely-in a former realm of thought, where every part and parcel of society, church, and school must move as one, at the same pace and in the same direction—or not move at all. Finally, to leave it up to others would simply be to substitute their authority for that of higher-ups—a move no more responsible and mature, far more blind and dangerous.

No, the moment has come to risk individual action. We may consult with colleagues, take counsel and comfort from their discernment and example. But no one can take the risk for us. We are in place, and for the progress and well-being of the church in that place we are accountable.[2] Monika Hellwig puts it as "catechetics here and now":[3]

> We need to go to work immediately, not waiting for experts to lay out any more paths or for administrators to give us the word, to undertake our own ongoing education as religious educators in whatever groups we can form in different areas. We need courage; we need one another's help. We need to work today toward the catechetics of the future. (p.70).

From this present date onward the years must see a decline in theoretical studies and an increase in practical applications, modest yet concrete. Time to get a move on: "Where can we begin? With ourselves. . . . When can we begin? Now."[4]

In consequence we may find ourselves not quite fitting in. We must accept being "different," singular, out of place. To be sure, we are not to set out deliberately to be different, as was once the fashion among some, yet we are not to refuse to be different either. Our actions should be inspired by the needs of our particular situation; we should not cast about to see what others are up to elsewhere.

Much has been made in other chapters of pluralism as a characteristic feature of modern society. Diversity evidently does not entail anarchy or chaos. Pluralism requires not simply diversity but also *equality* and *contact* among the diverse parties.[5] Therefore, while we are to accept being different from others, we must also accept their being different from us, and maintain mutual respect and contact. This kind of pluralism is becoming to our times. Imitation, on the other hand, whether us of them or them of us, is an outmoded style of work becoming a world already long gone.

It should be noted that pluralism on a grand scale, as in international society, is hardly at issue here. Diversity of that sort is literally of little concern: it reaches us only from afar and touches us somewhat intellectually rather than personally and proximately. There is rather a level or aspect of pluralism that can threaten as well as touch us. We may for instance find ourselves having to be different from the manner of thinking and acting exhibited by those we hold nearest and dearest, or perhaps wisest. We may find ourselves in a situation where in one and the same diocese or parish we see diverse styles of church life—a pluralistic mix of liturgical rites, religious practices, and doctrinal formulations. We might see in one and the same school entirely different forms of religious education. But this diversity befits the specifics of various faith-communities. It also accords with the specifications of social science, which provides that educative structures be designed to respond to the various elements in a situation. Therefore, as parameters are found to vary, so will structures. Therefore, a variety of educative forms is needed to serve a variety of educative needs, according to age and status, past training and present experience.

On these accounts we must abandon all thought of imitation and identity in service of maintaining one and the same program everywhere for everybody. The principle to keep in view while planning new programs is rather diversity in service of specific purposes and persons.

SERVICE TO FREEDOM

We are brought to conceive of religious instruction as a service to the faithful. This view has not often enjoyed support in practice, but our practice should rightly be renewed in its light.

Allied to service are the concepts of duty and right. These have traditionally been allocated as that the faithful have the duty to receive services which clerics have the right to give them. But we have the duty to give them the type of service which they have the right to receive. Insofar as each parishioner is concerned, he or she has the right to that form of instruction which best suits him or her. That is service. In an older view, religious education was occasionally thought to be in service of the school, the parish, or vocations to priestly and religious life; parishioners and students were seen as having duties to religious education. This entire perspective must be turned upside down until religious education can be seen as a service owed the faithful, who in turn have rights to enjoy and not obligations to discharge respecting it. This shift in perspective requires changing both our attitudes and our structures of education.

Attitudinal Changes

Service is not rendered to slaves but to freemen. Orders are not tendered to freemen but to slaves. Far and away the major change to make is in our attitudes regarding compulsion as a device to educate the faithful. To make of a given act or idea a matter of obligation is the most effective means to suppress the imagination of the educator and the motivation of the student. A matter of obligation is exempted from thoughtful concern for renewal. Obligation then is to be lifted as quickly as possible from all aspects of religious education so that we may all come back to life with renewed vigor and shape.

For centuries now we have had "Sunday obligation" and "Easter duty." However these might have been honored in tradition and practice, it was a catastrophe to have made the eucharist a matter of compulsion under pain of sin and worse. With one stroke, in the thirteenth century no less, the church laid upon the sinner's back the blame for strained relations between believer and liturgy, while relieving itself of the weight of pondering alternatives to the missing link between Christian faith and its expression in ritual. Compare the case of movies and their goers. Hollywood has made efforts none so strenuous as since the days when television and other entertainments emptied the cinemas of weekly-movie fans. But if a law were to be enacted tomorrow requiring of every American to attend movies on Sunday, the moguls would have no cause for exerting any imaginative efforts at all. To complete the parallel one need only think of the emptiness of church buildings and rituals.

As applied to our enterprise the lesson is even starker. By making religion class compulsory in a system already featuring students in compulsory attendance, we contrived to douse the emergent spark of educative genius. We might otherwise have been able on the contrary to kindle it among teachers of religion. But for generations passing, students were bound over hand and foot as hapless marks for the teacher's spiritless catechisms. Is it not now high time to release and inspire everyone? Should we not aim to enhance the freedom of persons in whose service we labor? No act, and no person, can be religious if it is not free. To impose faith is to frustrate its essence. To compel attendance in religion class is to frustrate its aim, and to erase by that act the very lesson being taught. This manner of operating is nonsensical.

A second attitudinal change follows from the first. If students are to be free, then we must start to consider them as responsible human beings just as soon as it is possible to do so. Where doubt arises or circumstance constrains, it becomes an educator to hasten rather than retard the process.

Education should enjoy a notoriety in this respect quite the opposite of that shown by society, civil and religious, which has taken curious positions on youth's coming of age. In certain states a girl can marry from age fifteen, but not before eighteen can she be permitted to view in "adult" films the sexual congress she is permitted to enjoy in life. Her husband can be enrolled in an army company to wage war at age sixteen, but only in company of a parent can he be allowed to witness the awful spectacle of violence in R-rated movies. The couple have the right to children but not to alcohol; they may become responsible parents but not drinkers. Meantime both spouses must pay taxes but neither can vote. In the church, a Christian aged seven or thereabouts is held to have attained the age of reason, as it is called, and may therefore be held responsible for sin. The Catholic church continues to recommend the sacrament of penance around this age. But whereas at seven years children are old enough to sin and repent; and whereas at twelve years they are mature enough to be confirmed in the Spirit and witness to the faith; nonetheless at age fourteen through eighteen years they are not yet grown up enough to have a say about attending religion class! These contrary positions can indeed be maintained simultaneously, but not without straining the mind.

We propose as standard against which to regulate our new affairs the question: Does this undertaking as planned promise to favor the student's freedom? To answer in the affirmative, one must have already denied four other propositions, each entailing an attitude too easily accepted as being in the nature of things.

(1) "Children belong to their parents." Children belong to nobody but themselves—or if you will, only to God—and this from the day of birth. It is true that over a period of years children cannot take care of themselves in certain vital respects, and so parents move in to take charge. That circumstance gives parents duties and not rights in face of the helpless child. Parents should ambition to make the child self-sufficient as rapidly as possible, since autonomy is the state which humans must eventually attain.

(2) "Children belong to the school." No more so—indeed less so—than to parents. As Christ remarked of the sabbath, it is the school that is made for the child. At times a school will suspend or expel a child for interfering with its operation or spoiling its high standards. That is a last resort and admits of failure. If the school fails in too many cases, it is not managing to care for the children and it were better, and more normally, closed down. Religious instruction should be organized so as to ease the functioning not of the school's affairs but of the child's freedom; he or she should be able to recognize in the way its structure is set up the great Christian theme of freedom for the person.

(3) "Freedom is to be given to people when they show themselves capable of handling it." This attitude is not only an error, it is the classic stance of a colonial power in face of clamors for independence. Freedom is not learned in a vacuum but in its exercise. Freedom must therefore of necessity be granted to persons *before* they can show capacity to use it worthily.

(4) "Education without failure." To grant freedom is always to run the

risk that it will be badly used. The entire myth of creation makes just that point. Dangers may indeed be circumscribed by depriving people of their freedom but this is obviously never a means to educating them. Our efforts to educate, and especially our ventures to create new approaches, will of necessity lead to failures and mistakes, to errors and even sins. These in themselves are evils, but we know them to be necessary evils in the education of a growing human being.

Structural Changes

Whatever moves we make toward facilitating the freedom of our students are sure to arouse questions and objections and even resistance on the part of parents, colleagues, clergy, and others in our entourage, not excepting students. Our respect for diversity as well as liberty, our promotion of personalism as well as pluralism, should guide our responses to these problems, preventing us from radical and brusque moves.

Chapters to come suggest some particulars regarding structural changes. Here the general point is that when we come to innovate, each of us should already have become familiar with the principles of organizational change and development. As an example, we know of several ways to introduce change into an institution. All of these methods may work results, but some of them are inappropriate to our enterprise. Study and reflection given to the findings in this field might help us to avoid the less seemly approaches, some of which—like the authoritarian ones—are the most popular and least fruitful, and to manage our scarce resources of time, money, and personnel in an effective way.

Our particular need for knowledge in this area has been discussed.[6] Within the limits of this book we can do little more than to urge professional training and study in the management of change. Training programs ought to be made available in plenty, designed for the use of religious educators, so that their manner of introducing changes might not arouse the antagonism and divisiveness that it has too often caused in the past. Coupled with this training, the field needs a comprehensive exposition of research findings applied to our particular endeavors. We need someone to do for theories of change what James Lee has done for theories of learning. Such a project would constitute a valuable contribution to our profession.

Every religious educator must at some time or other have wondered over our supposed right to force students into religion class. From the bare fact of a student's presence in a Christian school can we presume a disposition in favor of religion teaching? As for liturgies, can we rightfully schedule them as school-wide events for everyone's participation? One need only think of how we prefect such assemblies. If these questions have not so much as come to mind, the problem is all the more serious. The solution to these issues ought in every case to favor the side of the student's freedom. As the theory of values would have it, nothing can be a value unless freely chosen. By dint of imposing religion upon students so that they may lead good Christian lives, we only end up preventing religion from becoming one of their life's values.

EVALUATION OF CHANGE

"But it's all already been tried before!" How true an objection but how pointless. Yes, so many changes have been made over recent years that one does begin to wonder if anything is still left to be tried. One of the authors himself has experimented both here and in other countries, and was associated with some American experiments from their very start—for instance, Marist House, Family Learning, and En Rapport.[7] The following suggestions likely as not show that influence. But does the fact that a program has been tried before constitute of itself a suitable basis for not trying it again, here and now? There are more solid grounds for evaluating a proposal. Some have already been described in these pages. Here we may add general considerations as to results and structures.

Contemporary Results

New ventures should not be evaluated by criteria which apply only in days mercifully past. One ill-fitting criterion requires the venture to last forever as a permanent institution. While anything worth doing may be worth doing well, something may very well be worth trying out for now with no thought of making it a permanent fixture. We need to achieve results appropriate to time and place irrespective of success in perpetuity.

As an illustration, we may look to the situation of religious orders several years ago. This was a time of "search for community." A good number of small new communities flourished within or alongside more traditional ones in the same order and even sometimes in the same house. The newer groups tried to create a new life-style, to find a new sense of community life, work, and prayer. After three or four years it turned out that half the members had left, some returning to lay life and others to traditional religious life. This provoked some unkindly observers to remark that the whole thing was only a passing fad, since the movement did not last. True enough perhaps as an observation, but as an evaluation it appears to me most unjust. The new communities were in fact a success: they had not been formed so as to overtake an institution, to swell their own ranks, or to last forever; their success was found in the here-and-now of their existence. The same with our innovations in religious instruction: it is more important that we work to achieve results for now than to labor to assure the survival of our works.

No objection therefore can be made against undertaking a program which appears promising, merely on the grounds that it had once been attempted and then discontinued. The fact that it might have been abandoned where it was originated hardly signifies that it must have been a failure. The question is to examine the results it achieved in light of the objectives set. Achieving the result of establishment status is not a sufficient criterion; when an idea becomes an institution it may well negate the results it might otherwise have reached.

In this vein, we should undertake nothing to educate the young in beliefs and practices which on all accounts no longer find a place in contemporary life. Otherwise we give the impression of counting upon the young to rush in and repair the defenses erected against the menacing onslaught of progress. Think particularly of practices like individual confession. In olden days it assuredly played a role of first importance. In that epoch of Christian spirituality, religion was a private and individual affair, and confession was a time for receiving individual spiritual counsel as well as sacramental grace. But in our day the emphasis is on community rather than individual reconciliation. That is not to say, as some aver, that we no longer have the concept of sin, of separation from God's friendship and scandal to his people. Rather the act of reconciliation is conceived more as a community affair, an admission of faults at once more global and less frequent and fussy than in times past. Yet the impression given by certain parochial practice is of the wish to prepare the young for a church that no longer exists—practices and aims of very little educational value indeed. The same may be said of efforts to inculcate views of the church and ministry which take no account, seemingly, of current trends and changes. What was your response the last time a girl in your class wondered aloud about becoming a priest?

Structural Reforms

A contemporary program of religious instruction is a means to educate youth and adults for things as they might be made to become, and not only for things as they exist at present. Therefore, we hold as not even worth the trouble of a try any proposal which advocates change only on the procedural and not the structural level.

A good question to ask ourselves before embarking on some program is: "Just what change or improvement do we want to bring about in the church?" Asking this type of question represents a considerable advance over the type usually asked: "Just what works these days with the kids in religion class?" Religious instruction ranks among the better means that the church has at her disposal for contributing to her own change and development. That is what Lee has termed its prophetic role.[8]

And what did the prophets do? They were forever pointing out contradictions between the people's faith and activity, between the words they declaimed in prayer and the message they proclaimed in the way they arranged society. These are the sorts of things that we should undertake to point out—not by preaching or teaching them in class, but by arranging the educational situation such that the very structure we give to it bespeaks the lesson.

Now what does the structure of our schools do? On this point we have already been heard sufficiently, perhaps, so will cite two up-to-date assessments. The first is by a distinguished scholar:

> Alas, too many contemporary schools preach one thing and do another, preach civic due process and deny it to their own students, preach civility and treat students as cattle, preach scholarship but tolerate teachers whose major independent scholarship is a quickie analysis of last night's T.V. episodes, preach the glories of cultural pluralism and the school as "melting pot" while conducting public education in communities which are quietly, but ruthlessly segregated by race, or class, or income, or religion. Hypocrisy ranks with unfairness as the complaint of students about their schools.[9]

The second quotes from a student:

> A student is told to stay after school for talking in study hall. He asks the proctor if it can be put back one day because he has to work that night at the family business so that his father may go to night school. He is given a blunt, "No!"
>
> Another religion teacher tells us about the true Christian man who stops and helps anyone in need rather than being on time for his appointment. Why then, does a member of a car pool who is thirty seconds late for school have to stay after school because the driver of the car decided to wait for one of the members who was late?[10]

These passages indicate the work we have to do: to undertake a reform of existing structures so as to befit them to proclaim the Christian message and to "facilitate," as James Michael Lee would have it, Christian living. Just precisely this is John Westerhoff's conclusion too, from having observed the result of our structural negligence: "A tremendous gap has evolved between what we teach and what we are, what we preach and what we live."[11]

The goal to reach is by so living in change and by so working for change that we are brought as Christian educators to celebrate what we live, that is to celebrate change.[12] We celebrate the mystery of all that dies and comes to life, with Christ's own death and resurgence.

With these as guidelines we now make our way through the practice of religious instruction over the course of life.

As a device we mark off four periods and devote a chapter to each: infancy, childhood, adolescence, adulthood. To correct for this emphasis we give titles suggesting the dynamic continuity of life and the community aspect to an individual's emergence: the start of life, for example, is given as "enhancing the family."

As a design for each chapter we follow more or less closely one over-all plan, responding to three issues.

1. *What do we know about persons?*
   We will sample theoretical and empirical studies from disciplines like psychology and sociology. We pick and choose, trying out ways useful for our own purposes to conceive of persons-in-community at this stage. We take up a PERSPECTIVE: *this is one way to view life.*

2. *What do we want to achieve for them?*
   From this perspective we look into matters of theology and philosophy, catechesis, and education. We note useful suggestions and criticize certain notions and practices. Then, a PROPOSAL: *let us aim to do this.*

3. *What action can we take?*
   We describe a PROGRAM: *this is one way it can be done.* From the experience of having tried them out, specific steps are detailed, showing structure and procedure, laying out the rationale and implications.* By and large each set of suggestions comprises three interrelated components.
   a. *Group experience:* provision for community dimension and for the "process" aspect to education.
   b. *Individual study:* provision for personal dimension and for the "content" aspect to education.
   This is the dual-structure model. It has a little more verve to it in actual operation, as when persons-in-community come to the third component:
   c. *Community celebration:* provision for liturgical dimension.

From this point on, as we all learn with relief, things will be set forth in a less spartan manner most of the time. Let us start off towards the exploratory and suggestive and inviting venture. One wishes we could start off by turning to two different pages at once to read simultaneously about adults and infants. As we turn this next page let there seep into our mind this first line on adults:

Religious instruction for adults
> *must always be considered the chief form*
> *of religious education, the end towards which*
>> *children's*
>> *programs*
>> *must*
>>> *aim.*

*In every case, the sections on programs derive from DJP; they are translated by JTD.

CHAPTER 12

ENHANCING THE FAMILY

It has become a truism to stress the importance of the early years of life for nearly every last phase of the individual's development: moral, social, and linguistic; cognitive, affective, and psycho-motor.[1] Yet today we learn that—amazing to recount—we may actually have been understating the case.

PERSPECTIVE ON INFANCY

Current thought seems to suggest that we may be justified in laying even greater stress on the early years. On the one hand, they are important for the infant; on the other, they are important because of the family. Perhaps we may fruitfully adopt a new perspective that will reveal dramatic opportunities for religious instruction.

In *The First Three Years of Life,* Burton White observes:

> The experience of those first years are more important than we had previously thought. In their simple everyday activities, infants and toddlers form the foundations of *all* later development (p.xi).[2]

To begin looking at the child's educational development when she and he is two years of age is, in his view, *"already much too late"* (p.4). But whether or not one comes to conclude that "it's all over by three,"[3] the general point wins remarkable accord from among theorists of every persuasion and discipline, including for once our own.

The structuring and nurturing approaches finally come together over this matter. Each from his own perspective, James Michael Lee and John Westerhoff[4] give virtually identical expressions:

LEE:
> Early family life and background constitute the most powerful, the most pervasive, and the most perduring variable affecting virtually all phases of an individual's learning. Early childhood experiences in the home exert an enormous and in many ways an indelible influence on the individual's entire life (p.60).

WESTERHOFF:
> Obviously a person's most significant experiences are those in her or his family, particularly in the earliest years. . . . It is a primary group whose close, intense, and enduring emotional attachments are basic to all experiences and perceptions. A person's faith, world views, beliefs, attitudes, and values cannot be understood without reference to the family and to the early years of child-rearing (p.45).

For its part, the Catechetical Directory joins in the same refrain:

> The first roots of religious and moral life appear at the very beginning of human life. In the families of believers the first months and years of life, which are of the greatest importance for a man's balance in the years to come, can already provide the right conditions for developing a Christian personality (GCD,78).

> This is the time when all the important foundations are laid for determining how the person will relate to himself, other persons and to the entire created world. These foundations ultimately affect the person's ability to relate to God as friend in the state of faith (NCD,165).

If these quotations appear repetitive, a major point shall have been scored, for this convergence of views reflects an impressive achievement on several counts.

Social historians have only just informed us that the notion of childhood itself is, astonishingly, an invention of the modern era.[5] Moreover, the scientific study of childhood was begun within living memory. Some of our grandparents—and even parents—could not have read Dr. Freud, let alone Dr. Spock;[6] neither could they have taken courses in education or in psychology, sociology and anthropology.[7] Today the research on any one aspect of child development can scarcely be accommodated within a single volume, or brain. What now shall we do with it?

The importance of the individual's early years directs the educator's attention to the family. Here again we can observe a certain unanimity among scholars. A prominent education journal recently issued a special number entitled, "The Family: First Instructor and Pervasive Guide."[8] The very same is said, from different perspectives, by Lee, who speaks of "the importance of the family as the primary agent of religious instruction"; and by Westerhoff: "The first and most important socializing agency is the family."[9] It is in considering the family that we discover one opportunity to conjoin the structuring and nurturing approaches, both in the way that we conceive of our educational effort and in the way that we practice it.

The flavor of each approach may be detected in this conception of the family as educator, set forth by Hope Leichter:

> The family is an arena in which virtually the entire range of human experience can take place. . . . And so, also, can a variety of educational encounters, ranging from systematic instruction to repetitive, moment-to-moment influences at the margins of awareness (p.175).[10]

Here we may come to realize the necessity for adopting a perspective that will embrace the range of the child's experiences and the range of educational encounters within the family. On Leichter's view, even to understand those educational efforts that are intentional, deliberate and conscious, we must be able to consider realms wherein "the explicit shades off into the indistinct, the intentional into the incidental, and the focal into the peripheral" (p.202). On this conception we may perhaps effectuate a union of structuring and nurturing emphases in order to provide religious instruction for the infant and toddler. For, the appearance of the newborn marks not only a birth in the family but also the birth of the family. As he and she grows, so does the family and, for us, the Christian community called the church.

Everyone, then, we may take it, is agreed upon the crucial role of early family experience and education.[11] Unfortunately this accord is not matched by an encompassing theoretical conception such as was just suggested. As a result our practical dispositions may not be as opportune as they might, for in focusing upon one or another aspect they perforce miss the mark on the other.

FAILING THE FAMILY

We must acknowledge the pioneering programs set afoot in recognition of the stated importance of the early years. But we must also acknowledge that they have overall failed the family, and perhaps infant and parent as well.

Early religious education has generally followed one of two emphases. It has focused either upon the infant or upon the parents, while more or less neglecting the family. Perhaps as a result, most programs appear to have entailed an unrealistic model of both family and education.

Emphases

In one emphasis, efforts may be addressed to· finding ways of talking to the infant and providing her and him with special types of experiences that might evoke various sentiments for various purposes. For instance, a sense of wonder and awe might be evoked in an effort to prepare the infant to recognize the hand of God in creation, or a sense of contentment and warmth among kin to pave the way for a concept of community. Efforts in this vein have for effect most often to maintain the religious status quo; they are hardly the occasion for renewing the church. The proof comes in when the small child is afflicted with traditional practices. It then becomes apparent that he and she has been so carefully cultured only for the ease of bringing them to church on Sunday, for the readiness to recognize the priest as sole true minister, and so on.

Redirecting attention from infant to parents can often result in exploring new forms of church life. Here the adults are helped to renew the sense they give to their existence, the expression they give to their faith; they take on responsibility and initiative for playing a personal part in the great participatory act of making the kingdom of God come. On the other hand we may ask: but who and what are left out?

The majority of cases in practice to date, it must be said, follow the first of these emphases, often under an assumed title of nurturing. They largely consist of preparing the young child's mind and emotion for ulterior didactic purposes. They also prepare for school. Thus we have here not the nurturing of a young human but the tutoring literally of a preschooler, on the analogy of some religious Head Start. Just as some people provide sensori-motor exercises in hopes that the three-year-old will enter kindergarten already in advanced states of reading readiness and cultural disposition for school, so they will exercise the preschooler in adoration, in faith, in charity so as to dispose for church. On both counts the training—for so it is—readies the child for institutional life and role as these are currently pursued.

Good might yet come from these programs if redirected. But the scale of good is negated on balance when the models that underly the programs come to weigh in.

Models

At times a certain program becomes so ambitious as to reach the point where the only families it could possibly make contact with are those happening also to fly along in the wild blue yonder. The whole thing is unreal! What must they figure family life to be?!

One parish, for example, was observed to distribute to all parents a certain booklet which, if used in conjunction with the coordinator's sessions, was to aid their home efforts to assure preinstruction in religion for their small children. At year's end the parish called in the borrowed booklets. All of them were like new. One could tell at a glance that they had hardly been used at all during that year. On the following year, accordingly, the parish announced that only those families which actually made a request would receive a booklet. Three weeks passed. One family in eight asked for a booklet. The other seven had either forgotten to put in a request or had foreseen that they would never make use of the booklet in any case. What part may have been played in all this charade by publishers spotting an easy new market is a question arising out of darkest suspicions. The book only complicated a rightfully straightforward matter and froze an activity which ought to have been as lithe as life itself.

The absurdity of some ambitioning leads to a situation where only the more leisured of Christians can afford the "parish program." In effect it is not the parish families or children that profit, but the relatively affluent and educated among them; it is not the family that participates, but the mother—and only she who has the time, learning, and inclination. Once more it is the wealthy who inherit the earth, and when church projects are involved the result is not edifying. The working mother with several children already has more than she can handle to provide for her latest child, much less to execute an educational program such as some arm-chair theorists devise for her pains. Now it is she who without doubt stands most in need of parish support. She already feels uneasy and guilty for not being able to attend the nightly meetings, read children's fables aloud to her young ones of an evening, study the most recently acclaimed Guide to Child Care during the course of a quiet afternoon—do in sum as "good" parents do. Another model must be found.

The literature on the subject of religious education for the very young child shows a rather subtle traditional bias. Materials give off the curious notion that the infant emerges from the womb into an absolutely perfect entourage replicating the Holy Family. How does Daddy work, they ask; tirelessly and cheerfully, they reply. How does Mommy look after me? Constantly and lovingly. And why do they expend all this devoted care? Evidently because they love me as God must love me. Such a picture rather hastily paints over the vast numbers of infants born to unwed mothers, growing up with divorced parents, or relatives, hardly or never enjoying the father who works nights, suffers illness, beds apart, or rests in a grave. But that will remain the limited perspective so long as the focus is on children. By concentrating on them we forget the state of adults who surround them in reality. We must start off from the realities of family life however it is actually lived today. To be sure, we do not take this tack in blind acceptance of how things are but in faith that in this reality we are sure to find the face of salvation.

The model of education is no more real. Talk of an artificial family falls easily into plans for artificial education. It is artifice to act in a manner that one would never act were there no children about. It is artifice to perform religious acts contrary to or in the absence of belief, whether children are there or not. In no way does that mean that the arrival of a baby in one's home cannot constitute an occasion for improving conduct. All homes may do so, Christian or not. On the birth of his child, a father may for example be led to reflect on his heavy drinking and decide to cut down thereafter. But that decision is made for his own benefit and not for the child's future edification; the proof is that he continues to moderate his intake even when the youngster is later away from home on visit, vacation, or school. So too with Christian practices. A birth may be a moment of reflection for the parents as to, for example, the small place they accord to prayer in their life. They might then decide to pray before the evening meal and one night a week to kneel beside their baby's crib in thanksgiving over this new life they have been enabled to bring forth. The critical question is this: do they continue to give thanks for food and life when the child is absent? On this criterion one may judge whether their action is a practice aimed essentially at educating the child or expressing their faith.

One of the curiosities to be observed is that by causing so much attention to be paid to children, the church makes adults vaguely infantile; whereas by a reverse concentration of concern it might contribute to helping children grow more adult. Thus we should be more careful about our terms, emphasizing a person-centered rather than child-centered approach, structuring a natural rather than artificial environment, home over school, family over textbook nurturing. What then should parents do to give their toddler a good start in Christian education? To this question the response is: Nothing—absolutely nothing.

If it ever comes down to a situation where some program or other has to be offered for parents of small children, it should consist in counsel and exhortation to abstain from any effort or to make fewer rather than more in the area of moral and religious education. Sad to say, the source of many an error here is found in blind goodwill. When parents wish to begin formal religious training in the home, even in these our enlightened times, undue zeal can often lead to errors of two kinds. One error is to engage the tyke in endeavors of intellect. When he asks the very first question in a manner or matter unaccountably neglected in the otherwise splendid preparation the coordinator has given the parent, the parent falls back on explanations from his or her own youth. Hence it occurs to religion teachers amid their progressive lessons to hear from the mouth of babes opinions uttered about the fires of hell, the wings of angels, the whale of Jonah, the garden of Eden, and other colorful formulations of that old-time religion passed on to yet another generation by well-meaning elders. The other sort of error is to confound faith and morality just as was done in palmier times. Children are nicely enough told to do and not to do because God always knows when you lie, broken dishes and untouched zucchini cause the Virgin to weep and Asians to starve, a guardian angel hovers ever by even in most secret accesses, and the Infant of Prague is pleased when little children retire punctually and submissively. This unholy confusion is difficult to redress even in later life. The parish ought to turn parents away from formally instructing their tots in the faith.

Comparison is invited to another subject intimately bound up with family life and religious education. After years of bumbling about we know now full well that there is no such thing as truly good sexual education given in classroom groups according to an age-graded, cumulative, structured curriculum of information. The best information in this matter is not even absorbed if the child is not ready to hear it, and received distortions are notoriously resistant to correction. The best sex education is that which the individual child can of her and himself receive at home when sufficiently stimulated by the sight of parents' affectionate, even erotic, love-life clearly marked with a component of carnality, and when sufficient stimulation is joined by equal ease of asking questions as they arise. In this circumstance parents know no necessity for training in biology, anatomy, or medicine. The child can consult the specialists or the culture when his questions later so require. Enough for the moment that parents give him what he/she needs, and that is more than a piece of sexual information: it is a sense of sexuality, the sense which his parents have of it in truth and life; once the child grasps that sense he/she is well situated to act upon it of his/her own, whether to accept, modify, or reject it. The same goes for religious as for sexual education. It is by naturally experiencing the way parents live religion that the child will be brought to ask questions about it. By these questions will he and she introduce themselves with ease into yet another dimension of sensing life's experience, the religious dimension.

What should we aim to do at this level if, paradoxically, no formal instruction is to be given? Here is a proposal.

Religious educators ought to be of service by so disposing the structure of families as they are that they can benefit from the teaching moment presented by a birth in the family and so become a nurturing community capable both of raising the newborn in the faith and of raising up a newborn church.

And now, what are some steps to take by which this can be done?

FOSTERING THE FAMILY

We can make an approach to putting all of this into practice by considering two levels at which attempts can be made. At one level we have education *of* the family; at another, education *in* the family.

Family Education

Religious education in community context seems to be a subject of widespread preoccupation in recent years.[12] We will examine two exemplars of the family education movement. One springs from Protestant sources, the other from Catholic. The first is called Family Cluster and is associated with the name of Margaret Sawin; the second is Family Program, associated with Maureen Gallagher.[13]

Margaret Sawin appears to have been the first to give formulation to a family model of religious education, set forth in a 1971 report on her innovative Family Cluster approach.[14] The starting point is the recognized plight of the family today, in response to which no educational or social agency has arisen in particular. The family is not being treated as a unit. Yet one cannot respond to a family situation by dealing piecemeal with its several members in specialized groups; rather, all members must be dealt with at one time as one unit. Thus Sawin's Family Cluster includes divorcées, unwed mothers, grandparents—all the folks who in fact compose the basic social unit they think of as their family.

Maureen Gallagher's model is founded on somewhat the same basis but goes on to articulate a rather more specified program of religious instruction proper. The ambition behind Family Program is to constitute a total, self-sufficient program applying the recommendations of the episcopal document,

To Teach as Jesus Did. With this difference in emphasis, the two programs differ to some extent in organization.

Both programs call for a series of family gatherings lasting two hours each, held preferably in some church-related building. The Cluster rarely comprises more than six or eight families, while the Program handles up to eighteen. Family gatherings seem more existential in the Cluster, more formal in the Program: Program families spend the whole of the two hours in religious instruction of one form or another; those in Cluster spend one hour on instruction and the other on a friendly discussion and buffet. In the Family Program participants divide up into age-groups for the first hour of instruction. All groups study the same theme but at their own level: parents and senior high students, junior high, grade-schoolers, primary and preschoolers. Then the family re-forms during the second hour for an exchange over what was done in the first. In the Family Cluster grouping is by family, with one or several constituting a group; evidently either the intrafamily or interfamily group may be made up of dyads, triads, and so forth, ages and sexes combined. One trouble with both programs is the need for trained group leaders: five for the age-groups in one, up to eight for the family-groups in the other. Both models provide for some formation of group leaders. Psychological training and group-dynamics skill is stressed by Sawin; pedagogical training and subject-matter mastery is recommended by Gallagher.

It is safe to predict that these programs are going to enjoy great success in years to come. This is a matter for satisfaction as they certainly represent original ventures, rich in promise. Yet care must be taken lest they fall subject to the law of institutional entropy and be co-opted by other existing models of education. To this effect four suggestions are made.

In first place, neither of these family-programs must be hoped to constitute the one and only model, at least not for the moment.

Some may hail themselves as "Total Education" programs but this claim has to remain theoretical. Not all the faithful have arrived at the same level of readiness in this regard; some adapt better to more traditional formats. These needs as well must be respected and provided for in practice. Our tendency to simplify everything has resulted in monotonous errors over the decades as we put all of our efforts now into one solution, then into another. Piecemeal solutions may not work but neither will wholesale ones. The needs of our day, it must be repeated, cannot be satisfied save by pluralistic solutions. Hence, although the Family Cluster is attractive indeed it is not the last word: it befits neither all stages of a given family, nor all families at a given stage (e.g., those with preschool children).

In second place, the family "cluster" must not remain a semantical entity solely, with each family in the parish hall neatly tucked into its own corner.

Families must be clustered lest we betray the very insight of the cluster model. The family is as much endangered by its own temptation to turn in upon itself as by the world's sollicitation to break up and out. The family may well be a mini-society but it must not be transformed into a mini-ghetto. Sawin's program wisely provides that the nuclear family join a cluster of nuclei. One objective is precisely to enlarge its perspective, as when parents can better see their own children through contacting other children, while children perceive likewise among other parents. Sawin further insists that the decision to join a cluster must be taken by the family as a whole, for the whole to enter as participant; moreover the decision must entail a commitment to participate without exception in all sessions of the entire series. Hence the importance of every member's deciding—not just the parents, who would then drag the children along; not just the mother, who would then entice her husband to come along. Unmarried friends and relatives can also be invited to take a rightful place in the cluster on any of several grounds: their own needs and contributions in the program, their own association with the family outside of it. Expanding the nuclear family is important to this program both by reason of the tiny nucleus some families form and by the fact that infants beyond the age of fifteen months are nurtured not only by parents but also by "significant others"—especially adults in close association and acceptance. There is no necessary implication of dividing the family, some members going off to join another cluster, but it is necessary to enlarge the one single family for the meetings and activities by grouping three or four families together, for example.

A third suggestion is in reaction to Sawin's observation that certain clusters have lasted for three years and more. No such time-span should be regarded as necessarily model. Let the cluster endure, dissolve, or reorganize as needed; let the family join, remain, and quit when needed.

The cluster need not continue from year to year, and in the majority of cases perhaps it ought not to. If a given family would wish to join a certain cluster for one year every few years or so, that's fine. Man tires of all things, even the best, and a separation might betimes prove the only way to appreciate what one has. Group experience is not for everyone at all times. The family makes a considerable investment of affect when it joins a cluster; Sawin comments that some are too threatened even to join up, for fear of disclosure. A family might be less reticent if it were made clear that the experience would never last any more than x amount of time or meetings spread over a year's term—no matter what happens, even if everyone would want to continue on. We have to learn not only how to form and work in a group but also how to take leave of one. At times it takes as much courage and foresight to cut short an enterprise as it did to undertake it in the first place. In the case where everyone votes to continue the cluster it should change composition for the new term; members should be added, dropped, or replaced so that group life will enjoy a new dynamic. This is not a whimsical recommendation, nor should the educator give in to members' whims even if appearing desirable. To keep the group as is would only constitute one more subtle maneuver to escape the process of constant adaptation. This choice saves from change but condemns to petrification.

The last suggestion is to warn against encroachment by school-like mentality. Above all we should discourage dividing everyone according to age or level of schooling.

What is the point to a program of family education which first gathers the family together, next splits it up to educate members separately, and then puts everyone back together again to have coffee and go home? No program does quite this of course, but some do instruct family members in the same subject in different groups. And why? People of all ages, including little people, are perfectly capable of following with interest and participating with enjoyment in a given subject or activity. Not all the people, including this time big people, catch or comprehend every last one of the goings-on, and certainly no one's grasp is precisely like another's in any case. Yet in every case people can share in the excitement and happiness of their group.

Two experiences may be cited in this respect. The first occurred in a workshop on free graphic expression for people of all ages. In the same room at the same time were toddlers and teen-agers, adults and elders, all participating, no one languishing, each one getting something for himself out of the experience. A second case occurred in an adult discussion group. As baby-sitters were lacking, the children were welcome to stay if they wished, or to come and go as they would. Three-year-olds sat in mother's lap and boys of seven sat about. Impressed by adult seriousness, the boys spoke up occasionally, asking questions and seeming to have a deep understanding of what was being said. At one point the conversation turned to adultery and divorce. Several parents wondered if the children ought not leave the room but everyone stayed and the subject was discussed. At the end parents were surprised by the maturity of the boys' reactions to what they had understood. These two examples show what can happen when an activity or subject emerges from the group. But when either is prepared and imposed upon the group by an external agency, then the group must be divided up by age. One would go so far as to say that age-grouping is the surest sign that the topic at hand does not reflect the concerns of the family or group as such.

Education in the Family

The family cluster model is a first step in one right direction. But we must go further, to a model of family education within the family.

Religious instruction, we have maintained, must be considered as a service. In consequence we must reverse the customary flow of our enterprise. We are used to having people come to us as to the church. It is important that from time to time the church also go to them. Religious instruction of small children should take place at home. This has greater importance than one might at first suspect.

For one thing, the majority of folk do not talk in the same way as they do at home when they are assembled in parish hall or church. Imagine the response to the simple question, "Who is God?" posed to fifty people in a hall and to ten in a home. The same person will accordingly give two different answers: the one more or less fluent and firm in formulation, doctrinally proper and correct; the other more searching and hesitant, appropriate to personal experience of life. Which one do we aim to attain?

For another thing, we ourselves are sure not to talk the same way either. Religious educators have the gift of making people talk about things which do not interest them in the slightest, while leaving them to believe that what does interest them could not possibly make for a worthy topic of religious discourse. This talent is ours because here again we deem religious instruction a duty on their part rather than a service on ours. So as not to see them drift into waters that might unexpectedly turn into rapids, endangering our institution or competence, we take pains to steer them into carefully charted and becalmed waters. We invite them to "discuss" subjects which we have prepared. Whatever they might say, they will never have the last word, for we will seal it with a "that's good/interesting/not quite right/true. . . ." This act is easy enough in front of a classroom or lecture hall, but it is much tougher to pull off sitting around someone else's living room, not to mention over the drinks.

One objection comes easily to mind and must be cleared away lest it distract our attention further. If these gatherings are to be as small as recommended, how will leaders be found for them at a time when the number of priests available is already so drastically dwindling? Where will the priest find the time for all these home gatherings? This objection fails to hold, on three counts.

First, it rests on the false presupposition that the model is to be applied at one and the same time everywhere throughout the parish. The true premise has rather been that a program should be provided only for those whose growth it would facilitate. There would in consequence be few groups operating at any given time, and these can later go on to help other groups which arise.

A second false presupposition is that only a priest can do this sort of work. Of course laypeople and religious can do it too.

Finally, it is not a fact that prolonged training is needed to lead such a group. Under pain of panicking all involved, the expertise needed should be proportioned to the work done. Now, the group does the group work. About the only work for the leader is to set up a situation in which the group can do its work. Members must be able to freely speak their mind, encounter other views, and support each other in the process. It is the members who speak, encounter, and support—not the leader. Most of the situation is already assured by factors of circumstance of gathering, origin of group, and purposes of members. About the only expertise necessary to accomplish the rest is for the leader to be a good listener. This expertise is not unduly difficult to acquire or practice, though it is far subtler than imagined. The parish can train people in a good method of leading by listening. That is assuredly feasible without having to turn out a dozen finished therapists, teachers, or negotiators.

What the model comes down to, then, is a small home gathering during a limited period fixed in advance on matters chosen by the group itself.

Such a group is the necessary intermediary between the parish and the individual or family. Here the Directory has cleared the way wide open in speaking of home liturgies. The point could not be better put:

> The home liturgy possesses unique possibilities for catechesis and spiritual growth. Because the setting is, in a sense, so human, it witnesses to the Lord's love for all that is human. If the parish church expresses the transcendence of the Lord, the home speaks of his nearness. The home liturgy also reflects the simplicity and intimacy of the first eucharist, the supper of the Lord.
>
> Small group liturgies often involve participants who are well known to one another. Such liturgies are often the occasion for a deep experience of the union with God and unity among men that the eucharist symbolizes and effects. They provide a type of experience of liturgical prayer that overflows into subsequent celebrations of the liturgy even in large groups and into the family and daily lives of the participants. The wider communities of parish and universal church will benefit from the growth in faith and love that occurs in small group liturgies (NCD,193).

Nothing more is being proposed than to take this rich and hopeful text seriously.

Celebration of New Life

The basis for a new church is to be found in the new life appearing in the midst of family and family cluster. This new life calls for celebration. To share this persuasion let us consider the gifts of life and meaning.

In this epoch of contraception and abortion the birth of a child takes on new significance. More than ever before will the simple fact of being born and welcomed into the human midst come to constitute an event of grace. No longer undergone and suffered but come to willingly and gladly, childbirth surpasses the self in a baptism of humanity, signifying through the intermediary of life-accepting womb the wish of all humankind to go on holding, forwarding, and sharing life.

At that moment every parent may lay claim to the presence and service of a church attentive to life. Not only to baptize the child, the church will also come to hear the parents. For in taking the decision to have a child the parents mean to say something. They have a message to tell and the church owes to listen.

Parenting accrues status as a value when accepted by choice freely made among others deliberated. To give birth to new life is at the same time to give new meaning to existence. The parent wishes to accord not only life to a child but via the child a special sense to life, differing from the meaning he and/or she would otherwise confer upon existence. If childbirth is a moment inciting the gift of life and meaning, Christianity is a movement directed to both. The Christian is a being who gives to events, particularly to life and death, not a different content but a different sense: that which Christ has accorded them. The liturgy is that act whereby Christians associate to their existence the meaning which Christ gave to his own. Thereby have we part in his salvation and cause for our celebration. But as matters currently stand the liturgy can barely accomplish this process. It too must be brought to new life.

To celebrate requires at least three things. First it requires to live—that is, to act, experience, suffer, and love. Next it requires to live in awareness—that is, to think back over experience, assessing, judging, evaluating; for people of our day, experience accedes to formal consciousness through process of dialogue moreso than solitary reading or reflection. Lastly, this life-awareness must emerge from privacy of self and enter the public domain; there the community authenticates, plumbs, and confirms individual experience. At that moment the individual human being is carried quite beyond himself in an intensity of joy, openness, and willingness unknown to him in daily life. And it is here that liturgy proper comes in to give to this communally conscious'd experienced a special sense, the sense which for Christians is this: love wins out over death.

When and where better can this sense be grasped than in the midst of a loving family at home with a new infant life acclaimed by the whole family community? It is the privilege of every home welcoming a new arrival to constitute a little church by gathering the family cluster in an at-home liturgical celebration. It can be a strictly domestic affair: any and all gestures and materials can be used for celebration, and anyone at all can lead—father and mother or priest. To the hosts of course belongs the right to decide the rhythm, length, and form of their home celebration. The religious educator is present only in service to family wishes. He is there to ease their way to finding new sense in their life as a family, to help them gather, exchange, and celebrate with others in an access of new awareness, identity, and life.

What then of the religious instruction of infants and toddlers? They are not overlooked in this model. One of their own is the very occasion to celebrate; the whole family cluster is there to enjoy; and in the midst of all the activity the little ones are excitedly joined. Given the particulars of occasion, people, activity, purpose and result, these little children are already getting the very best religious instruction they possibly could. They have no need of anything else.

CHAPTER 13

AWAKENING TO THE WORLD

"I believe that churches should consider eliminating entirely their present Sunday church school classes for children from grades one through six." Having thus swept religious education out of the school, John Westerhoff[1] goes on to propose alternatives: "Let's begin to think about church education during these formative years by thinking of other learning possibilities." As we have seen, other possibilities are indeed being developed; family education programs, for example, are based on the view that the elementary-school child will find the best sort of religious instruction not within the classroom, but by participating in multi-family encounters over the year.

PERSPECTIVE ON CHILDHOOD

By and large, no one should have anything against giving religious instruction to a child. Then again, neither should one oppose withholding it altogether from a child. It matters little whether a child receives formal religious instruction or whether she/he does not.

The matter is not one of entire indifference either to us or to the child, but the difference does not turn on formal instruction. If during earlier years as infant and toddler the child has been able to experience moments of true religious life within the family entourage, then formal instruction will provide explicit terms for lessons already experienced implicitly. If the child has not had such experiences, then instruction will provide practically no meaning at all to him and her; at best they will have to memorize formulas out of goodwill but without good sense or much avail. Yet in either event the child is still going to have to pass through an additional experience, altogether new and different and even contrary. On that admittedly cryptic assertion shall be based these suggestions as to religious instruction at this age of life.

Religious instruction should not take place during the whole of childhood years, nor during the whole of any one year. The child runs the risk of being saturated with words about Christianity before he has had any experience of it independently. Three or four programs during the course of elementary schooling is more than enough. One program could prepare for First Communion, another for the rite of reconciliation, and the last one or two perhaps as a sort of overview of Christianity generally—who Christians are, what they

196

believe, how they developed over history. Evidently these aims do not require the effort of eight years long, nor indeed a year-long effort in any case. There is no need for year-round instruction. One can take the time needed to achieve the objectives and then leave off once these have been accomplished. Something like ten to fifteen sessions during the year should be time enough, instead of the 100 to 150 that the school now schedules.

Interesting consequences would follow. For one thing this restriction would lift restrictions. It would put the CCD very much at ease, lightening its burdens of programming, financing, recruiting, and status-seeking. The CCD is already accustomed at any rate to one session per week over a short year—November to February in some localities. For another thing the restriction would not impose a burden. It can easily be honored without scandal or expense, administrative complexity or professional preparation. For yet another thing it would represent a refreshing departure in educational reform. Progress is habitually conceived by the schools as an additive phenomenon: it adds rather than subtracts, supplements rather than supplants. Once a measure has shown importance, it is introduced in addition to everything already there; some program is laid on, some course squeezed in. The proposal here is merely to take something out. This operation is not traditional in the school, so it will require shifting a number of attitudes and approaches. Here we come to the most interesting consequences.

Catholic schools have long proceeded on the tortuous reasoning that since children take English every year they must take religion every year, and accordingly all year, five periods per week, fifty minutes per period. One tries to imagine what would happen if tomorrow our legislators were to mandate two hours of English instruction per day from grades K through twelve. We do not ordinarily leave a strong impression of having thoughtfully pondered the question as to just what is necessary for religious instruction on its own terms. The question has rather been one of envious and jealous ambitioning to do as the academic departments do: just as well that is, which in practice means just as badly.

In consideration for parity of time in the schedule, religious educators have paid an odd price. They now find themselves in the problematic situation of divising ways to fill up the time. Hence they must set year-by-year objectives for year-long instruction, irrespective of the necessity or suitability of either. Their aim, should it need specifying, is not to find time to fulfill the objectives of religious instruction but to find objectives to fulfill the time. These marvels of the mind transport us with Alice in Wonderland. But more imaginative yet would be the vision of religious instruction proceeding at its own pace towards its own objectives. These might not require—and indeed probably forbid— putting thirty or so children into a schoolroom for thirty or so minutes day after day, week after week, year after year.

These precautions observed leave a free body of children and teachers as well as time. Imagine what could be done then! This country does not lack for innovative ideas. It has long had programs associating parents, for a limited number of sessions, in the work of preparing the child for First Communion; ideally, these programs could be opened to the family-cluster dimension. The introduction of a new rite of reconciliation provides an ideal opportunity to leave our school manners behind in favor of devising a special program for the occasion, addressed to everyone at once—children and parents, adolescents and adults all grouped together regardless of age. This sacramental ritual will entail novel wording, various surroundings, uncustomary occasions, different atmosphere, and unfamiliar symbolism; in all of these respects adults as well as children remain untutored and in need of special instruction. Here is a splendid chance to profit by suspending regular instruction in the school and committing the teachers to programs focused much more on family, community, adult.

But, returning now to the facts of the matter, we see them come down to this: we can implement everything said and still not have solved the central issue, which remains the aim and form of religious instruction in childhood. We can reduce or eliminate school instruction; we can redirect the teachers and we can cluster the families. Notwithstanding all of that, children will yet need, as earlier noted, to pass through an altogether new and different experience that is in addition and opposition to whatever they may have enjoyed to that point. In effect, children come to us having been formed in a certain style of faith, one so structured as to prove incapable of being transformed without crisis into a faith of superior quality. From this circumstance we take our aim: it is essential that children lose their faith.

LOSS OF FAITH

The proposal for this stage may be formulated as follows:

The objective of religious education at a certain moment of childhood is to cause the loss of childhood faith, and to clear away its structural traces in favor of permitting another style of faith to emerge.

Our educative activity ought accordingly to consist in setting up situations which will promote the attaining of this objective.

To encourage efforts along this line, we plan to describe an experimental approach which can serve as one model and possibly stimulate thinking about alternatives. But as the proposal itself might appear paradoxical, we might first set out the reasoning behind it, falling back for the moment on a somewhat systematic approach.

A suite of propositions leads to the conclusion that our aim must be to help children lose their faith. The argument these propositions form is developed by means of evolving certain distinctions between faith and religion, in the main. Each distinction entails in turn a certain implication for religious instruction; these cumulate successively to compel the conclusion as specified. We set out the series under two headings: dimensions, and stages, of faith.

Dimensions

In our discussions of religious education, especially in settling upon instructional objectives, we are perhaps not always as attentive as we might be to the difference between faith and religion. To be sure, the two present much the same face and depend on one another; nevertheless they also show a number of crucial differences. If well understood, these facets would help us gain a better hold on the situation before us and devise a more effective plan for action.

In the first place, faith represents an essential element of religion, but only one of its elements. Religion is constituted overall of five dimensions.[2] These are the:

1. *ideological*—that is, religious belief;
2. *ritualistic*—religious practice;
3. *intellectual*—knowledge;
4. *consequential*—effects;
5. *experiential*—feeling.

Faith corresponds to the experiential element. We can appreciate at a glance that this last is private to the individual, whereas the others are rather more public and social. Faith, that is, is personal. Prominent students of religious experience characterize it above all in terms of personal intimacy and psychology:

- "a sense of reality, a feeling of objective presence, a perception of what we may call 'something there' " (James);
- an "experience of the numinous" telling us that we are related to another dimension of Being (Otto);
- a "peak-experience" within which the true self is found or "actualized" (Maslow).[3]

The first implication to note is that religious instruction must aim to disentangle faith from religion and situate its efforts on the level of strictly personal experience, viz., the child's faith.

In the second place we can conceive of faith as a personal process of integrating the other elements of religion. Faith is thus a dynamic.

While religion ordinarily serves to engender and sustain faith, faith in turn gives life and animation to religion. Without faith, religion would be dead. But it can happen that something of religion nonetheless outlast the disappearance of faith, just as the desiccated shell remains after the snail has departed.

On display in museums are the remains of many a religion deserted by faith of adherents. If like remains are not to be on display in churches and schools as well, Christian instruction must aim to keep faith alive, rather than to make religion survive.

Faith is further to be distinguished from belief, somewhat as the valuing process differs from values. Faith is a personal manner of adhering and understanding, whereas belief is an expression—individual, but most of all collective—of the result attained. If faith is dynamic, belief is static. Faith aims and lets fly at the target that belief constitutes; belief therefore describes limit to the trajectory of faith's flight, and in the end stops it dead: belief attained, faith loses movement and energy. Religious instruction must therefore disengage faith from childhood belief to restore its dynamic and redirect its movement towards more lofty targets.

A fourth point follows from these preliminaries. The nurturing approach, pursued in and through *community,* introduces the child more easily to religion than to faith. If members of the nurturing community are themselves imbued with a lively adult faith, freely given support and not constraint by the community, then the child will be able to feel something of this personal faith in his and her own experience. Otherwise the nurturing approach, as we have pointed out, might curtail individual experience by reason of markedly conservative if not actually repressive measures endeavoring to favor socio-religious concerns. Hence there is place for religious instruction to remove the child at one time and another from the protective atmosphere of nurturing which could prevent the emergence of personal faith experience.

In last place, faith is continually menaced by idolatry, that is, by degredation into religious ritual and routine. Two regressive aspects may appear. The faithful cease to engage in permanent quest and settle rather for permanent possession. They then immobilize faith by casting it in images which Old Testament custom called graven—false gods or idols. Static images are incompatible with faith. They are in fact marked by the feature of standing over and apart from the observer: exterior, objective, given. The image is found standing before me, not within me; I am presented with it ready-made, I have no part in making it come to be nor in its coming to be there. Faith, on the contrary, is enlivened by symbols. A symbol's features are interior, subjective, emergent. It exists in dynamic relation to me, a part of me and my active participation; it is symbol on my account: I make it be symbol, I symbolize. While images are mute and immutable, as it were, cast in bronze or frozen in stone, symbols are free to vary in connotation, if not in appearance, according to the movement and evolution of the cognizer's experience. The last implication of this series is therefore the duty of religious instruction to destroy the idols and dismantle the images of childhood religion, so that nothing false may remain to hold onto and search may continue in directions open to enactive symbolic processes of faith.

Stages

To this point we have spoken of a series of acts which in effect wrest faith from various embedding contexts freeing it to achieve a higher or more becoming level. The general phenomenon is called conversion. Whereas nurturing sustains the child's faith with religion, conversion separates it from religion and restores it to a place in personal experience. In order to keep pace with the overall evolution of a person's intimate experience, this wresting effect of conversion has to recur at several points over life's course. At each of these times the style of conversion will differ accordingly. Hence we are entitled to speak of styles or stages of faith.

We are already accustomed to thinking in these terms on an historical or phylogenetic scale. Roughly speaking we talk of faith's development from the Old to the New Testament, as peoples first converted to the Convenant, then to Christianity, with numerous stages inbetween and hopefully thereafter. When God wrested Abraham out of Ur, religion underwent a transformation astonishing for the times, yet it nonetheless rested upon the vision of a world ruled by the law of the talon, whereby one paid back in kind to neighbor. Different, and superior, was the vision Jesus brought out of the desert, wresting humans from tooth and nail and giving them the golden rule, whereby one paid back in kindness to neighbor.

As for stages of faith on an ontogenetic scale, we are on as sure ground but less certain of how to describe it.[4] "The life of faith passes through various stages, just as does man's existence while he is attaining maturity" (GCD,30). We may anticipate the matter by underscoring two fundamental presuppositions to stages of faith, howsoever distinguished.

The important reminder for Christian instruction is that conversion entails crisis. That is, the passage from one stage of faith to the next is eventful. But it is no more inevitable than it is uneventful. The passage cannot be made without some kind of upheaval, and it will not come about of its own natural occurrence.

We are not wont to think of conversion as a placid and common affair. Indeed we think it tumultuous and exceptional. But once someone establishes a scheme showing let us say, three or five developmental stages of faith, we tend to assume that its upper reaches must surely be attained in the course of development, the person more or less steadily and progressively passing from one stage to the next. And yet this very passage is what we refer to as conversion. Religious psychologists like Jung would affirm that the religious pilgrimage takes place in persons who undergo in every level of their being a struggle of meaning and value.[5] Now the struggle can surely be minimum in the case of passing from one stage to another in cognitive development, for example, when at issue is solely the transformation of logico-mathematical structures (as in Piaget's scheme).[6] But in speaking of faith we are dealing with a process of integrating all manner of religious phenomena: imitation of parents, for example, introjection of their attitudes and identification with their desires. To transform this mighty structure is a critical adventure which some people can not accomplish without high drama, and which others have never even dared to venture upon in all their forty or fifty years since child-hood.

The passage from stage to stage does not occur naturally of itself, nor does a higher stage simply emerge by subsuming its predecessor. Faced with the rudimentary level of student faith, teachers intuitively seek to "purify" it. But their attempts are misguided, for the objective is a dream. Faith at whatever stage represents an integrated structural whole. The studies of innumerable psychologists, sociologists, and anthropologists have amply demonstrated that to pass from one structuration to another, one must first destructure and then restructure. In Lewinian terms, the first step is: "unfreeze the preceding structure."[7] There then exists a state of astructuration, producing what the mystics termed the dark night, the void, the abandonment of soul. The third step is accomplished under stimulus of the person's interior development, necessitating a reorganization on a different model. This restructuration must then be solidified or "refrozen."

This process is well attested in the stories of dramatic conversions, though these represent only one of several styles. We recall for instance the interior agony experienced by Newman as he witnessed his Anglican faith being dismantled piece by piece. No more striking example can be given than that of the great mystics, of course. The successive passages which they record in their spiritual ascension are clearly marked by alternating steps of destruction, emptiness, and re-formation. Their experience is there to show that the passage to higher forms of faith is lived through precisely as a loss of faith. We too, and our young students, must go through this kind of experience in the course of life, each at his and her own level.

The point of the whole process is of course to attain maturity of faith. Adult faith may be seen to involve five major developmental tasks.[8] These are the progressive:

1. awakening of an historical consciousness;
2. development of symbolic functioning;
3. transformation of a magical and superstitious mentality;
4. reduction of moralism;
5. purification of belief beyond parental images.

The first task listed calls for special attention on our part since we have seen that contemporary human consciousness appears to be changing precisely in the opposite direction. The emphasis is on the present moment; the difficulty is to conceive of duration. Now even without special intervention the growing human being is certain to attain awareness of time eventually. But the process could take an excessively long time: we meet examples of young adults in whom the process is completed only in the thirtieth year of life.

Awareness of time dimensions has great significance for conceiving of faith, as we articulated chapters back. Now we see that adult faith is thought to require awareness of time and awareness of symbol. These have in fact been shown to be related: time and myth.[9] The power to construe symbol is linked to the perception of time. Next we must add a third term.

As time is related to symbol, symbol in turn is related to group. We can perceive a link between the emergence of symbol and the independent culture of a group. We had had previous acquaintance with the phenomenon of in-group symbolism, but we had imperfect understanding of it: jargon, fads, lingo, and jive in military, scientific, collegiate, and gang life. We had also known of the great epics and myths developed by various national groups over the misty past. The fact of the matter is that any group at all will develop its own level of symbol, myth, epic, providing that the group enjoys some measure of autonomous existence. We can now appreciate that symbol is sewn into development by two historical threads: the story of the individual, and the story of his/her group. Both must be engaged in any effort that aims to advance faith from childhood to adult stages.

Just such an effort now arises for consideration. With the aim of helping children to lose their faith, we should provide them with concrete steps to symbolic awareness.

ACCESS TO AWARENESS

For those who might esteem the nurturing or family-cluster approaches sufficient for the whole course of childhood, the following experimental approach raises some critical questions. Chief among these is the hypothesis on which this approach is based, namely, that it is incumbent upon the religious educator to provide children with an opportunity for losing their faith—with the evident rider attached that it is not within his power to be sure of providing the children with a more mature replacement for the lost faith.

The following approach, inspired by an idea of Jean-Pierre Bagot, has been tried with some success in France among children aged ten to eleven years, under the overall direction of Claude Lagarde.[10] The French character of the example certainly impairs its utility for American application in some respects, yet the usefulness of the program remains undiminished as an example of what might be done and as a spur to thinking about alternative approaches. Moreover, something of this flavor may already be seen here and there around the country, and perhaps it therefore represents a model which many American educators have been seeking to construct in one way or another. In any event, some such attempt must be made among children nearing the end of elementary school. To report but one attempt, then, we first specify its purpose, next its structure and procedures, and then its progression over the course of a year's trial. In last place we discuss some implications of the approach.

Purpose

The purpose is to awaken the child's powers in three domains:

(1) *Symbolic activity*, learning to internalize and thus relativize the image, in order to make it correspond to personal experience;

(2) *Time-dimension*, learning to step out of the present and conceive past and future—that we are influenced but not imprisoned by the past and have some hold but not entire control over the future; at the same time learning to accept the past without regret or remorse and to await the future without illusion or fear;

(3) *Communal life*, learning to discern differences and similarities among peers, to assume responsible part in maintaining community, to legislate and cooperate in its affairs, and so forth.

The symbolic domain deserves further comment. It is easy enough to work with since, as we have seen, every group of some intensity will develop its own symbols in any event. The problem comes in when specific symbolism is aimed at, in this case that of the bible and Christian tradition. Ronald Goldman saw the problem and Wayne Rood proposed an interesting solution in alternating between symbolic presentation and reenactment.[11] In general the difficulty has been met in one of two fashions: either by explaining to the child the nature and operation of symbolism; or by abandoning the child to his own manner of construing symbols as images. The first approach completely fails to work, while the second fails altogether to try. Children around the age of eleven can be introduced to symbolism on a most natural, personal, and hence deep level. They surely stand in need of some introduction.

When children are not in a position of having to recite their catechism they can utter the most amazing things about God and religion. We tape-recorded some of their talk. God was a sort of zombie made up of gas or ectoplasm rather finely spread so as not to take up room in our bodies where he lives. One child concluded that for God to be present in all our hearts, each one of us must have only a teeny piece of him. Another explained how Jonah escaped from the whale's belly because whales swim in cold water and so have a bad cough! A third child accepted that Jesus did indeed rise from the dead and that naturally priests and religious will too, but in his own particular case he figured it would probably take a miracle. We played these tapes to convince parents of the need for our type of approach. Their brightest children made an unexpectedly poor showing. Parents had no idea of how literally their youngsters took imagery and applied it without regard for its symbolic meaning.

Faith remained shallow, flat, two-dimensional; we proposed that an under-standing of symbolic levels would deepen and round it. On what procedure?

Structure

The program's overall structure consists in a series of three distinct group events in which all the children participate. Each event is structured in such a way that it is both different and separate from the others; no explicit connection or communication is made between one event and the other two. The individual child is left the equal possibilities of making a connection or not, and of realizing the lessons from any one or the whole of the series. Any trace of functioning in a teaching mode must be resolutely avoided; the program ought to function only via the manner in which the group experiences are structured overall. We shall call the three structures *Society, Theater,* and *Dialogue.*

Society is the first and most continuous structure. The children gather in groups of twelve to fifteen for a session of one-and-a-half hours once a week between October and April. The meetings must be given the tag of religion class, except that no religious instruction whatsoever shall be given. The teacher's role follows the well-established practices of group dynamics; he or she is there as a facilitator of group processes, helping the participants to discover their wishes and to take means to implement them. In addition the leader has the explicit role of proposing two ways of recording highlights in the life of *Society*—a photographic album and a written chronicle. The first consists of pictures, or even a movie, of various phases of life in *Society* during the course of the first semester, recording the diverse activities which the group might choose to engage in during religion class—whether tossing frisbees or drawing a map of the Holy Land. The second record is a chronicle of events in *Society,* made by keeping up four journals during the semester: *minutes* of every session, to be taken by members in turn, detailing all that is said and done—fights, projects, discussions, laughter, set-backs; *laws,* rules and regulations which the group adopts bit by bit in order to organize the chaos and get together on doing something constructive; *thoughts* which happen to strike one member or another; *art,* poetry, and song they may have produced or experienced and wish to share. That is as far as the leader will go to explain this activity.

Theater is the second event to be experienced, and occurs once a month. In this set-up groups of about seventy-five children at a time assemble to view a splendid slide-show on the Old or New Testament, or on the life of the church. It is essential that *Theater* not consist of the same groups as *Society,* nor that the same leaders appear in either. At no time should the way the two events are structured suggest to pupils that we want them to make a connection between the two. Moreover, if they do in fact fail to make the connection we remain indifferent to the matter; we make no effort for them to "catch up." As it happens, the connection proved to be made in every case over three years' trial with this approach. If it were not to have been made, we would neither have tried to provoke it; we would have consulted the model and either improved it or abandoned it.

Dialogue is an event which follows directly upon *Theater*. It comprises two twenty-minute sessions of various groups made up of five or six children each time, together with some mothers. The mothers receive no special training but the caution never to teach or to correct notions which appear in the discussion. Their assignment is to help the children to talk about the pictures which they have just seen. The goal is solely to permit the children, by talking about what they have experienced, to get a better hold on it and to make it their very own, in whichever form it may have come to them. It is through dialogical exchange that experience arises to consciousness.

The overall structure is pictured in Figure 1. The scheme shows one student being exposed to two concomitant structures, drawn with no channel or link-up passing back and forth. In the measure that a connection is actually made, we are entitled to say that it is the work of the person involved, who has thereby opened himself to a new dimension of individual experience and faith. For how many students, one might ask, is this in fact the case? How do things unfold or develop over the course of a year's experience in this structure?

Progression

Life in *Society* is excessively trying for children and leader. Evidently it is impossible to arrive at group cohesion in any speedy way. Quarrels and factions arise, and the children are surprised that their teacher does not step in to quell them. A number of children are scandalized by the sight of their teacher's passivity—not intervening when needed, not speaking of God and Christ, not starting class off with a prayer. Their childhood religion is shaken, and they complain to their parents. (Needless to say, parents must have been apprised from the start as to the nature of the program, lest they too be surprised and scandalized, and go on to limit the program's effectiveness by unduly supporting the perplexed child; parents must be asked to examine themselves beforehand to see if they can in this event support the program instead.) Certain children will come up and request leave to quit the program, and it is granted them straightaway. This unexpected turn of events most often brings the child to come back anyway. Most try to salvage the situation by throwing themselves into some "religious" activity which in past years has proven to bring them the most security with the least personal involvement: they will trace a map of Palestine, they will bake a few communion wafers, they will make a colored banner; in general, they will execute whatever little

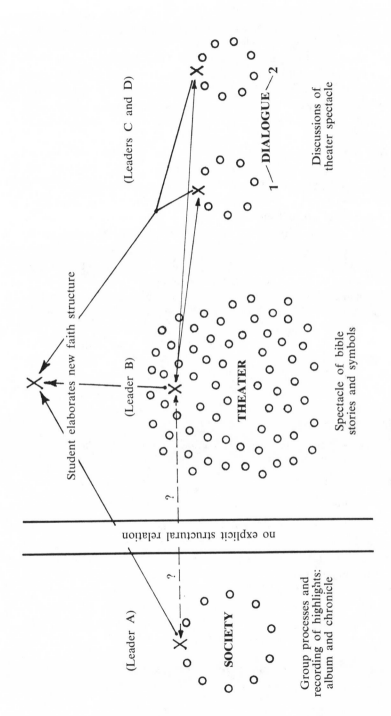

Figure 1. Structure of Program for Late-Elementary-Schoolchildren

niceties have been pleasantly passed off on them as religious instruction these days, for fear of really getting into it.

During all of this first time, the leader is alert to soothe the genuinely overanxious or tearful child. But otherwise he and she is careful to refrain from impinging upon the group's obligation to regulate its affairs on its own. It is the group that confronts and must resolve a number of problems in *Society:* to decide on religious activities in common, to devise rules for living together, and so on.

The first signs that things are easing up begin to appear in *Society* around Christmas, when the leader suggests that for semester's end the group might like to look over the photos and accounts of their early sessions together. This activity seems to rip away a veil covering the past. The children accede to a vision of time as it affects them and their group. They begin to recall earlier hopes, tantrums, proceedings; they see themselves dressing, looking, and behaving as of old. For certain children the experience represents the first time in the group that they form an awareness of their own personal history as intertwined with the collective history of the group.

But it is another one or two months still later before the effects of the whole scheme begin to show. During their discussions in *Society,* certain pupils begin to make allusions to what they had done in *Theater* or *Dialogue.* We remind ourselves that these children are now saying these things in an altogether different setting, to a different set of classmates and teacher. From this point it is not long before they will start, again with no suggestion on the part of any adult, to use outright biblical symbolism while speaking of their very own experiences. The effect is striking indeed. Imagine a ten-year-old throwing off this remark:

> Sometimes, you know, when we're all here like this everybody talking, I get the feeling like the Jews in the desert.

Or hear another one saying:

> What I wanna be when I grow up, it's like the Promised Land.

Even here the leader does not interpose himself in any way. He knows that this kind of language is just starting to show through on the part of a few children only. The rest hardly even notice it. Such talk will recede and then pop up now and again amid all the activity.

Eventually the time comes when all the children can be seen to pick up on symbolic references and allusions to what everyone at one time or another will have experienced in *Theater* or *Dialogue.* At that moment, near the end of the year, the leader makes two moves aimed at solidifying or "refreezing" the new structure.

First the leader has the children reflect on the meaning of their group chronicle, still being kept all during the course of the year. Looking through their various records, the pupils have no trouble grasping that any group with a history behind it, whether *them,* the *Jews,* or the *church,* feels the need to document its past in a "chronicle." They see that a group of people finds it necessary to make laws to ease life in society. They see how a group treasures its collections of poetry, literature, and song, which had kept them going during the rough times they had together.

The second move profits from the new excitement the children show in handling symbols. The leader now has them write their own history, or some part of contemporary history, in symbolic terms. Elsewhere of course the reverse is customary: biblical symbolism is first explained, and necks are thereafter craned to spot it in some corner or other of the pupil's experience. Our procedure is to invite the child to write down something of his life, making use of whatever symbols he likes from the bible. An illustration might be helpful.

In one of our groups, the children started talking about a miracle which had just taken place at Lourdes; the daily papers were making the most of the story. It so happened that these children were just at the point where their talk in *Society* quite frequently contained symbols seen in *Theater.* The leader suggested that they get together to tell the story of this modern-day miracle, not as the papers had it, but as if they were ancient scribes from Testament days. That was the extent of the leader's comment. Here is the account rendered:

A certain woman was gravely ill. The physicians had all proclaimed that she could not be healed. Wherefore she decided to betake herself to Lourdes. There the priest told her to pray and fast for all of three days and then to lower herself into the pool for seven days in a row. The woman went off to pray and fast. And on the third day behold she saw an angel in her prayer who said to her, "When thou seest a serpent come out of the water, have confidence thou shalt be cured." Thereupon she went and bathed seven times, and on the last day she saw beside her a serpent of great size rise out of the waters. She was sore afraid—but remembering the angel's word, she got out of the pool, and found she was healed.

One can be unsure about the evocation of scripture here,[12] but certain of one thing: these children at age twelve had discovered the nature of duration and distance, and had learned that the symbol is a remarkable instrument for expressing thought. The symbol permits communication over time and distance, not because of what is it in itself, but because it is linked to a history of events and themes which recur in the life of humanity generally and every one of its kind.

One reason for describing this alternative, experimental, and admittedly particular program is to show two important propositions.

First, an approach in practice must be founded upon theory. The importance of this point has been illustrated by citing the case of J.T. Dillon, who brought to bear a body of theoretical views operationalized in practice (cf. ch.4). Similarly with our program here. At its origin lies all that previous chapters have discursed upon—conceptions of time, community, dialogue, cognitive processes, structure, and so forth.

Secondly, the approaches available at present—nurturing, structuring, family education—are not suitable or at least not sufficient for the particular tasks at this stage. Following upon the child's earlier welcome into the community, his training and nurture, this program represents the experience of weaning, which permits the ingestion of solids and promotes the growth of strength. The child is weaned from childhood faith and community to permit his access to a more mature way of believing and belonging. In effect the program is also equivalent to the process of initiation into adulthood which ethnologists have described for various cultures.

We know of course that all change and progress entails risk. In this case certain pupils seem to have had a presentiment of the coming break and, fearing perhaps the more responsible awareness sure to ensue, they betook themselves to the safety of traditional practices; moreover, they pronounced the year a waste of time and betook themselves to other schools, where things would be done "right," or at least not so wrongly. We ought not to take umbrage or offense at this reaction: nobody has to grow up as we say, take the path we indicate, thrive in the atmosphere we provide. At least there was opportunity to choose; some merely profited by choosing to say no, as others said yes. And of what worth is a yes, if no cannot possibly be said? Are we to be more successful religious educators than Jesus Christ himself?

What is more bothersome than our failures is the misguidance we seem to get from the Catechetical Directory. Progressive enough in its recommendations for the religious education of preschoolers, this document threatens initiative at the elementary level. Here its psychology is general, its methodology ambiguous. But its position is clear and firm against reducing the amount of instruction over the span of childhood, or omitting "formal schooling and the work of a teacher" (NCD, 225). This point alone is able to arrest ventures such as are suggested in this chapter. But still more recommendations step on the brakes and our toes as well, such as the goal of instilling in children a basic grounding in doctrine (225).

Strangely enough, the Directory also makes a number of good points along the way: to combine children from public and parochial schools; to lift the child out of the unique influence of the family circle; and to invent proposals beyond what is listed as suggestive and not exhaustive of reasonable programs (182,184,225). Now these remarks would seem to support aspects of this venture and others.

Finally, one would hope that religious educators can succeed in threading their way through the maze of the Directory's section on liturgy for children (194). These paragraphs constitute a classic example of starting with praiseworthy premises and mysteriously nudging them to deplorable conclusions. It is true to think that liturgy is beneficial only when there exists a group, a communal experience, and reflection on that experience. It is false to think that a mass of grade-school children assembled for Mass constitutes either a group, an experience, or a liturgy. The individuals barely recognize one another on sight, rarely meet up with one another otherwise, strictly divide by age, sex, and level for classes, and hardly reflect on their communal experience, if indeed they do have such. On these grounds alone the situation defies liturgical sense. But there they are, in the hundreds, gathered for an hour's "celebration" in which they are to "take active part," says the Directory, by decorating the altar, carrying up the offerings. . . . Such liturgies are a parody. Better to omit them altogether. In our program the children themselves requested a liturgy, one only, during Holy Week. One can be sure that this one eucharist for the dozen or so who had worked and lived together for five eventful months exceeded in value any ten Masses vibrant with artifice and "adapted" to the children's level. It is a crime to treat children as childishly as we sometimes do.

These reflections are deliberately made in order to show how important it is to consult the Directory and to surpass it. The Directory is there to foster our labors, not to frustrate them. Programs and ideas, whether in print or in practice, we must always consider as subject to improvement.

CHAPTER 14

VENTURING ON CHANGE

Of religious instruction in adolescence we may say that at no other age do we make greater efforts, face more troubles, and enjoy less return. What sort of people are these youngsters? What sort of religious instruction makes sense for them?

PERSPECTIVE ON ADOLESCENCE

Today's adolescents represent the very first generation to be wholly defined by the changing consciousness of man as described in chapter 7. The cohorts of ages thirteen to eighteen are entering upon, and constituting, an entire new world. Those with which we have been faced to now had all been formed in another mental universe; today's adolescents no doubt cannot think in terms and processes proper to that older world. How then do they proceed?

Thanks to our previous reflections, we are in a position to divine something of the new mentality of adolescents. We may suppose, for one, that their mode of thought is rather more global than linear. This feature likely permits them to get a serious hold on new knowledge without passing through a programmed or serialized presentation of subject-matter. We may also suppose that we will find a better hearing among them if we speak in terms of authenticity more than fidelity, of immediacy more than deferral; and, further, if our terms seem to promise happiness rather than work, and fulfillment of the person rather than satisfaction on the job over the long run. The dignity and rewards of labor we can scarcely conceive to stir their interest. They are more likely to rally around respect for humanity and the worth of all things most conducive to its spirit, as for instance community, conviviality, communication. Finally we might not expect them to be assured so much as confused. The world is diverse and shifting, proffering at best a problematic context in which to situate and identify both self and others. Classic styles of pinpointing the world and orienting one's self in it are suitable enough in a cartographic frame of reference, but what is to be done in a kaleidoscopic frame? Confusion, we may think, is the great problem of adolescents today.[1]

On the specific matter of religion, the age of adolescence has been thought a time for religious conversion. It is at this age for instance that the call was once widely heard to the religious and priestly life.

212

Nowadays observers suggest that conversion in adolescence is more likely to develop around experiences of an entirely different kind, attendant upon such things as ingestion of drugs and interest in demonism.[2] Distinguished educators like Robert Havighurst draw the attention of religious educators to three especially significant subgroups: hippies, radical social-activists, and the "uncommitted" youth (p.719). He and Barry Keating[3] report six conclusions from studies (in 1966) on the religion of youth:

1. Youth are concerned about what they do with and about their religious beliefs;
2. Youth reflect the values of adults;
3. Youth tend to have a small world of concerns;
4. Youth's priorities of concern tend to differ from what adults expect;
5. Religion is a factor in the life of youth, but religious knowledge and activities are not consistently related to their day-to-day experience;
6. The adult image of the religious concerns and values of youth tends to be one of "hedging" and "drifting" (pp.714–715).

These points will be taken into consideration in the program to be suggested.

The Catechetical Directory is most intriguing in its give-and-take approach to adolescence. We shall prefer the "give."

Taking note of the fluidity and inconstancy not of adolescents but of adolescence—that is, our social definition—the Directory suggests that two stages mark this time of life: the accession to conscious spiritual life; the emergence of life decisions. Although no one can specify when these might develop, once the individual has fairly entered upon the second he/she begins to be an adult (NCD,168,169). These suggestive notions parallel much of the thought behind the program to be described.

As to specifics of approach, the Directory wisely abstains but does iterate certain "principles" regarding freedom of choice and education in groups. "Religious education is never manipulation or coercion" but "an ongoing invitation and ongoing assistance" (161); if persons are not responding as planned, the program may still be appropriate: "Faith is a free response; the program does not compel it" (183). The role of community looms larger in adolescence, partly because of the declining influence of family, partly because of the need to experience life as lived in the wider community of adult believers (168). We should give "priority" to situations that provide "more interaction and personal involvement" and to techniques for experience and reflection upon it: value clarification strategies, group discussion and prayer, and communication skills are specifically mentioned (181). Perhaps the favorite word respecting adolescent religious education is "variety"—of models, approaches, curricula, methods (e.g., 224).

The Directory giveth and the Directory taketh away. For instance, with the right eye we read of the requirement for diversity, variety, plurality, and the avoidance of conformity and uniformity; with the left eye we read of curricula set, standard, coordinated, diocesan-wide, and of religion departments not too loosely constructed around too many individual options. One finger waggles at us lest we coerce, force, manipulate students; the other pushes us to persuade, motivate, and encourage CCD attendance because, realistically, the kids will not present themselves just because they like the program. The outer ear hears of declining family influence and the need to provide experiences in the adult community, but the inner ear catches how much more influential must be the institution of school, and beneficial the classroom instruction. These are cited not to make much of them but merely to reflect the genius of this text which can, within one and the same paragraph (e.g.,224) encompass not only both the extremes but numbers of middles, delivering itself of the whole with such ineffable finesse that all parties can think themselves unambiguously either sustained or stranded in their views. As a colleague used to utter in opinion: "I doubt if the contrary be not the case" (Leo Srubas).

The proposed view can be characterized in terms of an invitation to choice and change, that is, to alternatives.

INVITATION TO ALTERNATIVES

Invitations will go out first to all of us. Otherwise we risk the embarrassment of having to recall those sent out to adolescents, should their educators meantime decline. We can ponder alternatives to tradition in two senses: other things to do; other ways of doing things.

It is to be feared that in practice, save for the unlikely intervention of exemplary creative effort, many of our programs will take place within a school context and the majority of them will take the traditional form of courses and classes for freshmen, for sophomores, etc. This situation is one for concern, on any number of awful grounds. We shall raise just two: to have a traditional religion program in Christian high schools is, first, a scandal, and second, an absurdity.

It is a scandal of Christian schools that they should claim to be established in order to serve the spreading of the gospel while yet establishing their operations on imperatives from other claims. Religious instruction as once practiced is dying all about, save in the bastions of academe, where it survives by protection—and compulsion—of law. Yet it consumes the strength and energies of many a creative priest, religious, and layperson who could doubtlessly expend their forces in more productive sectors and endeavors. The results they achieve, while certainly not insignificant, are not perhaps as correspondingly immense as the efforts they put forth. Part of this circumstance must derive from having subjected Christian instruction to the imperatives of school administration: regulations and schedules, class size and room usage, grades and credits. Not the demands of religious instruction but those of administration and, naturally, of coaching, are considered essential. Here the hidden curriculum teaches more lessons than the religion program—and contrary lessons at that. Any trace of good samaritanism, love of neighbor, or other Christian proprieties which might finally have made faint appearance in the morning's religion class are sure to be obliterated twice over in the afternoon's football practice: "Kill 'em! Hit 'em hard! Knock 'em down, and then hit 'em again!" are variations on themes literally pounded home by coaches, chanted by student bodies, cheered by young lovelies, applauded by alumni, Christians all. Some compassion must be spared for those who continue to labor against this mighty tide, their efforts thwarted not by foes of Christian life but by the very establishment which should have been their strongest support. This situation may deserve to be called absurd, but absurdity of another sort is next in mind.

One of the functions of religious instruction is to render explicit that which has been experienced beforehand as implicit. On this view the mystagogic catechesis of early times would give a complete explanation of the sacraments once the initiate would have experienced tasting the joy of the sacred mysteries. On this view also tenants of the nurturing approach, and we too, are led to withhold formal instruction during the first eight years of life, while the child is experiencing a taste of Christian life and liturgy in the family. The instruction to be given subsequently (see ch. 13) will make explicit all the religious experience that the child will have by then lived through to age twelve or so. Wherefore: to embark immediately thereafter on a program of formal religious instruction is useless, and even absurd. It will have nothing to make explicit; or it will make explicit precisely those childhood experiences which the adolescent means to leave behind. For formal instruction to reassume sensible character, the growing human must be left for some years running to amass another store of experiences, theories, trials and errors. No particular time-span can be assigned this process. On that account, the programs which we ought to set afoot for adolescents must never have age as a specific consideration.

In what terms shall we formulate the problem at hand? A useful summary may be that we are looking to find a content adapted to an audience. Each of these two parameters can be regarded as either rigid or fluid. Combining the dimensions we have altogether four options to examine in solution. These are identified in Figure 2.

Regimentation is the traditional solution. It aims to find an appropriate content for a fixed audience, indeed a captive one in compulsory attendance. For example, the principal assigns twenty-five seniors by alphabet to a certain teacher who is to give them a one-semester course on Christian Marriage and Family. The solution is not entirely rigid, for from time to time the course title will shift as new subjects are sought which might miraculously befit this audience. The solution raises a number of problems, of course, but solves one major problem, viz., administration. This solution is preferred by administrators, as the problem it solves is administrative whereas the problems it

CONTENT

	Rigid	Fluid
Rigid	Regimentation	Venture
Fluid	Selection	Chaos

AUDIENCE

Figure 2. Options for Religious Instruction

raises are not: these are left to the teacher and students to work out. The first solution is familiar, and it is hopeless.

Chaos represents the opposite case. Everything is chosen to be elective, that is, unforeseen and unplanned. This is the solution often recommended in the absence of thought, on grounds that the only alternative to organizing everything (i.e., regimentation) is to leave everything unorganized. The solution is to abdicate and prepare nothing; the outcome is that nothing results.

Selection clearly defines the content beforehand but not the audience. The audience is defined on the basis of personal choices among the given contents. The setup is something like a cafeteria of religious instruction. A menu is listed; diners consult it and select what they will. This solution appears to be in line with the Directory's remark to the effect that everyone must be hungry and eat at least something. However, exceptions can still be permitted.

Venture, on the other hand, clearly defines the audience but not the content. For example, a teacher is put in charge of fifteen sophomores but refuses to decide a priori just what they shall do together. The content will emerge as the fruit of group processes; the teacher's role is to watch over the ripening of the group.

The last two solutions can be seen to overcome, each in its own way, the difficulty of adapting a defined content to a fixed audience. A number of schools have sensed this advantage and have attempted to replace *Regimentation* with one of these last. This attempt is made in error, for one solution will not substitute. The first solution can be replaced only by the simultaneous adoption of both the *Selection* programs and the *Venture* groups. The presence of one is necessary to the success of the other; the neglect of one leads quickly to the extinction of the other.

As an alternative to present practice. the following is proposed:

> *Christian institutions which aim to provide instructional service to adolescents ought to feature the entire suppression of all courses, classes, and programs designed for specified years or groups, to be replaced by the simultaneous establishment of two structures: one in which adolescents are free to follow a*

content that is defined; the other in which they are free to define the content that is to be followed.

This proposal aims to put into practice the notion of religious instruction as service to the individual's development in freedom, and the notion of dismantling the school-like apparatus ("deschooling") presently encumbering the enterprise and distracting it from its proper objectives, procedures, and results. How can this be done?

PROVISIONS OF CHOICE

In place of present courses, two structures can be established for simultaneous operation: Programs for selecting one's way and Groups for venturing upon it. Liturgy enters in to confirm in change.

Programs: Selecting the Way

Christian schools, parishes, and other establishments aiming to educate their clientele have the duty to offer instructional services as numerous and diversified as possible. This is a general principle of service owed all the faithful. The principle requires a variety of programs differing in length and depth, dimension and level.

These programs should vary in length and depth. This feature requires leaving off the habitual blinders of the school paradigm whereby the only foreseeable treatment of subject-matters is by blocks of ordered information dispensed within a given grading period or semester. On that view, someone wishing to inform himself on Holy Orders must first endure a series of presentations on sacraments preceding Orders. In fact, as events often turn out, the period may elapse without the class ever having neared the end of the sacramentary: Orders may not even be "covered" except perhaps hastily and sketchily, while the student's questions are honored with either, "We'll get to that later," or , "We don't have time to get into that now." But on the suggested feature, the school must give proof of outstanding imaginativeness and suppleness. Varying time must be devoted to various perspectives of a subject. That is, to an issue is allotted a one-hour lecture, to a topic an evening or weekend seminar; to a theme is given a mini-course, to a domain a semester. The same subject should also be proposed under varying perspectives according to clientele. That is, for those who for one reason or another desire at this point in life only a certain limited bit of information on a given subject, a short or restricted form of program should be made available, along with a more expansive form on the very same subject for those who wish to delve into it for personal reasons related to that subject.

The programs should also differ in dimension attained, to respond to various aspects of personality. Certain programs will be of a rather more cognitive nature, comprising intellectual facets or introducing methods of thought, be they exegetical, historical, theological. Other programs will be more oriented to the affective domain, featuring occasions for intimate experience of prayer, encounter, self-discovery and the like during a weekend or evening session. Finally, other programs yet will be more activity-oriented, offering a chance to work in service of unfortunates after a training period and followed by an evaluation phase. These three dimensions are presupposed in Christian life (TJD,14). But they must not be supposed each and all to be salient at every given point in the life of any given Christian. Programs for all of them must always be available to all Christians, who can then severally avail themselves of whichever service they happen to require at a particular moment in their individual life.

The programs should as well differ in level, such that participants may be empowered to discover something of value according to the stage at which they happen to find themselves at the time. Thus, for example, certain programs will give an overview of religious cultures—Islam, Buddhism, etc. Others will give mini-courses in Christian theology—information on sacraments, commentary on scripture, discussion of church social doctrine. Still others will offer formation in Christian spirituality—kerygmatic activities presupposing a rather deep commitment of participants.

With so many variable features, all programs ought to be clearly described in some sort of prospectus made available to interested parties. To this purpose religious educators must exert themselves to acquire the skill of defining and describing instructional objectives. Objectives which are utterly clear in everyone's mind provide sensible grounds not only for the teacher's activity in a program but also for the participant's choice among programs. In brief, it is not sufficient to announce a course on prayer, for example, to be taught by so-and-so at such-and-such time and place. Specifications must be given as to what aspect of prayer shall be dealt with, in what manner, and to what purpose—to name but a few requirements. What shall participants expect to be doing in the program, and what can they reasonably anticipate to achieve by doing it? Are they to hear a rundown of the history, forms, or conditions of prayer? Are they to be trained in meditative techniques—if so, which ones in what way? Are they to learn to recognize prayer, to value it, to know it, or to practice it? And so forth. Excellent manuals are available to help the educator specify all these points and more.[4]

Two additional features need no mention in the prospectus, for they are to be assumed as prerequisites in every case without exception. Programs are to be free of compulsion to attend and pressure to conform.

The programs should be optional and open to all. This feature is actually the indispensable condition for the model to function. The various offerings may be enriched by associating teachers and students from neighboring schools, including public schools, as the Directory recommends. The programs ought to be open to the participation of parents as well, and of local parishioners generally; those who find themselves free and interested should be able to join in. Christian instruction is thereby shown to be a service not restricted to young people alone but rightfully available on a permanent basis throughout life to anyone who would partake of it. Part of this service may well be offered through the good offices of the school. But religious instruction does not *belong* to the school, nor does it belong only in the school or for school children.

In last place but of first importance is that these programs should have nothing machiavellian about them. We mean to negate all possibility of anyone's entering upon a program in good faith that it shall prove to be as announced—informational, for example—and then feeling pressured into belief, conversion, or commitment. We do not intend to say that the instructor must maintain an aloof neutrality over every issue at hand—that is not only not necessary, it is not possible. The teacher may of course give his own point of view even in a purely informational program. But what cannot be tolerated is that the educator should take improper advantage of the situation in which for particular and personal reasons the individual is led to join in the activity. Proper advantage is to satisfy the reasons for coming; improper advantage is to capitalize on the reasons by peddling an entirely different bag of goods. That is called manipulativeness, and would cause us to lose all credibility in the sight of the young generation. More importantly, it runs counter to the essence of religious enterprise. Other enterprises have other essences, but we undertake to be responsible religious educators, not entrepreneurs out for a killing or salesmen out for a commission.

Once having set this model in motion one will observe at the start a pronounced decrease in the number of students participating, compared to the number attending mandatory classes. But if the model is maintained steadfastly for two or three years, one will notice a change in pattern. Attendance will evidently never rise to 100 percent at a time, but it will tend to situate in the area of 40–50 percent. We may figure that over the four years of high school, since different students will now and again attend or abstain, something like 70 percent will eventually participate. The crucial distinction does not lie in rate of attendance so much as in level of participation and quality of learning. In the traditional course, everyone attends but fewer participate and still fewer, we may perhaps surmise, benefit. With elective and purposeful attendance the entire educative situation is transformed. If attendance is at 70 percent, we may not unfairly assume an equivalent level of participation and learning.

If, on the other hand, attendance does not show increase over an initial low, we have three causes to investigate. The students may be distrustful, indifferent, or unreachable. School may already have lost all credibility in their eyes:

so much have they been duped in the past that they are not about to believe that we will deliver as promised, nothing more, nothing less. Or school is disqualified in their eyes: everything that goes on is so inconsequential that they do not even trouble to inform themselves about our various new offerings. Or lastly, school is irrelevant in their eyes: they are so entangled in their own problems and concerns that nothing from the outside can possibly motivate them. None of these explanations is meant to imply that these youngsters might not be benefiting from other programs in other places, such as the parish, youth groups, and so forth. No one program can possibly assure the entirety of the church's pastoral effort or population.

As for our own proposal, this program must at very best be complemented with a second, permitting in fact the first to function.

Groups: Venturing upon the Way[5]

The very same population and place open to the first structure must also be open to a second. Here students are given the chance to join in groups for free discussion. Instruction aims to facilitate free expression of self and hence processes of formalizing experience, clarifying values, and searching for identity. The complex and turbulent experiences of life at adolescence are sorted out and given formal shape, content, and meaning. The slow unfolding of a group permits students to perceive and accept individual differences as well as similarities among members. The group process also contributes to peeling off layers of security acquired by the end of childhood, motivating the student to inquire into this or that program which might then help him to reorganize his world (see Figure 3).

Group sessions can vary in length, frequency, locale, and so on. If membership is small, the sessions may be held during regular class time; if too large, the class may be divided, each group meeting once a week with the teacher. Sessions may be scheduled over a long weekend or as a three-day retreat, and so forth. Naturally, the members must all be aware of the nature and purpose of these groups. These are such as to render yearly participation quite unnecessary. Once the word gets spread around, most students will want to participate in a group at one point or another during their high school years. But once or twice at most would be quite sufficient.

However they may vary, all groups must be left free to unfold at their own pace and direction. They must not be programmed: they have no ideal to attain, no path to follow. The process will depend on the degree to which the group and each member is involved. The leader is careful to refrain from intervening in the process by lecturing, correcting, teaching; he refrains as well from setting up mock situations for group activity—role-playing, problem-solving, and the like. These techniques are appropriate to task-oriented groups and other circumstances, but here their only effect is to

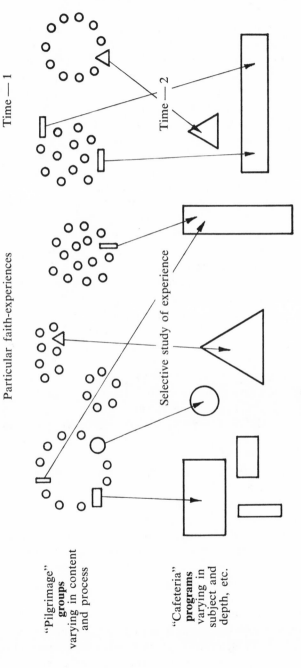

Figure 3. Dual-Structure Model for Adolescence

A student joins in a group during Time-1 and in group process clarifies his values, builds up identity, and so on; at some moment his experience reaches a point which motivates him to enter a program in order to study a well-defined subject appropriate to the experience he has had. His friends from the group do not necessarily join him in his particular program; they may also desire to join that program, or they may join another one, or they may do nothing.

distract the group from the task which is to be defined and accomplished by the group itself.

This is not to say that the group has no content and the leader no role. Rather, the orientation of both is to the group process, whereas the orientation of programs is to the content. The criterion is the type of language used. A precondition of these groups is that the only sort of discourse admissible in its proceedings is the language of the members. Problems, issues, topics, and concerns will arise; solutions can arise only within the same framework—that is, the group's resources of experience and knowledge. The leader's role is to facilitate the group's discovery and deployment of its resources. Now the leader may of course speak. But his talk must be restricted to the linguistic register of the group; he may not use a tone or content foreign to the group's experience, as for example appealing to outside authority to resolve some group question or adopting an official tone to overwhelm less weighty group contributions.

If everyone is to be free to express himself, the group must evidently be small enough, perhaps six or eight members altogether. It is pure mockery to claim to have free discussion in a group of thirty people. Even if the teacher permits people to speak out freely, the group will not.

The case is quite different with the programs, which may enroll as many as 150 participants in a single session. There the task, the content and the process can be handled by lectures, audio-visual presentations, and the like; these are traditional enough as to be familiar. But the groups are so different a matter that we might not perhaps be altogether prepared to operate them as required. Some added developments may reveal more of their spirit.

The groups are an essentially verbal enterprise. They repose on the idea expressed by scripture as, "the mouth speaks out of the abundance of the heart." The groups are needed because the mouth does not always speak what the heart intends: some of what is spoken is not intended, and some of what is intended is not spoken.

If it is true that our values are made transparent by our speech, it is not true that everything we say has this quality to it. There are several levels of verbal expression. At times we merely give off *utterances,* that is, sentences about anything at all—as when we talk to fill up the silence, avoid solitude, dispel fear. At other times we issue *pronouncements,* that is, sentences about some things—as when we recite facts and theories. Then at times we make *disclosures,* that is, sentences about ourself—as when we speak our mind, express ourself, talk personally. Only on this third level do we engage in clarifying values, forming identity, shaping awareness. Here the group leader's task is not to dispute content but to encourage the use of language to bespeak self.

The corollary holds that speech does not always give exact expression to intent. As meaning passes through the stages of formulation, it encounters factors which may enhance or hinder: fluency, education, experience. Between conception and expression, then, meaning is diffracted, eventually emerging somewhat off course though still within range. Figure 4 pictures the process. As an example, a young person can perfectly well say, "I want to go off and become a sailor," without at all being attracted to life at sea. His

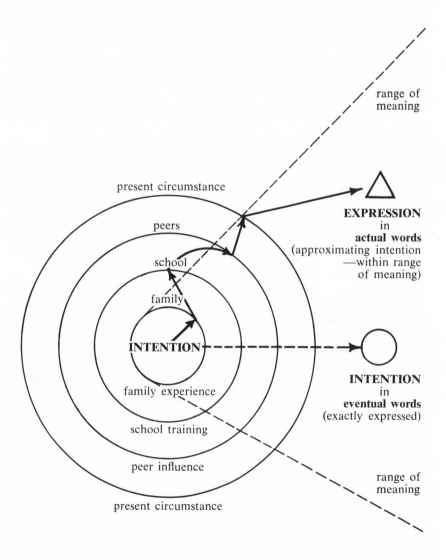

Figure 4.
Diffraction of Meaning
From Intention to Expression

intended meaning is that he wants to leave home; he does not know how or toward what; he recalls having run into a sailor who lived quite afar from everyone; the solution appears, but the meaning is shifted:

I *want to* (go off/leave home) (and)
become (a sailor/independent).

Similarly she might well say, "I hate Christ," while not at all hating him. She had put her faith in Christ; she then encountered a bishop who neglects the poor in favor of the rich, a priest who sires a child by mother superior, and Christians as selfish and unvirtuous as any to be seen. Her meaning is then expressed:

I *hate* (Christ/people who: abuse my trust/prove me naive)

We can appreciate how important it is that this young person be able to express her thoughts until delivering herself of her exact intention, and hence how important that the teacher must *listen* to her successive formulations without intervening prematurely. The very same goes for questions. Answering the question first formulated rarely will satisfy the question he intends—to which in any event he may already have the answer or could derive it, if only he would know the question!

In consequence of the mismatch between intention and expression, the youth's attention is focused on "a small world of concerns," restricting exploration of personal thoughts and values. Work with adolescents, has enabled us to identify three dimensions on which attention is restricted to one point only; as result, an instance (e.g., the present) is construed as a class (time-continuum) and hence other instances are overlooked (past, future). Figure 5 specifies dimensions and points.

As example, a youngster might conceive his problem only in present terms ("I don't have the money for a car"); or she might experience persistently in a cognitive mode ("I think, therefore I am, wherefore I think I am in love with you"); or they may live an in-group life only ("What are all of us guys gonna do now that school is out?"). The work of the group leader here is not to bring relevant doctrine or advice to bear, but to enlarge the field of awareness by de-centering attention from one sole fixation to free it to survey the other possibilities. Thus he invites the one youngster to admit causes and consequences into his problem-solving; the other she encourages to express feeling as well as thought; another they reinforce in use of first-person phrases.[6]

What can come of a group discussion maintained at this level? Here again a basis is found in a traditional saying: "Man is at bottom a religious creature." Often enough it is by failing to show our humanity that we fail to see the religious dimension of our being. Via their exchanges in these groups and with no outside help, students eventuate, certainly not in discovering dogma, but in piercing through to the world of faith. This achievement is produced in either of two fashions.

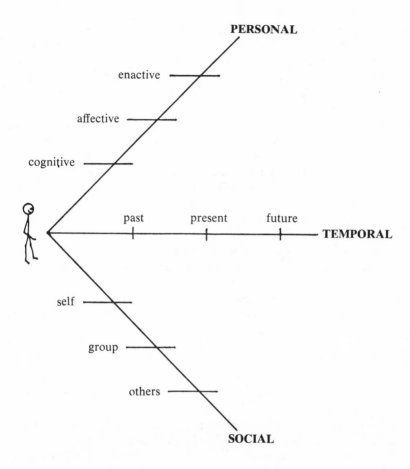

Figure 5.
Dimensions and Focuses of Attention

One way is reminiscent of Socrates' famous view that learning is remembering what we already knew (e.g., *Meno*). It will occur for example to some youngster in the group to say:

> You know, like I must've heard/read/said that like a thousand times before, you know, but I only never like really *got* it till now, you know?

Often enough this sudden grasp gets hold of some ancient Christian formula—the command to love one's neighbor, the promise of resurrection, the import of communion. All the pieces had been there all along, contributed by church, family, and school. But they had never made a piece; they had no structure to organize and sustain meaning. Searching his or her experience with the help of the group exchange, the person begins to emerge anew, recognizes the pieces for what they are—elements of a potential structure—and then proceeds to interrelate them into an organized whole at once cohesive and vibrant, personal and meaningful. The situation which we have provided in educational service to them has permitted them to experience revelation at work in their own life.

The other method comes about when the discussion reaches a frustrating dead end and the group despairs of making its way out on its own power. At this point it turns to the "leader," but not really to have him lead the way out or pull them out. The students sincerely ask to know how he or she has resolved the problem in their own personal life. They are calling upon him and her to bear witness in truth, and bear it they must. In one sense, this is the only moment of truth: when the teacher's personal testimony is solicited by the group. Otherwise, it is suspect.

In neither event has the youngster received didactic instruction. Yet in both he and she has acceded to a new level of interior life. It is by reason of arriving in this new territory that they bring themselves to enroll in one or another "program" now, to become acquainted with the lay of this land, its flora and fauna, its limits and possibilities. Far from having to "motivate" them, the program-teacher will have a time of it merely keeping apace.

Finally we may consider objections to the overall model. One is aware of numerous ones, all having to do with the difficulty of putting it into operation. The rejoinder will be both theoretical and practical.

In a theoretical vein, the model incorporates the two major approaches to instruction. The groups have a nurturing function, which aims to give rise and sustenance to new being. The programs have a structuring function, which aims to give shape and strength to development on a specified dimension.

In a practical vein, the model permits—one would say favors—beginning in a limited sector of operation. Several schools have started with this model for juniors and seniors, leaving underclassmen to more traditional fates for a while. The matter is of no great consequence. The model is presented only as an alternative, especially designed to be coherent with the body of theoretical views articulated in this book.[7]

One practical advantage to the model is that it permits teachers to finesse a problem which they otherwise seem unable both to avoid raising and to achieve solving. This problem features a desire to be at once student-centered and teacher-centered, respecting the processes unfolding in the group but nonetheless intervening when opportune. Teachers may sidestep this problem since the model sets up one opportunity for intervention genuinely called for (programs) and another, separate, opportunity for respect genuinely called for (groups). No step along the way can be taken without active consent and request of students. They in effect regulate the teacher's intervention in their own passage from one world to another. And yet even so, as experience has shown, they still manage for all that to complete the passage, nonetheless.

Liturgy: Confirmation of Change

Viewed in the light of the model just described, the sacrament of confirmation can be seen to assume special significance.

This sacrament has long been accorded theological ambiguity and pastoral hesitancy: on what grounds is it differentiated from baptism and conferred at adolescence? Explanations have not always been clear, ranging from the putative need to extend the sacramentary to a symbolic seven, to the supposedly greater outpouring of the Spirit. These of course have not sufficed for confirmation to enjoy a specificity all its own. One source of ambiguity may be the neglect over past centuries of the viewpoint whereupon sacraments show two aspects: one in virtue of which they work an effect upon the individual, the other whereby they reflect upon the community in context of which the sacrament is given. In this sense sacramental virtue marks the person and attains the church. In the eucharist, for example, persons conjoin and thus constitute the church; when a baby is baptized, the church is inseminated.

Would we be extending this view overmuch to look upon baptism and confirmation as celebrating the same reality under two aspects? Whereas baptism would concern the individual aspect, confirmation would concern the community, in the manner of celebrating the effects that redound to the church from having welcomed into its midst the newly-baptized member.

From this perspective, confirmation ought to acquire some serious stature—which it has assuredly not enjoyed for half a century. We are dealing with an event which is supposed to be the sacrament of personal commitment, of Christian maturity. Well now, make a few inquiries among Christian acquaintances: how many of them remember their confirmation day? The sacrament, like the episcopal blow it features, has become a matter of routine administration. What does this sacrament change in the life of the Christian? One truly wonders. By the ceremony itself Christians are taught, à la hidden curriculum, that the church does not quite know just what it is about in giving the sacrament and so is not about to make a big to-do over it. And yet the verbal lesson that is preached on this occasion, as well as taught in preparing for it, is that the confirmed receive the fullness of the Spirit and all its gifts—prophecy, tongues, fortitude, witness, and the like. By the mouth of the newly-confirmed Christian the Spirit speaks; possibly the first to be addressed is the church itself. And so, what more marvelous invention than this sacrament could the church imagine for continuous introspection and renewal?

The sacrament of confirmation would provide the church with an institutional means of safeguarding the possibility of renewal under the moving power of the Spirit. By confirming someone the church would be confirming his and her right to speak, to edify, and to reform: for it recognizes in this person the grace and gifts of the Spirit. In practice this viewpoint would entail three things. Confirmation would have to be given on mutual deliberation, not automatically at a certain age. Either the person manifests the desire to be confirmed and the church agrees to confirm her and him, after a suitable period of preparation; or the church invites a person to receive the sacrament and she and he accepts. On what grounds ought parents assume once again, as at baptism, the role of instigator and proxy?

The moment of confirmation would have to constitute an occasion for parish introspection and change. The Spirit is to go forth within the young and they shall prophesy (Isaiah): what will the parish do in response to this voice? As the parish proclaims in the sequence at Pentecost, the Spirit makes straight what is crooked, makes right what is lacking, and so on; his coming into the young at confirmation ought normally to produce just these effects. But the parish must set up a situation in which these effects are permitted to arise. To confirm the young, the church must embark on a path of renewal beforehand.

Lastly, confirmation would have to see the confirmed Christian be granted a real responsibility as well as voice: not pious amusements such as carrying the incense or decorating the altar, but weighty enough part in pastoral and financial decisions. If such responsibilities must await the age of sixteen, seventeen, or older, then confirmation must await that age. One observes that certain Protestant parishes include teenagers in their councils of elders.

And one dreams of the day when the ceremony of confirmation will include concrete realizations of its sacramental import. One imagines a ceremony during which candidates present to the parish their brief for helping it become more prophetic and loving, more attuned to the gospel. One envisions candidates giving the homily and distributing communion. On that day we would in truth see that the Spirit is a spirit of renewal, that the sacrament is a confirmation of change.

For all of that to occur, our youth must have been educated in a fashion which would permit them to accede to personal choices and to personal comprehension of the language-forms in Christian usage. Religious instruction would thereby manifest itself as being truly prophetic for the church, as is its duty to become.

CHAPTER 15

FLOURISHING THROUGH COMMUNITY

"Catechesis for adults," proclaims the Directory, "must be considered the chief form of catechesis. The focus of catechesis in the United States must now center on adults" (GCD,20; NCD,84).

By these ringing declarations our efforts and concerns are now beckoned, not to say wrenched, away from habitual emphases, to a wholly novel perspective and practice. "Adult religious education must always be viewed as the end toward which children's programs aim" (NCD,172). Our bishops see it as "the culmination of the entire catechetical process" and situate it "not at the periphery of the church's educational mission but at its center" (TJD,43,47). No statements could be more distinct and no viewpoint more different by contrast to the world in which we have accustomed ourselves to think and act as religious educators.

We have here then a perfectly clear view of the place of adult instruction in the overall scheme of religious education. But we may revolve the question to ask, what is the place of Christian instruction in the overall scheme of adult life? On what grounds do we center first and foremost upon adults? What forms and objectives are conducive to the flourishing of life? Our first task, as before, must be to inquire into what is known about this period of life.

PERSPECTIVE ON ADULTHOOD

About infancy, childhood, and adolescence our knowledge, however tentative, is impressive. We have a mass of data and concepts: on the stages and phases, steps and passages through which an individual grows in respects intellectual, moral, social, physiological, and behavioral. We can see neonate become baby and infant, toddler become child, and pubescent adolescent. We conceive that shortly after (or before) leaving the teen-age, a human individual enters adulthood. And then—what?

To put the matter brusquely: so far as we know, having become an adult the person ages and then dies. That is, the next discipline under which the new adult is studied is gerontology, followed by thanatology. Hence we know the stages in infancy, childhood, adolescence—and death, "the final stage of growth."[1] But what field occupies the space between pediatrics and geriatrics? What do human beings do during the half-century between the age of twenty, when they are expectedly adult, and seventy, when they might expectedly be dead?

It is implausible that between adolescence and senescence human beings merely stay adult, but we do not have many names for what else they might become—"midolescents"?[2] Where does "human development" go when humans get to be adult? They must grow in some other wise than older and weaker. Through which developments do they pass? What might distinguish adults aged thirty from those in their fifties and sixties? To answer questions such as these,[3] we may turn to a current symposium on adulthood, which begins by summarizing the state of our knowledge as follows:

> Despite the growth of interest in the human life cycle, we still know far too little about the "stages" of adult life, not nearly enough about the transitions from adolescence to adulthood, and surprisingly little about middle age, let alone senescence. We are insufficiently informed about how concepts of adulthood have changed over time, about how adult behavior is culturally conditioned, about the relevance of work, leisure, and family to adulthood (p.v).[4]

The problem remains to develop methods and concepts that will make the study of adulthood as common, and fruitful, as the study of childhood.

This circumstance is not at all cheering, given the chief emphasis that we are to place upon religious instruction of adults. Nonetheless, we are in possession of a certain amount of knowledge—clues and glimpses perhaps—that may guide our efforts. Here we may select for special consideration an emerging view of adulthood.

Life during adulthood, as with earlier periods, comprises a succession of events in such clear relief and import as to be called stages. Despite the paucity of research this matter has not gone unnoticed. As usual, the poets seem to have anticipated and expressed the matter before anyone else. The Bard:

> And one man in his time plays many parts,
> His acts being seven ages. [As You Like It, II.7]

Psychologists have recognized it, as Erikson does by his last three stages in the life cycle; educators too, as Havighurst by his developmental tasks in early adulthood, middle age, and later maturity; students of religion also, as Fowler by his stages of adult faith.[5] These theoretical efforts are being joined by current empirical studies seeking to identify stages in adult life.[6] From our own perspective we note that the Directory, in "earnestly affirming" the priority of adult education, specifies as one of its reasons:

> The adult, moreover, must successfully pass through certain periods of life which are full of crises. Although these crises are less obvious than those experienced by adolescents, they are not to be considered less dangerous or less profound; in these

times the adult's faith must be constantly illumined, developed, and fortified (GCD,97).

How might we conceive of these stages?

Here we find ourselves in a curious plight as compared to our discussions of education, and family. There we met with the possibility that our multiple concepts (e.g., socialization versus education) might too finely distinguish and falsely dichotomize an essentially singular reality, making two separate things out of one. We therefore sought an encompassing or wholistic conception to give us perspective. Now we seem to encounter the reverse. Perhaps our plight here is that our conception of adult life is so encompassing as not to distinguish multiple realities that fairly intrude themselves upon our attention and justly claim our educative concern. We therefore seek particular concepts to give us perspective. Happily nowhere does our purpose exceed our capacities, for we neither can nor need elaborate a theoretical model within which all terms are nicely articulated and systematically related. It is enough to suggest some more or less random examples of stage-like events during adulthood, and to indicate, in general terms, the significance of these for our task as religious educators.

As to the importance of adult stages, we may consider each of them to entail at least three quite obvious features. First, the individual is taken out of habitual, familiar context and thrust into a strange complex of circumstances. Second, the person must resituate self in consequence, making the strange understandable, making of circumstance a context. Third, any such step is a crisis. Between losing the familiar and reacting to the novel, the person lives an ambivalent and likely painful moment, indeterminate in promise and issue, opportunity and utility. These features may exhibit themselves in varying degrees of intensity and import but the dynamic appears to be invariable: meaning must be accorded anew.

Conceive that each stage brings a person to a new landing, so to speak, giving a new appearance to existence and requiring that a new sense be given to it. This new sense may in fact be a continuation of the preceding one; it can approximate some one sense that dominates the whole of development; it can be a different, novel meaning. But old sense or new, a distinct act of according meaning, of construing life, is required at the new stage. Once-familiar meanings abruptly show themselves inadequate or inappropriate for some time. A thoughtful and purposeful action is called for.

Thus the passage from one stage to another always involves a kind of crisis, justly so-called. We have all heard tell of the "middle-age crisis," but there are numerous others, we may be sure, and public discussion as well as scientific study is seeking to make some of them plain and even predictable.[7] The crisis in all of them, we can think, is that old certainties, comfortable views, reliable principles and habitual reactions appear to fall apart or otherwise to suffer impairment. For a time the person is lost. Then a light dawns to illuminate a perspective that he and she might eventually wish to adopt. The perspective might involve accepting and accommodating, overcoming and benefiting, relaxing in and adjusting to the limitations of new circumstance. On the other hand, the alternative might involve adopting a yet more rigid stance, a determination to reject developments as they have befallen, to give oneself over to bitterness and regret and to give one's days over to fruitless efforts to fly in the face of realities and to recover former circumstances. On the face of it, the first of these leads to growth. When the ideal perspective of growth beckons, the adult has need of new learning and educative assistance, to clarify perception and confirm intuition, to support choice and strengthen resolve, to formulate and effectuate the response he and she means to undertake.

Certainly we can conceive of this new stage to come about rather reasonably and even mildly, partaking of a steady development unfolding over the course of years, or evolving in part from the person's prior dispositions for the future. Yet in other, perhaps more frequent, cases, events erupt rudely, unexpectedly, wantonly, brusquely. They fall to one's lot undeservedly. One haps upon them without provocation or preparation. These are the events that shake one's whole life, suddenly throwing into disarray the edifice so carefully constructed over the years, disrupting the network of relationships, the lattice of plans, hopes, and certitudes: a child is found cold dead; cancer is discovered; alarms sound, projects fail, without rhyme or reason. What can the person do? where to turn?

What precious, indeed priceless personal offerings could we make at times like these! At very least we can provide that the distraught person be able to join with others in sharing, examining, and resolving his and her plight. Perhaps they might find something of what they particularly need in the way of a supportive group within which they can take hold and see, bit by bit, the world, others, and God in a different light fetching the response of personal reconversion and emergent life.

Not to put a fine edge on it, we may identify four rubrics and some examples of stage-like events in adult life. These are neither systematic nor exhaustive but illustrative of the kinds of events that come to mind in considering the ordinary course of life and the opportunities it presents for religious instruction.

States. One type of event inducts the individual into a somewhat prolonged period of time during which he and she lives a qualitatively consistent life different from that before and after; that is, a stage of life properly so-called. We have for example young adulthood, maturity, and aging as stages in the life-span. On other continua, we have the interpersonal states of courtship and/or cohabitation followed, let us say, by marriage and parenthood, the nascent family, mature family, departure of children, and a new marital life style; we have the more or less individual states of mind and body, moving from the formally educated to the experientially educated to the wise, reflective, and prudently communicative person, or to adult-parent on the birth of a child and adult-independent on the death of a parent; or again through menopause and climacteric, or from acuity to senility; and states as worker, from aspirant to apprentice to master, a shift perhaps to another job or career, and then retirement and another type of productivity; or again the states of consumer or earner, or yet as *socius,* from sought-after, desired, enjoyed to ignored and neglected and isolated.

Disruptions. A second type of event represents mere intrusion and temporary adjustment or living-through, as accidents, illnesses and depressions; periods of mourning and suffering, failure and success.

Occasions. These include participatory events such as achievements of one's children or friends, their growth, entrance into institutions, sacramental, educational, and social; various regular events of church and society.

Transitions. A last type of event has the character of the first two without eventuating in a state of life nor yet constituting a horrendous blow, as for instance any change in one's life circumstances, status, residence, and locale.

This series indicates types and specifics we might wish to think about for adult education. For the more serious and perduring of these eventful experiences, we find a striking expression in a letter by the poet René Daumal to his wife Vera; published only after his death, these lines seem to capture the subjective quality of coming to such a pass as we originally described.

I am dead because I lack desire;
I lack desire because I think I possess;
I think I possess because I do not try to give.
In trying to give, you see that you have nothing;
Seeing you have nothing, you try to give of yourself;
Trying to give of yourself, you see that you are nothing;
Seeing you are nothing, you desire to become;
In desiring to become, you begin to live.[8]

Rare are the words that could so simply render the experience and so directly compel our concern.

ISSUES IN ANDRAGOGY

How then shall we most fruitfully conceive of educational efforts so as to befit individuals during adulthood?

Concepts

Some basic considerations come to our aid from various sources of educational and catechetical thought.

From research on adult learning[9] we know that personality is apt to be less supple than in earlier years; adults tend to show more stability and more resistance to change. Whereas young children are still more or less susceptible to the influence of formal education, numerous adults carry with them painful memories of their school experiences or normative views of adult dignity that tend to make them steer clear of situations looking like school and are immediately put off by features academic and pedagogic. Not unnaturally, adults do not like to be treated like (school-) children. Further, adult opinion may tend to have deeper roots and be held more tenaciously than is the case with children, but also the views tend to be more diverse. Hence a group gathering of adults can permit a more educative interchange than the commonly homogeneous group made up of children.

From the study of adult education any number of practical points can be garnered.[10] For example, one of the standard texts[11] in the field enumerates four facets of adulthood that relate particularly to education. First of all, adult self-concept tends to move away from dependency as the person becomes self-directed in life. In addition, the reservoir of experience accumulated by an adult represents an increasing resource for her and his learning. Moreover adult "readiness to learn" becomes increasingly oriented to the developmental tasks the adult continues to face. Lastly there is a shift in time-perspective, and with that a decreasing tendency to postpone application of knowledge. Hence we might think of adults as continuing to encounter new circumstances and to experience new concerns. Their focus shifts from subject-centered to problem-centered learning.

From philosophy of adult education[12] come stipulations that the needs of participants be emphasized over subject-matter, and that programs be voluntary and cooperative endeavors. Resources and activities arise only in response to the adult learner's needs, and the whole is set in a circumstance designed to be appropriately responsive to the status and concerns of participants. Especially meaningful are "problem-centered" or situation-oriented programs in keeping with the milieu in which they are operated.

From official documents we learn of a series of matters pertaining specifically to adult religious education.

Rationale [GCD,92;NCD,172;TJD,43,47]. Four reasons are given for the primacy of adult education. First, adults' maturity (preparation, experience, and development) enables them to hear, to benefit from, and to respond to educative effort, and deserves Christian complement. Adults also have responsibilities and tasks to achieve both in church and society, especially those of executing the church's mission of justice and peace and fostering the faith of the young through example and teaching. Third, their faith and person must be sustained through the crises of life. Lastly, the great changes in contemporary times merit that adults be helped to function more effectively, to realize their full potential, and deepen their community.

Functions [GCD,97; TJD,48]. Adult education is to evaluate and explain, in the light of faith, contemporary changes and current issues affecting religion and morality. It also has the function of showing the relationship between "temporal" and "eccesial" duties of adult life. Finally it must develop "rational foundations" for adult understanding of faith.

Content [NCD,173]. Three general domains for adults are first, traditional study of scripture, liturgy, and theology; second, ways and means of nurturing the faith of the young; and last, information and skills to enable them to bring about justice and peace in the world. Specific topics are also pointed out as required by the times and the challenges it presents to the faith: Christian concepts of suffering and of personal freedom, and a sort of atheological "education in the process of change."

Methods [NCD,174;TJD,44]. These documents stress the flavor rather than the specifics of adult methodology. They hold it essential that provisions for adults recognize and respect adult needs, adult status, and the resources adults bring to the effort. "Basically, this means adults will play a central role in their own education" (NCD,174). Adults will participate at every stage, identifying needs, planning ways to meet them, teaching one another, and evaluating the program. The whole must emphasize self-direction, dialogue, and responsibility. As one salient aspect of adult education should be "personal reflection upon life experiences," methods should include discussion techniques, group dynamics and communication skills; education-in-group must be considered "requisite" for adults (GCD,76).

Occasions [GCD,96;NCD,169]. The moments in adult life particularly calling for religious instruction are specified in much the same way as we have discussed. One occasion is the period of decision and crisis, when religious instruction might assist the person to live out life decisions and to live through life crises. Another is "principal life events" such as marriage and illness, "times when people are moved more strongly than ever to seek the true meaning of life" (GCD,96). Two other occasions are given as changes in life circumstances, and special events in church and society.

Groupings [NCD,93,177]. Our attention is called to married people and to parents, especially those without partners. Minority groups are also singled out, whether formed on a socio-economic basis, or an ethnic, racial, and cultural one. Lastly, all manner of "special interest groups" are identified: the aged, young single collegiates, and workers, the widowed and divorced, the retarded, the physically handicapped and emotionally disturbed, immigrants, and the imprisoned.

This précis is enough to indicate the constituents of adult education, and to show how from several perspectives certain themes emerge again and again to catch our attention. These will be taken into consideration in the program to be suggested. Here we may pause to comment on a few selected points of criticism.

It seems that most observers underscore the difference between adult and child education. But in some essential respects, the difference is not all that considerable. Both cases, for instance, are subject to the same general laws of learning and teaching. In fact it is a hope that childhood education will in a few years' time begin to take after adult education, at least with regard to teaching methods. We will then have come full circle in one major development. In a first phase, adult education, having appeared later on the scene, tended to imitate child education. At present adult education seems to be separating off, for its own greater benefit. In future the two will tend to approximate each other once again, with the added feature that child education will have profited from discoveries made in adult endeavors. In any event, experience has shown that childhood educators who at one time or another have worked, even part-time, among adults cease to entertain the same views as before with respect to teaching children. They seem to come back from their experience with a much more articulate and sophisticated viewpoint. If for nothing else than this advantage, all religious educators should be encouraged to do some work with adult groups in addition to the children they teach. Their teaching practice will likely emerge transformed thanks to this new experiential perspective.

As for our American Directory, we register a particular note of disappointment over its ambiguous and ambivalent attitude respecting the importance of adult education. Now, as noted, nothing could be clearer than the ringing affirmations it makes about the primacy of religious education for adults. Yet one is nonplussed to encounter equally clear statements to the contrary, affirmation countering affirmation. For instance, having first noted that "the focus of the church's catechetical activity" for the past century has been upon children, the Directory states: "The focus of catechesis in the United States must now center on adults." But in between these two statements, and in fact introducing the latter one is the phrase "without weakening" the focus upon children (84). How can you center focus upon a new point "without weakening" the center of focus upon a prior point? For another example, the Directory speaks of "child-centered" emphases in terms of "obstacle" to adult education, which is acknowledged to be in embryonic state; whereupon: "But until adult education is sufficiently developed and provided, the religious education of children and youth will suffer" (182). Therefore, "it should be given first priority in terms of assigning personnel, funds, and time for the task" (172). But the earlier terms of must and focus, centrality and priority later become "emphasis is given to adult education"—while similar education for children and youth is "never questioned," "without weakening," and "continually strive to provide" (178,225).

The Directory may shift emphasis to the man on the moon for all of that, as long as the shift is rhetorical rather than practical.

Perhaps such give-and-take is inevitable in a document representing not only a first draft but also the collaboration of many and diverse persons from various constituencies. Yet the force of it is to vitiate the writ for adult education. If it is to be vitiated, why build it up in the first place, save spuriously? Simple souls such as we who read the document can grasp it if it would but say, "Adult education has second-place and childhood has first-place," or the reverse, but the Directory says both and it says them at the same time. Collaborative effort or no, the text must not require hermeneutic analysis but give forth its meaning when read; alas that after hours of exegesis this text will not yield.

Should this point bear stressing, or the horse more beating, let it be clear that on this matter the Directory's half-heartedness shows not by rhetoric alone, nor only after close inspection. A superficial reading does not at all leave one with the impression that adulthood has been emphasized. To the utter contrary, one sees at a glance that it is adolescence which receives the most expansive consideration of all the periods of life, and a pedantic count of the lines of print confirms the impression and specifies it in terms of nearly half the total discussion.[13] In the section on "organization and structure" of catechesis by age-levels (221–226), adolescence alone accounts for almost 60 percent of the lines, whereas infancy and adulthood *together* account for a mere 10 percent—these negligible episodes of life "when all the important foundations are laid" (NCD,165) and to which "should be given first priority" (172). To adulthood, a period comprising some 70 percent of the life-span, is devoted fully 7 percent of the lines. Thus does the Directory show that "religious education embraces the person's full life-span from infancy to death" (164).

It is perplexing to see so much made of childhood and adolescence when everyone already knows so much about them and (because?) we all have uncountable edifices, methods, materials, programs and whatnot for them, and to hear so little about organization and structure and resources for adults, when hardly anybody knows anything about them and next to nothing is ready and forthcoming to provide for their religious education.

Models

What exactly do we wish to achieve for adults? What educational model will befit these aims? Such questions are not a matter of principles of psychology or pedagogy (or "andragogy"), nor can they be settled merely by agreeing to accord priority to adult education. Rather their answers are determined by our mentality regarding adults and the services we esteem them to need. The framework to be suggested here embraces community-cum-individual development. We may set this framework off by considering a competing mentality, that of institutional service and schooling.

Persons may be of several minds as to the particular form of educational service to provide adults. One mentality endeavors to assist people who are considered incapable of helping themselves. They are therefore given that which one conceives good to give them. A service structure is set up and the unfortunates are invited to come and receive its good offices. After a time disappointment sets in as these people do not show themselves to profit maximally as planned from the excellent services, provided after all for their own good. In general the institution is seen apart from the individuals it is to serve, as having virtue and merit of its own accord. This sort of mentality puts a brake on progress.

Another mentality esteems individuals to have on the contrary the perfect capacity to make steady progress on their own, to get a grasp on their problems and to make useful efforts to educate themselves. Their only need is for some outside agency ready to facilitate their endeavor. On this view the worth of an institution accrues from the value placed on it by participants insofar as their advancement is fostered. This mentality on adult education promotes progress.

But other views on institutional service also come into play. On the whole they assure that a more traditional, school-like approach to adult education might unfortunately have the greater chance of being implemented in practice.

For one thing, current vocabulary and practice may bias us. When we think of education for adults, it is likely in terms of courses and curricula and school. For example, a significant proportion of adult education programs consists in preparation for the General Educational Development test (GED), on the basis of which some three hundred thousand adults per year are granted *high-school* equivalency certificates.[14] The upshot is that much of "adult" education gives instruction in high-school curricula with objective to pass a high-school test; adult performance on the GED is evaluated against that of high-school seniors and is certified by a high-school diploma. Partly in reaction to this youthful and scholastic bias, a new test has appeared recently, the Adult Performance Level test (APL), proposing to measure competence in areas of adult functioning in contemporary society. But initial reactions to the APL within the field of adult education suggest that the APL will now merely replace the GED: in its turn shaping programs and objectives so as to certify that a given adult has knowledge and skills equivalent to those of a high-school graduate.[15]

For another "bad example" we have the influence of earlier efforts and future personnel. Those who will be charged with ventures in adult religious education, just as was the case with older ventures, are already involved in childhood education. Priests, coordinators, and schoolteachers will tend, as in the past, to extend to adults their present occupations among children. Thus adult education takes place in *night* school and *extension* courses. That tends to color the entire venture as remedial education. Religious instruction for adults will aim to make up the deficiencies or omissions in past schooling, to give courses which adults should have taken or remembered if they hope to be suitably prepared of course for day-to-day living.

Finally, the whole affair will tend to be systematized. An outlay of personnel and resources on adult education entails a shift in habitual emphasis. It will be made on the basis of plans well-laid, conceived in offices and departments, bureaus and boards, researched and analyzed by means of expensive surveys, questionnaires, consultants, and computers. Print-out in hand we will then maintain that our programs represent a tailored response to adult needs. This position cannot be maintained for long. Evidence will shortly pour in that once again only the leisured, affluent, and educated participate in the programs. A new model will have been constructed at great labor and expense only to reproduce the same old elitism and all the tired defects of the school system.

If we are to devise a new and appropriate model, as indeed we must, then we should see to it that the model is a new instance not of an old but of a genuinely novel and fresh approach.

The proposal is:

A dual-structure model must be devised, one that makes simultaneous provision for community and individual development.

As to the individual component, the general approach has been limned in the discussion of stages and crises in adult life. As to the community component, we need to develop a number of points before going on to specify a program.

One useful model for our purpose is contributed by a prominent adult educator at Chicago, Cyril Houle. In *Design of Education,*[16] he distinguishes four designs of adult education: the problem-solving system (Dewey), the university-extension program (Tyler), the group-dynamics approach (Lewin), and the community-development model (pp.10–23). As the principle of the last, Houle gives the following:

> The focal idea is that a community (which may be variously defined in geographic or social terms) should be helped to act collectively to solve some problem which affects the lives of all of them (p.21).

The community-development model appears to incorporate Dewey's emphasis on responding to felt problems, and Lewin's emphasis on group process apart from content. It also seems to bear resemblance to a nurturing approach in that it provides for people of all ages to share activity over a common concern.

It is essential to differentiate this model from social service. In social-service programs the participants are on the receiving end of all manner of suggestions, lessons, and advice given by those who assume a traditional stance of superiority over the lowly of circumstance; it is the functionary who possesses knowledge and autonomy as well as status and authority. In the adult education model, the participants should be conceived to enjoy autonomy and responsibility over their own affairs.

Now it so happens that the church counts a number of members who are well placed to understand education in a community-development scheme. These people just happen not to be known as educators. They might be known as social workers, for one, operating in some such setup as Catholic Action. One may even take some comfort at the thought that these agents are not known as educators, considering the scholastic bias we tend to show when speaking in educational terms. All we need do is to accept that the activity of these agents is truly educative, and we may then set ourselves to working with them and borrowing their methods. There surely is little reason for adult education not to cooperate or to benefit from the example and experience of other existing schemes of action merely because these might lack the label of education. They do not lack the substance.

Religious instruction can find itself left behind in favor of other enterprises which prove more effective and progressive agencies of change and development. We must be clear as to the steps to take to advance our enterprise in seemly ways, that is by measures designed to achieve our proper objectives rather than to guard our ancient preserves. One sensible measure for progress is to work with and to borrow from other enterprises active in the church, or elsewhere, when these offer something condign to our highest purposes.

A number of adult educators appear to view something like a community-development model as the most promising and befitting format for adults.[17] The locus of learning is no longer the classroom but the community; the educator is more of a change-agent than a didact; the method is group discussion and action rather than transmission of knowledge from the one to the many; the content is the pressing problems in the participants' experience rather than a potentially useful and intriguing text. These contrasts describe far more than a theoretical distinction. The question is of some moment in practice, and good-willed people can sharply divide on the answer, as can be seen in reports of diocesan and neighborhood disputes over which approach to follow.[18]

We take a case in point of realities we face.

Realities

Nearly all the themes and specifics we have discussed—both desirable and otherwise—find illustration in the design of adult education within one of our largest cities. We will cite from a journalistic account by Judith Barnard[19] as one example of how theoretical notions can appear in practical form and public discussion.

An early step in reorganizing adult education in this major city was taken around 1966 with the redefinition of the city's seven junior colleges as "community colleges." That was eventually to mean that these institutions would provide, in addition to the two-year college program, special programs for adults in their respective neighborhood communities. The Master Plan set forth by the state in 1971 mentioned the concept "tailored to the needs of communities and individuals," while that of the city, in 1974, specified not a poor man's university "but an agent for community change" (p.102). Adult education was defined by the city as "education and training for citizenship responsibilities in a democratic society" (p.104).

What structural form was given to these ideations? With one fell swoop all adult programs were gathered up and plunked down into an existing school system, the city colleges. Thereafter the system comprised in all three components:

1. *College programs:* the regular two-year course for high-school graduates, leading to the A.A. degree.
2. *Urban Skills Institute:* remedial education for adults, consisting primarily of two programs, the GED and ESL (English as second language), leading to high-school certification.
3. *City-Wide Institute:* continuing education for adults.

The rest of our story bears on the third component. But we may note that to this point adult education as a whole has been nestled with a school system, while one of the two adult components is devoted to remedial, high-school equivalency programs. Moreover we observe that the existing school system has now been assigned yet several other roles in addition to its already manifold functions.

To continue our little case study we need to understand one or two facets about the organization of the City-Wide Institute. It is an umbrella for all programs of adult continuing education. These programs emanate from seven Centers for Continuing Education (one for each "community" college). Each center is headed by a dean, with a president administering the whole of the seven-centered institute. The case under study turns on two factors, each of which is significant in light of our previous discussions and, as it turns out, not unrelated to the other.

First of all, this entire organization—the City-Wide Institute, one of three component parts of the entire system and the one with the largest potential clientele—is reportedly awarded 0.6 percent of the system's overall budget of $132 million.

Second, two styles of programs have emerged, recognized and labeled as "traditional," and "community-oriented" (or "radical"). The style of program depends partly upon the dean of a respective center, for this administrator has considerable discretion to design and execute programs as he or she sees fit. Now, the deans differ, their centers differ, the neighborhoods in which they are located differ; accordingly, the programs have differed. We

will examine some of each style, the community-oriented, and the traditional.
For "community-oriented" programs, as they are labeled, we visit the
center run by Dean A. The neighborhoods within Dean A.'s purview are not
of the most easy in the city. She says:

> Continuing education is the only place for the poor, those damaged by society or our
> educational system, older adults who've been largely ignored (p.110).

While the better educated, more affluent population has knowledge of and
access to educational resources and government services available for free—

> Powerless people don't know these things; in effect they have no resources, cer-
> tainly no choice of resources. What we want to do is give them a voice in the city,
> an action base (p.110).

To this end Dean A.'s center offers, among others, three programs.

One program consists of courses taught, say, at the community college.
Some of these are: community organizing through the use of film and discussion; pragmatics of community control of schools; community management of
inner-city buildings. One course, called "Issues at the Work Place" is led by a
labor lawyer and a union organizer, and includes such topics as health and
safety, pensions and wages, race and sex discrimination, and union problems.

Another program is the "adult alternative high school," established in
response to the observed GED failure rate of 70 percent. Interestingly enough,
this school rents a deserted Catholic girls' high school in a depressed
neighborhood. The director describes the "students":

> These people were at the bottom . . .—they had nowhere to go. Here they're told
> they can take hold of their own lives, not just have things happen to them (p.105).

Apparently this message is lived up to, for one of the courses in this school is
"Governing Board." In it, twenty-five students, together with the director
(all having one vote each) create new courses, set school policy, and interview
prospective teachers—or "facilitators" as they are called, "to wipe out the
image of someone up high dispensing wisdom to the ignorant down below"
(p.105). Another course is "Group." Unfortunately in our eyes, but undoubtedly of merit in theirs, this course is mandatory. But its curriculum seems
ideal, at least as worded:

> In this class we share with one another responsibilities, feelings, ideas. It is an
> opportunity to develop leadership skills, group communication skills, a sense of
> trust and openness with the group, the ability to express your personal feelings with
> others, and to share theirs with them (p.112).

A third "community-oriented" program offered by Dean A.'s center is
Peer Group Education. Its aim is self-development, and its locale is an enormous, forbidding housing project. "Can you handle your life or will you be
handled by others?" is the question set for it by the director. Within the

project peer groups were established that after two years "became, almost, extended families," observed the director:

> They learned what it meant to work together, to form friendship bonds, to stand together so that each had a better self-image. They weren't alone any more. (p.105).

The women began to work together on plans for improving their lives in the project. In Dean A.'s evaluation of this program, these were the things achieved:

> —How to live with themselves, how to reach their aldermen and legislators, how to cope with public housing, how to bring up children in an atmosphere of gangs and poverty, how to get back to school if they or their children wanted—all the things they communicated were the really valuable things (p.110).

This is indeed impressive. If these three programs did proceed on and then achieve the half of their claims and intents, they must surely be taken as admirable instances in practice of the notions we have reviewed as desirable for adult education.

The other, contrasting, style of adult programs is labeled "traditional." Our source gives less information on this type but we are told of some to be found in the center run by Dean X: courses of lectures by outstanding city figures; instruction in crocheting, self-hypnosis, typing, and preparing tax returns. We are further told that the higher administration speaks of these as "model" programs. A second series of programs is directed by the president of the entire system, and these too are "model," and teach "useful knowledge": public service programs of training for police and fire personnel, building and sanitation inspectors. These courses, according to the president, "are the ones that will bring real differences to the lives of [citizens] in ten or twenty years..." (p.106). Finally, a third series is directed to industrial manpower needs. That is, the traditional programs appear to bear on city government, industrial employment, and "productive leisure."

The two contrasting styles of programs, traditional and community, do not, by all reports, share equally in the esteem or resources of the system. It is not to our interest to enter into the details of this particular case, sorting out the sources of personality conflict, organizational politics, philosophical divergence, and so forth—although all of these are to be cited. Suffice it to say that tensions exist and that, for whatever particular reasons, Dean A.'s programs have not won highest support. More pointedly they are reported to be losing their funding.

For whatever the reason, when governor and legislature slashed allocations and city administrators slashed accordingly, the swath passed more sweepingly through Dean A.'s center than through Dean X.'s. The new budget for Dean A.'s programs has provoked the observation: "These are precisely the programs scheduled to die" (p.109). Her staff has reportedly been reassigned, leaving one clerk-typist behind, while her office lease was not renewed for the coming year (rent of $4000). By contrast the budget reportedly allots one-half million dollars to another program described as favored by the administration. "And that may be revealing," adds the author of the article:

> Executive commitment in the City-Wide Institute is given to a program that isolates people, feeding them packaged information without their participating in the lively, often disorienting, occasionally disrupting, potentially earthshaking experience of group discussion (p.112).

The author's conclusion continues as follows:

> To the extent that they succeed . . . continuing education programs that emphasize attitudes, perceptions, higher self-esteem, and an understanding of the uses of power are antithetical to the role of community colleges vis-à-vis business, industry, higher education, and a quiet populace (p.113).

To be sure, whatever the merits in this particular case, the issues in most all cases could not be more clearly rendered. To see them in operation is instructive.

What lessons can be drawn for our own enterprise? The story was told to give an illustration, even a parable, of how things go in reality. We have seen distinct and contrasting positions. From these we can conclude regarding such issues as: multiple functions of the school, or other institution; scholastic roles and biases; emphasis on participants' needs, responsibilities, and self-directions; orientation to present and to problematic experience; methods of group and community education, such as dialogue and communication skills; allocation of resources; tactful change-making within organizational structures; and so on.

We too must take up position on the issues. We too must be prepared to struggle with competing notions and personages, not the least within our own selves. We too must give a try at translating notions into practice, evaluating the try, and trying again. It is an educational enterprise for everyone. Can we in religious education assume warrant for exempting ourselves, our colleagues and superiors, from the like?

In light of lessons drawn, considerations and conceptions earlier reviewed, we face the question: How might the best of these be given practical form over the course of life?

COURSE OF LIFE

The proposed model for education over adulthood, as with other periods, is a dual-structure one, consisting of programs and groups. Programs entail responding to life-events, while groups focus on developing life together. The results of these appear in liturgy, celebrating life together.

Programs: Responding to Life-Events

By and large these are the very same programs as were specified in the chapter on adolescence. There we detailed the main features and requirements of this structure; these remain in force here. We also noted as a general principle that the programs should be instituted in service to all parishioners, adult as well as adolescent; we remarked that they should be open to parishioners generally, not restricted to the adolescent school population. School or parish center might therefore schedule a number of programs during the evening hours, when either group might be free to attend. We ought also to point out that participation is an individual, not a parental, filial, or familial affair; if family members do participate, each must do so on his or her own grounds—mutuality of presence in a program must remain mere happenstance. Now if the parish center schedules a given program, the school need not; why duplicate efforts and exhaust personnel? We can perceive that a single prevailing structure may be established, offering a diversity of programs: some in school and some in parish center, during afternoon and evening hours, for adolescents and adults indiscriminately.

But apart from these similarities and identities, certain programs can be designed especially for adults, while others especially for adolescents. The nature of these programs will of course be determined by concerns specific to the two periods of life, but again they are not by any means to be restrictive or exclusive. Yet since the programs must be problem-centered, it stands to reason that the life-events to which they respond would make them particularly appropriate to only one population. Hence we may consider the content of programs which, in addition to those befitting either age, might well befit adults in particular.

Three general types of programs may be conceived to respond to events specific to adult life. One type focuses on issues of concern which may arise; another concentrates on transitions likely to be made; a third deals with states of life. These programs should be formulated in terms of problems and not subject-matters. On this provision, those who experience a certain problem will stand a good chance of seeing their needs met, and the program itself will be used as well as useful. Otherwise it is to be feared that participation will be restricted to the intellectually curious, to untiring regulars of parish activities, or to those with good but vague intentions as to deepening their knowledge of the faith.

What might be some issues of concern to adults? Certainly not something on the order of "The Gospel of St. John." But this gospel does respond to problems of love and friendship, for example. Thus a program might be announced as follows:

Our (such-and-such problem/issue/concern) with friendship: the gospel of John as one source of answers.

Similarly, one alludes to no problematic by listing a course on "Liturgy in light of Vatican II." But the following title may well attract those who genuinely experience a problem in this area:

Recent (problem) in our parish: the eucharist as a way of understanding and solving it.

The key is always to include specific reference to the people involved in the specific problem.

Now, a meeting called on "Children and Drugs" can only degenerate into lamentations over children and drug-pushers, while failing to address problems experienced by the parents—that is, by the participants who experience a problem with children and drugs. Their problem will not be the same as the children's, and it is to their problem that adult education should respond. Anyone at all can rant indignantly and fluently over the drug-problem—which is after all not *his* problem. But when it comes to a pointed problem that he really feels because it truly perplexes him and he personally has to resolve it, his talk is altogether a different matter—baffled, befuddled, halting, and anguished. Thus programs do not deal with "*the* problem of" but "*our* (problem) with our children who take drugs." Consider the difference in problems denoted by "Death and the Christian" and "I am dying of cancer" or "my child has just passed away."

Whatever issue is involved, the title of the program ought to word it in such wise as to indicate the nature of the problem as it might likely be experienced by one or another handful of parishioners. These will then know to join the program. And they will know too that the others who show up are not about to exchange lofty views on some removed matter, but will inquire together in a genuine attempt to come to some sort of satisfying terms with a truly disconcerting problem that they must personally solve.

What are the various transitions occurring in adult life? As these are more predictable than the specific issues, programs may be scheduled as a matter of course: for example, becoming engaged, entering the service, moving to a new job or neighborhood. While these indicate the transition they naturally do not give strict definition to the content of the program; specifics will be elaborated once the participants have gathered. What the program guarantees is that an educational structure will exist to respond to events in the life of some parishioners or other during that year. We can predict and provide for transitions without knowing in advance who might eventually make this or that transition. As the transitions are sure to be made, a program for those who wind up making it should be assured.

What are the various states of life at this period? In some cases they follow directly from the transitions made. As the church has anciently seen its role to sanctify states of life, it may well be urged to take notice of the newer states become more frequent in modern times, for which it might do well to institute a quasi sacrament. Old age or late maturity for instance has become more widespread. But other important states have developed, meriting to be marked by some sort of celebration, some sign that the Christian community accords them significance and supports those embarking upon them. Think of the moment of retirement, for example, when the person is cut off from the network of relationships in the workaday world and has to carve out some new purpose to everyday life. Think too of widowhood considered as a state in which one might wish to remain. And think of that period when all the children have gone off and left the family home empty for the first time in decades, giving parents occasion for new purposes and styles of life as a married couple. These and other states might well be the focus of special weekend programs, sponsored perhaps by several parishes together as a service to these particular members.

Along this line the church can be urged to give new consideration to familiar states. It might reinvigorate its service to matrimony and reinaugurate its service to the catechumenate.

Preparation of young people entering the married state is in process of change, but the change must extend well beyond the point of the marriage ceremony. Not so very long ago the church still considered its duty finished if it had prepared the couple to receive the sacrament and to know its obligations. "Pre-Cana" classes led up to the ceremony, and that was about it— save perhaps for a Cana Conference some 25 years later, where the couple could renew their vows and restudy their obligations. Married people were to have the usual support of the other sacraments; if the marriage failed, the blame was their own. But married life is such a piece of masterful achievement that the church should show at least as much concern to service it as to prepare for it.

Marriage entails, at least implicitly, the spouses' willingness to enlarge the human family through giving birth to children. Now to bring children into the world is, at least implicitly for Christians, to bring forth children of God and thus to enlarge his kingdom, the church. The church should take care to welcome children and their parents into its midst. The welcome should start at the moment when a young couple declare themselves before the Christian community to be man and wife, constituting a new cell in the church. Their entrance into the larger body should take place via a a small group of friendly marrieds who may serve as a kind of godparent to the new couple. This is the occasion for the church to regard these couples as constituting a mini-community with the right to celebrate home liturgies over a given period of time.

Actually the introduction of couples or individuals into the church might feature many practices of the ancient catechumenate. It is surprising to see how little this important service has been developed in the United States.[20] It regards those who for one reason or another (say, marriage to a Christian) show a desire to come to know Jesus Christ. The general idea is that they first learn of him in a small group of ordinary, nonspecialized Christians who ensure his early socialization and first nurturing in the church. Rendering such a service to the initiate is obviously a source of great personal and community enrichment on the part of those who provide it. A church which provides for a catechumenate is a church which provides for her own enrichment.

Groups: Developing Life Together

This second structure, to repeat, must be established in addition to the programs, which would otherwise rapidly expire. Unfortunately few parishes set groups in operation alongside the programs; hence many a parish has a rickety structure of adult education, with very little point, participation, or profit to it.

Insofar as these groups are groups, they share the same features as those described for adolescence—or for childhood, for that matter. But that does not mean that the particularities of adolescent groups characterize adult groups as well. As groups they share the same group nature and process, but they are not to be one and the same groupings. Programs, on the other hand, as we have just seen, may in large part be one and the same, with adults and adolescents together studying the same topic. But each must belong to its own kind of group, since purposes and experiences will differ. Thus the overall model comprises first, programs: some of which pertain to adults, others to adolescents, and still others to both; and second, groups: one set for adults, another for adolescents, none in common.

Adult groups can hardly be as formally organized as groups for adolescents in school. It is better to have different types of group-structure potentially at hand, and then to activate one or another as occasion warrants. Three sorts of groups might be useful: action, friendship, and inquiry.

Action groups come about in response to some social need or issue requiring group action: a problem in the school, a parish anniversary project or financial crisis, a special liturgical event. Action groups will flourish if people see that they make for initiative, responsibility, decision-making—and results.

Friendship groups are constituted less for action than for amity. People form them for mutual support, comfort, and other emotional returns. For example, families with small children get together, or young marrieds with those a trifle more experienced. Friendship groups interact rather than act, one might say.

Inquiry groups spring up over a topic or question which has not or cannot be satisfactorily dealt with in one of the program presentations. People join the process of group inquiry in order to exhaust a topic found intellectually demanding.

Parish officials should view these groups as having great educative value and importance to the life of the parish. They should have a conviction that groups are the stuff and tissue of parish life; without them the parish suffers from lethargy or anemia, each member lolling about in place awaiting his individual salvation to be handed him. The sensitive official can detect the need and even implicit existence of these groups before they are formally organized. If one but listens carefully, with patience and open mind to what parishioners express, he begins to perceive a certain commonality of desire and purpose among these few overheard here, those met with over there; they are in effect expressing the desire to take part in this or that group, were it only available. But these expressions often go unheeded for want of official esteem for group education. In truth, service to these groups should lie at the very heart of parish education. Religious educators have as an important task to promote the life and growth of these groups, and to help them accomplish their various undertakings.

The maturing process whereby the group becomes part and parcel of parish life may usefully be viewed as unfolding in several stages.[21] At the start members are somewhat unequal and their relations awkward and unbalanced; some have more say, less weight, and so forth. Under the leader's sensitive skill, members then become more or less equal and their interchange fairer; everyone, regardless of age or status, may have a say and be counted. At this stage the group resembles a type of democratic assembly, where proceedings are still rather formal and legislated. The next step is when democratic relations give way to dialogue. Each member begins to sense that what the other is saying can be of some usefulness to himself. After some time in this atmosphere of dialogue, the question comes to mind: "How does it happen that I get some of my best ideas from somebody else in the group?" Now the group is ripe for the emergence of inspired interchanges touched by awareness of the presence of the Spirit. These exchanges arouse the feeling that mutuality and communality are due to members' sharing in one Spirit and one faith.

Over the course of this evolution the leader takes care to reflect the state of the group and to draw its attention to the process. It will so result that the action group becomes interested not just in getting results but also in inquiring into the reasons and foundations for its action. The inquiry group in turn perceives that in the process members are getting to know and like each other better, and so the pursuit of inquiry starts to be characterized by an atmosphere of friendliness. Friendship groups for their part discover that they cannot continue simply getting together but need to take up some kind of activity related to outside concerns and people, if they are to stay together as a group. Finally, certain members of all groups come to the point where they feel the need to participate in one or another program of instruction appropriate to their particular experience. The motivation to move from group experience to program study is exactly the same as that in adolescent education.

Perhaps we can now appreciate more fully how it is that a parish is enlivened by these groups. Imagine what one single educator could achieve: he could devote himself to training and serving a single group of ten to twelve leaders; these in turn would each work with three or four groups. We might better appreciate as well how some of the best educators in this respect are the experienced workers in social and community programs. These professionals are skilled at setting up situations which dispose people to set to work for themselves, cooperating, building, seeking information, and finding solutions.

It should therefore be immediately apparent that a first step is to get professionals together for mutual exchanges and planning. Schoolteachers by and large know only how to construct courses, give instruction, and handle disciplined groups in protective structures. Their projects for nonschool or nonyouth education need to be reviewed at the planning stage by those more experienced with other educational levels, milieus, and approaches. Conversely the teachers' experience is needed by nonschool professionals whose skill does not include instruction and the like. Each cadre brings its own expertise in theory and practice to the joint effort. Both ought to be represented in every undertaking at the level of adult education.

Liturgy: Celebrating Life Together

If this proposal succeeds in enhancing parish life, it will assuredly redound to enlivening parish liturgy. Liturgy is celebration of Christian life.

Our liturgies at present are rather feeble in celebration. There must certainly exist some form of Christian life in the parish during the week, but one may wonder about the degree to which this life is consciously shared, expressed, and evaluated. Come Sunday, there is not the time to achieve the entire process during the 10:15 Mass.

Direct efforts on the liturgy are powerless to restore the Christian life of the parish. The liturgy is the natural fruit of an active, conscious, shared Christian life. Direct efforts should therefore be put into groups aiming to develop life together. If these groups are formed, then the programs will fill, parish life will flourish and liturgy will flower. There will indeed be something to celebrate.

And so with the liturgy there is completed the face of Christian education in all its dimensions: instruction, service, liturgy. This is a far cry from attempting to incorporate into religion class the unassimilable features of community service, group development, and liturgical celebration. When our pastors and teachers make attempts to squeeze these encompassing dimensions into the tiny box of the schoolroom, they undoubtedly manifest enormous good will and effort. But also they make stupendous avowals: that everything in sum depends on religious *instruction,* and this in turn on the school; that everything must be cast into the mold of instruction and the model of the school;

that everything not partaking of that world can safely be ignored if it cannot be absorbed—including the people who are not in school or who will not return there to be instructed. This sterile and benighted circumstance must not be permitted to continue. We make it and we can unmake it.

CONCLUSION

It is in a way a curious book that we have written, neither wholly theoretical nor wholly practical: we wished to avoid writing a piece of fiction for another world and, equally, a maintenance manual for some antique machinery. To be sure, theory and practice have continually flourished in our enterprise, the both of them—but not together, as we have seen it; we have ventured to weave them together. There has issued this hybrid. We would that it motivate readers to inquire into practice-*and*-theory—in theology, anthropology, history, pedagogy—all the while making it their rigorous study to articulate the mutual relations between these two awfully disjointed dimensions of the human endeavor.

How difficult it yet appears to put even these modest suggestions into practice! In appearance they may be viewed as insurmountably difficult, whereas in fact they are easy enough to implement. Ecclesiastical establishments are not peopled with the venturous of spirit. Caution and remove in the face of adventure are hallmarks of the profession and handicaps to renewal; arrived at the moment of revolution, the functionary is likely to demand credentials, memos, and timetables until the moment is safely past.* As these attributions are less than kindly and meritorious, we enjoy the option of holding them undeserved except by others. Yet they hold a mirror up to us, reflecting the procrastinations, nullifications, and abjurations, the maneuvers, feints, and parries with which we are wont to heed the call to action. The fact remains that church officials number temperaments undisposed to change.

There is another manner of conceiving this difficulty which at first glance appears to obfuscate but in final result precipitates change of one kind or another. This view is to esteem that the church already suffers from the progress it has contributed to. Indeed, by the instruction it has dispensed and the reforms it has made it has rendered the faithful measure for measure more autonomous, responsible, and participatory. But hand in hand with this development comes dissatisfaction over existing institutional arrangements. At this stage some decision must be made. One position is to maintain the faithful

*James E. Dittes, "Psychological Characteristics of Religious Professionals," in Merton P. Strommen (ed.), *Research on Religious Development* (Hawthorn, 1971), pp.422–460.

in that state of dependency customary down through the ages; in this case religious instruction has no need of reform, quite the contrary. The alternative is to accord adult status. As a result the entire face of the church undergoes dramatic uplift, and religious instruction accordingly. This development cannot unfold without arousing anxious and disquieting reactions.

Perhaps change would be made the easier if experimentation were more widely accepted. The Council opened the way to this direction, whereupon others promptly closed it off. Experimentation is sure to produce error, and even the apostles were said to be afraid of that. In response Jesus made a remark that applies just as aptly to our own situation. He stated in effect that you have to let the chaff grow with the grain. He also indicated that a tree is known by its fruits. And so, reforms inspired by the Spirit will eventually resonate among God's people while others will fall flat and dissipate in due course. We read in Acts that if an action comes from God it will triumph; if from man it will fail in the end.

In this regard, the company of Christian believers has always and everywhere included devotees of experimentation. These are members of the ministry and of religious orders. Oddly enough though, the bold-spirited thrusts of olden days may be traced time and again down through the system to their present tame and inoffensive form in some hulking institution. By allowing themselves to settle into the status quo with such accommodating alacrity, religious faithlessly beshadow their founding lights. Indeed the majority of founders had at least one or two bones to pick with hierarchs of the time; they succeeded in launching their ventures not thanks to the authorities but only in spite of them: new projects could not be viewed as fitting into the framework of the epoch.

To relate this matter to our own subject, chances are still there for the taking, as once were taken, to follow the promptings of the Spirit. Here is a source of renewal. Here also is one of the pressing needs of our time, to restore prophetic spirit to religious communities. A country which can list a couple hundred thousand religious should have no trouble making structural reforms—no trouble that is, if instead of joining the serried ranks of the Old Guard, each man and woman among them would respond to the Spirit and become on his or her own ground a prophet, calling and making for ventures as imaginative, innovative, and disruptive as possible.

Perhaps now at the end you will have appreciated the metaphor worked into the structure of these pages. It intends to recall Christ's death and resurrection. This is the message we are charged to proclaim. This is the mystery we are invited to live. And the mystery is this:

Only can the new arise to life
but that the old must first
be made to die.

Neither entire decline nor fulsome resurgence now marks the days of our life and work. We move about, not in the gloom of Friday or the glory of Sunday but amid Saturday's darkling and hesitant glimmer. So we pray the Lord: errant and purblind we yet turn our face expectant in the dawning of his morrow.

APPENDIX

1977 SYNOD QUESTIONS

Here are listed selected questions posed for the 1977 international synod of bishops, answers to which may be found in the text of this book. Apart from the numbering, the questions are given as they appear in the document, "Catechetics in our Time."*

1. What main remarks can you make on the responsibility of your Christians for catechetics?

2a. In your country, to whom is catechetics mainly directed? Who, on the other hand, remains most outside?

 b. What are the main experiences of catechetics that tries to respond to the needs of the Christians of our time?

3a. What consideration is given to children and their education? And what consideration does the Christian community give to this matter? Does the Christian community also pay attention to the very youngest, up to the age of four or five?

 b. In what way is catechetics for children evolving? What are the positive aspects and what are the worrying points?

 c. How does the Christian community participate in the tasks of catechetics for children? How do parents participate?

 d. What is the relationship between catechetics for children and the stages of their liturgical and sacramental initiation?

4a. What are the main problems that the world of youth poses to catechetics? What are the main preoccupations?

 b. What orientations and dominant choices characterize catechetics for young people in your country?

 c. In particular, what are the most important themes of catechetics for young people? What are the primary objectives regarding education in the faith?

5a. What are the difficulties that may be created by the break or lack of understanding between the rising generation and the Church in your country?

 b. On the other hand, what are the particular points of convergence between the Christian message ard the rising generation?

6a. What positive features for catechetics can be drawn from the cultural situation in your country? What are the difficulties?

 b. How is catechetics approaching the problem of ecumenism?

 c. In your country, is an effort being made to renew catechetical language and teaching methods? With what results? What are the difficulties?

7. What are the most important experiments now being conducted in your country

*Synod of Bishops, "Catechetics in our Time with Special Reference to Catechetics for Children and Young People." For the use of the Episcopal Conferences. Theme for 1977, International Synod of Bishops. Washington, D.C.: United States Catholic Conference, 1976.

255

for a positive solution of the relationship between catechetics and social situations?

8. How does catechetics in your country intend to promote liberation from social, political, economic and moral conditioning?

9a. Is there catechetics in the schools in your country? How is it understood? With what result and with what limitations is it carried out?

 b. What steps do you take to catechize children and young people who do not go to school?

10. In what way does catechetics educate children and young people for an image-dominated culture?

11a. What models of Christian education should today inspire the renewal of catechetics?

 b. Is it not necessary to learn to distinguish with greater maturity the aim, content and methods of catechetics today from those of other times?

 c. Should not one learn to distinguish the task of catechetics from the task of a pure and simple theological and doctrinal teaching?

 d. Which aims of catechetics are of most concern to you?

12. What do you think should be done in order that catechetics today may demonstrate the originality of Christian salvation?

13a. What methodological orientations do you recommend for catechetics for children and young people respectively?

 b. What more strictly didactic aspects seem to you important for catechetics in our time?

14. What orientations and programs [have been] introduced to foster the coresponsibility of the whole of your church in catechetics?

APPENDIX TO CHAPTER 9

Two texts are reprinted here for the reader who might otherwise find them hard to locate. The first is a summary of recommendations from the Conference of Bergen (1970) held by the Office of Education of the World Council of Churches. The applications to religious instruction are transparent. The second text is an official letter written by Paolo Freire on the matter of these recommendations.

Recommendations of the Council of Bergen

a - We propose that the overdependence of education upon schools handicaps effective education and that we must develop alternatives to schools.

b - We propose that education everywhere needs to recognize consciously the choice which it has to make between domestication and liberation. In our understanding, it must serve the liberation of persons and peoples to become agents of change towards freedom and help them to recognize and resist the dehumanizing and repressive forces that operate on them including those within the educational system itself.

c - Because educational systems often reflect authoritarian structures of power, we propose that there must be broader participation in making educational decisions. Only by so doing the decision-making processes use well the increasing pluralism and better organize the conflicts of competing interests.

d - We propose that present authoritarian practices which heighten the differences between the educator and the educatee and build upon the distinction between school learning and life must be replaced by those which bind educator and educatee together in a common activity of learning and of transforming the reality with which they are faced.

e - Because an elitist approach to education harms the dignity of individuals as well as the needs of societies, we advocate the democratization and equalization of education in the deepest and broadest sense. We therefore support radical development of alternatives to elitist schooling.

From *Seeing Education Whole,* Geneva :World Council of Churches, 1970. pp.107–111.

From *Seeing Education Whole,* Geneva : World Council of Churches, 1970, pp.102–103.

Letter from Paolo Freire

I have just read Martin's letter in which he comments on different aspects and moments of the Bergen Consultation, discussing among other points, the statement which I made on the impossibility of a neutral education.

If I have rightly understood his analysis, I think that it is necessary for me to try to clarify what I mean by "the impossibility of a neutral education."

First of all, it no more depends on my point of view than on anyone else's wish. To say that education cannot be a neutral action is to state a concrete fact, the critical perception of which is an essential part of my attitude with regard to the educational process.

However, this critical perception does not define education as a practice in which educators fail to respect not only the expressivity of the educatees but also their right to *choose* and their right to learn how to choose by the practical method of choosing.

Education cannot be neutral because it is always an action either for the "domestication" of men or for their liberation. While in the former sense it is solely a domesticating practice, in the latter sense it is a procedure in which the educators invite the educatees to know, and to "unveil the world" in a critical manner.

In the domesticating practice, there must be a dichotomy between those who manipulate and those who are manipulated. In the liberating practice, one does not find subjects who liberate, and objects which are liberated. There is thus no dichotomy.

While the former process is prescriptive, the latter is dialogical. Education for domestication is an act of transferring knowledge; but education for liberation is an act of knowing in which educator and educatee together become cognitive subjects, mediated by the knowable object they are seeking to know.

The "domesticating" educator is always the educator of the educatee. The "liberating" educator, however, has "to die" as the unilateral educator of the educatees in order to be born again as the educator-educatee of the educatees-educators. Not only this, but he has to propose to the educatees that they "die" as unilateral educatees of the educator so that they can be born again as educatees-educators of the educator-educatee. Education for liberation is impossible without this mutual "death" and this mutual "new birth."

This is not to say, however, that the educator can totally disappear as an inductive presence. This induction is always implied when education is used as an ideological instrument for the preservation of the status quo, as well as a method for transforming and knowing reality. In "liberating" education, however, the initial induction gradually gives way to a *synthesis* in which the educator-educatee and the educatees-educators become together the subjects of the educational process.

The most important thing for the educator for liberation is to be warned that he is preparing for "death" at the very moment in which he initiates the educational process. Only with his "death," whose process he has to start himself, is his "new birth" possible on the one hand, and that of the educatees as his educators on the other.

He is an educator who has to live the deep significance of Easter.

If he cannot be a libertarian, he cannot be an authoritarian either. He has the difficult task of discovering how authority and liberty can exist in harmony, and of living this harmony.

APPENDIX TO CHAPTER 10

British and Canadian Approaches to Religious Instruction

Noteworthy approaches have been formulated in response to particular situations in contemporary Canada and Britain. In both of these countries religious instruction has traditionally been given in state schools, thus posing a problem in far different terms than in the United States. For example, there the reform of religious instruction is a matter ultimately determined moreso by legislative than by ecclesiastical authority. Moreover, it is hardly a question of whether or not religious instruction shall be given, or whether it will have this or that degree of structure. Rather the question is one of how intimately and forcefully students may be involved by the efforts of the state to teach religion. Elected legislators do not dare repudiate a system which has been in practice for centuries, one which has proven its worth and gained not only the sympathies of the populace but also the status of a cultural value. Yet at the same time it is realized that the students who receive this instruction as a matter of course cannot all be at the same level of receptivity, disposition, and motivation.

In response comes one proposal from the Ministry of Education in Québec. Norman Ryan, head of the Catholic division, proposes a system of nonpartisan instruction in religious content. As part of their general education program, students are to be offered the choice between courses designed to provide religious formation and those which treat of religion as a facet of the culture, with no thought of converting or indoctrinating them. In Ryan's estimation, such a plan constitutes neither a move to rescue an increasingly deteriorating situation, nor a maneuver to ensure attaining the goals of religious instruction under another guise.

In the analogous circumstance of Britain, four approaches are proposed. R. Rummery* analyzes these as "educating in," and "teaching *that,* or *how,* or *about.*" The first approximates the nurturing approach. The second represents traditional practice based on the supposition of Christian faith among students. "Teaching *about*" is restricted to stating the facts about religion without in the least implicating the student. Lastly, "teaching *how*" is another purely descriptive and phenomenological approach, presenting the state of religion as it actually is in society, including the opposition it meets with but also the commitment it attracts; however at no time is the teacher permitted to detail steps for joining the religion or enhancing its prospects.

Rummery manifests his preference for this last, "teaching *how*." The scheme is based on the thought of Ninian Smart** and has been the object of studies by the University of Lancaster's Project on Religious Education. Rummery observes that, despite certain omissions and differences, the principles embodied in this approach make it akin to the catechetical model of education in the faith and to Babin's model of

---

*R. Rummery, *Catechesis and Religious Education in a Pluralistic Society* (Australia: E.J. Dwyer, 1975), pp.163sq.
**Ninian Smart, *Secular Education and the Logic of Religion* (York: Faber and Faber, 1968).

cultural development (pp.181,191). Over this choice of strategy I could not disagree more with my colleague. If we take the Lancaster-Smart model as a sort of preformation in faith—exactly what Ryan proposes to forbid—unfortunate results will follow. We will continue to take manipulativeness as a basis for instructional models, and we will continue to snake our way into the dead ends of the mid-sixties. That is, we will neither have advanced our practices and conceptions, nor resolved our problems, the very ones which conspire to frustrate our enterprise—as I have taken pains to demonstrate in the text (Part One). Above all, if religious educators come to view such a model as after all rather suited to a pluralistic society, which the U.S. evidently is, then I fear we shall dispense ourselves from giving some hard and fast thought to the problems actually entangling us in this country.

Now in actual fact these proposals may be quite legitimate for Canada and England. They constitute a response on the part of state officials who must take everything in their respective societies into account and go on to salvage circumstances as best they can. In this light the responses may be seen as respectable and worthy—though I remain skeptical of the provision for neutral, nonpartisan teaching (hardly a viable position nowadays when nothing is "value-free"). In any event, their goal is to maintain civil society, whereas ours is to enrich the church. In this light we must see that our own efforts in the United States become far more pioneering and creative (-DJP).

NOTES

Chapter 1. EMERGENCE OF CHANGE

1. An additional consideration behind the choice of 1955 may be noted. It was around that year that Monsieur Piveteau made his first visit to the United States.
2. Compare these contemporary discussions: J.J. Kane, "Catholic Separatism." *Commonweal,* 26 June 1953, 58 (12), 293–296; Donald B. King, "Catholics and a Ghetto Mentality." *Catholic World,* 1956, 183, 424–427; John Tracy Ellis, *American Catholics and the Intellectual Life* (Walgreen Lectures, 1955). Heritage Foundation, 1957.
3. Gerard S. Sloyan (Ed.), *Shaping the Christian Message: Essays in Religious Education.* Macmillan, 1958.
4. Exceptions include the journal *Lumen Vitae,* published in French and English, and a number of works by Gabriel Moran translated and published by Editions Ligel.
5. See Adolf Exeler, "French Catechesis." In Josef Goldbrunner (Ed.), *New Catechetical Methods.* Notre Dame, 1965. Pp.123–134.
6. For historical background, see Michael Donnellan, "Bishops and Uniformity in Religious Education: Vatican I to Vatican II." *Living Light,* 1973, 10, 237–248.
7. Sacred Congregation for the Clergy, *General Catechetical Directory.* Washington, D.C.: United States Catholic Conference, 1971.
8. William W. Jacobs, "A Survey of CCD Materials." In J.T. Dillon (Ed.), *Catechetics Reconsidered: Readings in Catechetics for High School Teachers.* Winona, Minn.: St. Mary's College, 1968. Pp.164–177 [from *Ave Maria,* 22 April 1967].
9. James Micael Lee, *The Shape of Religious Instruction.* Notre Dame, Ind.: Religious Education Press, 1971. P.306; *The Flow of Religious Instruction.* Religious Education Press, 1973. P.189.
10. See: Frank B. Norris, "The Catechetics Course in the Major Seminary." In Johannes Hofinger and Theodore C. Stone (Eds.), *Pastoral Catechetics.* Herder & Herder, 1964. Pp.213–225; Gerard S. Sloyan, "Seminary Training and Religious Education." In Sloyan (Ed.), *Modern Catechetics: Message and Method in Religious Formation.* Macmillan, 1963. Pp.291–303.
11. Canon Carr, *The Lamp of the World: An Outline of Religion.* Rev. and enl. by Joseph B. Collins and Raphael J. Collins. Newman, 1941.
12. Rudolph G. Bandas, *Religion Teaching and Practice.* 2nd ed., rev. New York: Wagner, 1939 (1st ed., 1935). P.12.
13. *Manual of the Confraternity of Christian Doctrine.* Rev. ed. Washington, D.C.: Confraternity of Christian Doctrine, 1941. Pp.20–21.
14. Joseph H. Ostdiek, *Simple Methods in Religious Instruction.* Bruce, 1936. P12.
15. Mary Rosalia, *The Adaptive Way of Teaching Confraternity Classes.* St. Paul, Minn.: Catechetical Guild Educational Society, 1955. This is one of several

editions of the hardy manual first published in 1943, of which a reviewer then stated: "Whoever cares to learn how best to teach religion will often consult this book." John V. Matthews, *America*, 29 April 1944, 71, 106. A "Post Vatican Edition" was published in 1966 as *Teaching Religion—The Adaptive Way*.

16. Pierre Babin, *Crisis of Faith: The Religious Psychology of Adolescence*. Herder & Herder, 1963; E.T. Clark, *The Psychology of Religious Awakening*. Macmillan, 1929; Ronald Goldman, *Religious Thinking from Childhood to Adolescence*. London: Routledge & Kegan Paul, 1964; G. Stanley Hall, *Adolescence*. 2 vols. Appleton, 1904; E.D. Starbuck, *The Psychology of Religion*. Scribner, 1900.

17. National Conference of Catholic Bishops, *To Teach as Jesus Did: A Pastoral Message on Catholic Education*. Washington, D.C.: United States Catholic Conference, 1973.

18. Patrick J. Sloan, *The Sunday School Director's Guide to Success*. Benziger, 1909.

19. M. Berenice Trachta, *Catechetics Today: A Manual for Training CCD and Parochial Teachers of Religion*. 1st ed., rev. San Antonio, Texas: Confraternity of Christian Doctrine, 1963. Virtually the identical paragraph appears in the 1950 edition of Rosalia's *The Adaptive Way*, p.v.

20. For example: Hall, *Adolescence;* Starbuck, *Psychology of Religion*.

21. Ostdiek, *Simple Methods*, p.101.

22. Brothers of the Christian Schools, *Living with Christ: High School Religion*. 4 vols. Winona, Minn.: St. Mary's College, 1945–50.

23. For an influential example of this view, see Francis H. Drinkwater, *Teaching the Catechism: An Aid-book for Teachers*. London: Burns, Oates & Washbourne, 1936.

24. Confraternity of Christian Doctrine, *Proceedings of the National Congress . . . Boston, 1946*. St. Anthony Guild, 1947.

25. Johannes Hofinger, "The Formation our Catechists Need." In Sloyan, *Shaping the Christian Message*, pp.221–242.

26. Ostdiek, *Simple Methods*, p.10.

Chapter 2. TRACING A PATH

1. R.M. Rummery, *Catechesis and Religious Education in a Pluralistic Society*. Australia: E.J. Dwyer, 1975.

2. Jean-Pierre Bagot, *Royaume, trésor caché*. Editions du Châlet, 1971; Jean LeDu, *Catéchèse et dynamique de groupe*. Editions Mame-Fayard, 1969.

3. Robert R. Newton, "Current Educational Trends and Strategies in Religious Education." *Religious Education*, 1972, 67, 253–258.

4. Wayne R. Rood, *Understanding Christian Education*. Abingdom, 1970.

5. Harold W. Burgess, *An Invitation to Religious Education*. Notre Dame, Ind.: Religious Education Press, 1975.

6. To name but two: Robert R. Boehlke, *Theories of Learning in Christian Education*. Westminster, 1972; James R. Schaefer, *Program Planning for Adult Christian Education*. Newman, 1972.

7. Represented in the influential work of Louis E. Raths, Merrill Harmin, and Sidney B. Simon, *Values and Teaching*. Merrill, 1966.

8. Ian P. Knox, *Above or Within?* Notre Dame, Ind.: Religious Education Press, 1977.

9. Luis Erdozain, "The Evolution of Catechetics: A Survey of Six International Study Weeks on Catechetics." *Lumen Vitae,* 1970, 25, 7–31.
10. Gabriel Moran, "Catechetics, R.I.P." *Commonweal,* 18 December 1970, 99, 299–302.
11. Gabriel Moran, Gerard Pottebaum, Mary Perkins Ryan and William J. Reedy, "Catechesis for Our Times." In J.T. Dillon (Ed.), *Catechetics Reconsidered: Readings in Catechetics for High School Teachers.* Winona, Minn.: St. Mary's College, 1968. Pp. 6–13 [from *The Bible Today,* February 1967]. "The question also needs to be asked: as competent catechists become available, should not their first work be with adults and especially, perhaps, parents, rather than children? Or, at least, with parents as well as children?" (p.13).
12. Matthew J. Fedewa, "Evolution of an Experiment." In Dillon, *Catechetics Reconsidered,* pp.54–62 [from *Catholic High School Quarterly,* January 1967].
13. See Warren G. Bennis, Kenneth D. Benne, Robert Chin, and Kenneth E. Corey (Eds.), *The Planning of Change.* 3rd ed. Holt, Rinehart & Winston, 1976.
14. For example: Michael Novak, *A New Generation: American and Catholic.* Herder & Herder, 1964; Herbert W. Richardson, *Toward an American Theology.* Harper & Row, 1967; Donald J. Thorman, *American Catholics Face the Future.* Dimension, 1968.
15. Richard A. Schmuck and Matthew B. Miles, *Organization Development in Schools.* Palo Alto, Calif.: National Press Books, 1971.
16. Donald Klein, "Some Notes on the Dynamics of Resistance to Change: The Defender Role" In Bennis, Benne, Chin, and Corey, *The Planning of Change,* pp.117–124; and Alvin Zander, "Resistance to Change—Its Analysis and Prevention." In Bennis *et al.,* 1st ed., 1961, pp.543–548.
17. Savio Warren, "Help for the Insecure Religion Teacher." In Dillon, *Catechetics Reconsidered,* pp.191–197 [from *Living Light,* 1965–66, 2 (4), 30–39].
18. Raths, Harmin, and Simon, *Values and Teaching,* p.75.
19. For example, Carl A. Elder, *Making Value Judgments: Decisions for Today. Teacher's Manual.* Merrill, 1972.
20. Pierre Babin, *Options.* Herder & Herder, 1967; *Methods,* Herder & Herder, 1967; *The Audio-Visual Man.* Pflaum, 1970.
21. James Michael Lee. *The: Flow/Shape/Content of Religious Instruction.* Notre Dame, Ind.: Religious Education Press, 1971, 1973, in preparation; Gabriel Moran, *Catechesis of Revelation.* Herder & Herder, 1966.
22. *LIVE, Grade 1, Teacher's Manual,* and *ACT, Grade 3, Teacher's Manual.* Benziger, 1968, 1973.

Chapter 3. TURNS FOR THE WORSE

1. Harold W. Burgess, *An Invitation to Religious Education.* Notre Dame, Ind.: Religious Education Press, 1975. P.23. It must be stressed that Burgess' account of the "traditional" approach has a different purpose, and hence tone, from that in the text, although some of the same points are made.
2. Klemens Tilmann, "Origin and Development of Modern Catechetical Methods." In Johannes Hofinger (Ed.), *Teaching All Nations: A Symposium on Modern Catechetics.* Herder & Herder, 1961. Pp.81–94.
3. Josef A. Jungmann, *The Good News Yesterday and Today* [1936]. Abrid. ed. Sadlier, 1962; *Handing on the Faith: A Manual of Catechetics* [1955]. Herder & Herder, 1959.

4. Josef Goldbrunner, "Catechetical Method as Handmaid of Kerygma." In Hofinger, *Teaching All Nations*, pp.108–121. The steps are: preparation, presentation, explanation, recapitulation, and application.

5. Mary Rosalia, *The Adaptive Way (A Confraternity School Year Religion Course)*. Washington, D.C.: Confraternity of Christian Doctrine, 1950. Pp.7–12. Citing the influence of the Munich Method, Rosalia gives these five steps: orientation, presentation, assimilation, organization, and recitation.

6. M. Berenice Trachta, *Catechetics Today: A Manual for Training CCD and Parochial Teachers of Religion*. 1st rev. ed. San Antonio, Texas: Confraternity of Christian Doctrine, 1963. Pp.104–105. Trachta also cites the influence of the Munich Method.

7. One version of Herbart's five steps runs: preparation, presentation, association, generalization, and application. Johann Friedrich Herbart (1776–1841) was appointed to occupy Kant's former chair at Königsberg in 1809, and is not to be confounded with the Herbart Method as it was derived from him by German followers, understood from these by American students, translated by these and spread about in America. The master analysis is given by Harold B. Dunkel, *Herbart and Education*. Random House, 1969; and *Herbart and Herbartianism: An Educational Ghost Story*. Chicago, 1970.

8. Jungmann, *Handing on the Faith*, pp.80 sq.

9. André Boyer, "Primary Religious Education and Primary Teaching." In Gerard S. Sloyan (Ed.), *Shaping the Christian Message: Essays in Religious Education*. Macmillan, 1958. Pp.150–169.

10. Gerard S. Sloyan (Ed.), *Modern Catechetics: Message and Method in Religious Formation*. Macmillan, 1963. Chapter 5: Maria de la Cruz Aymes-Coucke, "Teaching the Very Young 'In Spirit and in Truth': Kindergarten, First and Second Grades"; Chap.6: Eva Fleischner, "The Religious Formation of Children in the Second, Third, and Fourth Grades"; Chap.7: Anne Norpel, "Religious Education in the Intermediate Grades"; Chap.8: Mary Nona McGreal, "Growing up in Christ: Religious Education in the Seventh and Eighth Grades"; Chap.9: Mary Virgine Pugh, "Special Problems in the First Two Years of High School"; Chap.10: James E. Kraus, "Religious Formation in the Last Two Years of High School."

11. Trachta, *Catechetics Today*, pp.78–79.

12. Rosalia, *Adaptive Way*, p.v.

13. Erik H. Erikson, "Identity and the Life Cycle." *Psychological Issues*, 1959, 1 (Whole No.1); also, *Childhood and Society*. 2nd ed. Norton, 1963. Chap.7, "Eight Ages of Man."

14. Wayne R. Rood, *Understanding Christian Education*. Abingdon, 1970. Pp.382–383.

15. Department of Education, Green Bay, Wisconsin, "The Green Bay Plan." Introduction by Reverend David Kasperek [with text]. *Notre Dame Journal of Education*, 1973, 4, 113–132. The elaborate chart of this plan is reproduced and explicated in Richard Reichert, *Learning Process for Religious Education*. Pflaum, 1975.

16. As quoted, with italics, in Trachta, *Catechetics Today*, p.75.

17. Sacred Congregation for the Clergy, *General Catechetical Directory*. Washington, D.C.: United States Catholic Conference, 1971.

18. National Conference of Catholic Bishops, *National Catechetical Directory*. Huntington, Ind.: Our Sunday Visitor Press, 1974.

19. E.T. Clark, *The Psychology of Religious Awakening.* Macmillan, 1929; E.D. Starbuck, *The Psychology of Religion.* Scribner, 1900.
20. Pierre Babin, *Crisis of Faith: The Religious Psychology of Adolescence.* Herder & Herder, 1963.
21. Ronald Goldman, *Religious Thinking from Childhood to Adolescence.* London: Routledge & Kegan Paul, 1964; also, *Readiness for Religion: A Basis for Developmental Religious Education.* Routledge & Kegan Paul, 1965.
22. For examples: Jacques de Lorimier, Roger Graveline and Aubert April, *Identity and Faith in Young Adults* (French Canada). Paulist, 1973; James DiGiacomo & Edward Wakin, *We Were Never Their Age.* Holt, Rinehard & Winston, 1972; Martin L. Hoffman, "Development of Internal Moral Standards in Children." In Merton P. Strommen (Ed.), *Research on Religious Development: A Comprehensive Handbook.* Hawthorn, 1971. Pp.211–263; William A. Koppe, *How Persons Grow in Christian Community* (Lutheran Longitudinal Study). Yearbooks in Christian Education, vol. IV. Philadelphia: Fortress Press, 1973; Strommen, *Lutheran Youth Research Survey. Manual.* Minneapolis, Minn.: Lutheran Youth Research Center, 1971; also, *Profiles of Church Youth: Report on a Four-year Study of 3,000 Lutheran High School Youth.* St. Louis, Mo.: Concordia, 1963.
23. André Godin, "Some Developmental Tasks in Christian Education." In Strommen, *Research on Religious Development,* pp.109–154. P.148.
24. David Elkind, "The Development of Religious Understanding in Children and Adolescents." In Strommen, *Research on Religious Development,* pp.655–685. P.682.
25. William B. Williamson analyzes "need" as a normative term, and "meeting needs" through an educational program as "actually a value judgment"—a prescriptive move, rather than a descriptive one as some theorists of Christian education may represent it to be (p.67). *Language and Concepts in Christian Education.* Westminster, 1970. The allusion to "Real Needs" is cited by Williamson from Edward Farley's caustic review of "educators turned mystagogues" or "a kind of inside dopester": "Does Christian Education Need the Holy Spirit? Part I: The Strange History of Christian Paideia." *Religious Education,* 1965, 60, 339–346.
26. Lawrence Kohlberg, "Indoctrination versus Relativity in Value Education." *Theology Digest,* 1973, 21, 113–119; Kohlberg and Eliot Turiel (Eds.), *Recent Research in Moral Development.* Holt, Rinehard & Winston, 1974.
27. Jean Piaget, *The Moral Judgment of the Child* [1935]. Free Press, 1965.
28. Compare titles such as: Thelma C. Adair & Rachel S. Adams, *When We Teach 4's & 5's.* Philadelphia: Geneva, 1962; Dorothy LaCroix Hill, *The Church Teaches Nines to Twelves.* Abingdon, 1965.
29. Charles Burke, "The Religion Discussion Method." In J.T. Dillon (Ed.), *Catechetics Reconsidered: Readings in Catechetics for High School Teachers.* Winona, Minn.: St. Mary's College, 1968. Pp.199–202 (from *LaSalle Catechist,* March 1967). P.199.
30. One source of "practical help" that came highly recommended at the time suggested that the four principal techniques to be mastered by the religion teacher were: how to show a picture, tell a story, ask a question, and, lastly, how to use a piece of chalk. Aloysius J. Heeg, *Practical Helps for the Religion Teacher.* Part I: *Practical Methods for Practical Catechists;* II: *How to Teach the First Communicant;* III: *How to Teach Religion in the Primary Grades;* IV: *How to Teach the Apostles' Creed.* St. Louis: The Queen's Work, I&II, 1940; III&IV, 1944.

31. Examples of: a book, George H. Adkins, *Tools for Teachers*. St. Louis: Bethany Press, 1962; a series of chapters, Wayne R. Rood, *The Art of Teaching Christianity: Enabling the Loving Revolution*. Abington, 1968. Pp.80–144; a chapter, Trachta, *Catechetics Today,* pp.107–136; and paragraph headings, Pugh, "First Two Years of High School," pp.220, 224.

32. Jungmann, *Handing on the Faith*, p.229.

33. Savio Warren, "Help for the Insecure Religion Teacher." In Dillon, *Catechetics Reconsidered*, pp.191–197 [from *Living Light*, 1965–66, 2 (4), 30–39[. P.197.

34. Ferdinand Kopp, "Discussion Techniques." In Josef Goldbrunner (Ed.), *New Catechetical Methods*. Notre Dame, 1965. Pp.82–97. P.97.

35. Pierre Babin (Ed.), *The Audio-Visual Man*. Pflaum, 1970 [All quotations refer to chapters written by Babin.]

36. Pierre Babin, *Methods*. Herder & Herder, 1967. Chap.6, "Students' Questions."

37. For instance, Babin's mentions of the role of student questions in the "discovery" of revelation, in self-expression and freedom, find analogues in book-length manuals devoted to student questioning as essential to "discovery" learning, personal development, positive self-concept, and individual creativity: Arthur A. Carin & Robert B. Sund, *Developing Questioning Techniques: A Self-concept Approach*. Merrill, 1971; Francis P. Hunkins, *Involving Students in Questioning*. Allyn & Bacon, 1976; E.Paul Torrance and Robert E. Myers, *Creative Learning and Teaching*. Dodd, Mead, 1970. Similarly, Charles A. Curran regards the learner's question "as a form of cautious, beginning self-investment" (p.194). *Counseling-Learning: A Whole-Person Model for Education*. Grune & Stratton, 1972.

38. François Coudreau, "The Catechesis of the Church Understood through the Celebration of the Liturgy." *Living Light*, 1965, 2 (3), 6–17; Jungmann, *Handing on the Faith*, p.223; Mary Perkins Ryan, "The Liturgy and Catechetics." In Sloyan, *Modern Catechetics*, pp.23–44; William Scherzer, "Liturgy and Catechetics: Inseparable Partners." In Johannes Hofinger & Theodore C. Stone (Eds.), *Pastoral Catechetics*. Herder & Herder, 1964. Pp.48–65.

39. Sister Romain, *Tell My People*. Fides, 1965.

40. Joseph Colomb, "The Use of the Bible in Teaching the Church's Faith." In Sloyan, *Modern Catechetics*, pp.1–22; Gerard S. Sloyan, "What Should Children's Catechisms Be Like?" In Hofinger and Stone, *Pastoral Catechetics*, pp.33–46.

41. Thomas F. Mathews, "Manicheans in our Midst." *Living Light*, 1965, 2 (1), 124–134. Pp. 126, 127.

42. On these models, see Didier J. Piveteau, "Vers demain." *Catéchistes*, 1973, No.95, 401–406. The distinctions are taken from Gilles Ferry, *Technique du travail en groupe*. Editions Dunod, 1970.

43. Pierre Babin, "Le Point." *Catéchistes*, 1974, No.100, 563–572. P.567.

Chapter 4. VENTURES OF PROMISE

1. Alfonso M. Nebreda, *Kerygma in Crisis?* Loyola, 1965.

2. See Carl R. Rogers, *Client-Centered Therapy*. Houghton Mifflin, 1951.

3. The text emphasizes neglect in practice of Nebreda's work, which is not at all to say that it was without influence; interestingly enough a student of Jungmann's, Johannes Hofinger, dedicated to Nebreda his *Evangelization and Catechesis*. Paulist, 1976.

4. Gabriel Moran, "Catechetics, R.I.P." *Commonweal*, 18 December 1970, 99, 299–302.

5. Didier J. Piveteau, "Biblical Pedagogics." In James Michael Lee and Patrick C. Rooney (Eds.), *Toward a Future for Religious Education*. Pflaum, 1970. Pp.93–114. P.109.

6. Gabriel Moran, preface to Hubert Halbfas, *Theory of Catechetics: Language and Experience in Religious Education*. Herder & Herder, 1971.

7. Gabriel Moran, "Religious Education—Community." *America*, 30 January 1971, 124 (4), 86–89.

8. Sidney B. Simon, *Meeting Yourself Halfway: 31 Value Clarification Strategies for Daily Living*. Niles, Ill.: Argus Communications, 1974; Simon, Leland W. Howe and Howard Kirschenbaum, *Values Clarification: A Handbook of Practical Strategies for Teachers and Students*. Hart, 1972; Merrill Harmin, Kirschenbaum and Simon, *Clarifying Values through Subject Matter: Applications for the Classroom*. Minneapolis, Minn.: Winston, 1973; Kirschenbaum and Simon (Eds.), *Readings in Values Clarification*. Winston, 1973. Simon, Hawley, and Britton. *Composition for Personal Growth: Values Clarification through Writing*. Hart, 1973.

9. Delwin Brown, Ralph E. James and Gene Reeves (Eds.), *Process Philosophy and Christian Thought*. Bobbs-Merrill, 1971; Ewert H. Cousins (Ed.), *Process Theology*. Newman, 1971; David Griffin, *A Process Christology*. Westminster, 1973; Leon McKenzie, *Process Catechetics*. Paulist, 1970; Edgar H. Schein, *Process Consultation*. Addison-Wesley, 1969.

10. Benjamin S. Bloom, et al. (Eds.) *Taxonomy of Educational Objectives: The Classification of Educational Goals*. I, *Cognitive Domain;* II, *Affective Domain;* III, *Psycho-motor Domain*. David McKay, 1956, 1964, 1972. On the importance of the affective domain in religious instruction, see: Robert T. O'Gorman, "The Nature and Meaning of the Affective Domain." *Lumen Vitae*, 1971, 26, 81–88.

11. Carl R. Rogers, *On Becoming a Person*. Houghton Mifflin, 1961. See also Rogers, *Freedom to Learn*. Merrill, 1969. Chap.12, "A Modern Approach to the Valuing Process."

12. For examples: Sidney B. Simon, "Value Education." In John H. Westerhoff (Ed.), *A Colloquy on Christian Education*. Pilgrim, 1972. Pp.158–177; Bert S. Gerard, "Values Teaching: The Hidden Agenda in Religious Education." *Religious Education*, 1974, 69, 219–227; Brian P. Hall, *Value Clarification as Learning Process:* I, *A Handbook for Religious Educators* (with Maury Smith); II, *A Sourcebook for Learning Theory;* III, *A Guidebook of Learning Strategies*. Paulist, 1973; Hall, *The Development of Consciousness: A Confluent Theory of Values*. Paulist, 1973; Louis M. Savary, *Integrating Values: Theory and Exercises for Clarifying and Integrating Religious Values*. Pflaum, 1974. The National Catechetical Directory specifies "value clarification strategies" among priority techniques for adolescent religious education (para.181).

13. J.T. Dillon, *Personal Teaching*. Merrill, 1971 (*Educación Personal*. Buenos Aires: Editorial Guadalupe, 1973. Trans. R.Alcalde; *Eux et moi, le risque d'enseigner*. Paris: Editions Fleurus, 1974. Trans. P.Castan); John F. Murphy, *The Catechetical Experience*. Herder & Herder, 1968.

14. It is interesting to note that while Dillon's work, for example, has been translated into European tongues, the majority of European ones of that same period have not been translated into English; examples from France and Belgium would include: Pierre Bagot, *Royaume, trésor caché*. Editions du Châlet, 1971; Marie Joelle Dardelin, *La Liberté de croire*. Editions Ouvrières, 1969; Jean LeDu, *Catéchèse et dynamique de groupe*. Editions Mame-Fayard, 1969.

15. J.T. Dillon, "Discussion of *Options* by Pierre Babin." *La Salle Catechist*, 1967, 33, 170–174. P.170.
16. J.T. Dillon (Ed.), *Catechetics Reconsidered: Readings in Catechetics for High School Teachers*. Winona, Minn.: St. Mary's College, 1968; and, for example: "The Role of the Religion Teacher." *La Salle Catechist*, 1966, 32, 206–214.
17. Compare the title in French translation, "le risque d'enseigner."

Chapter 5. ENTERPRISE AT REST

1. Gabriel Moran, *Design for Religion: Towards Ecumenical Education*. Herder & Herder, 1970. P.25.
2. In connection with the term "casuistry," it is interesting to note that a reviewer in *America* found Van Caster's contribution to *Experiential Catechetics* "less than lucid"—"after eight years of college and graduate study I was left wondering what he could possibly be talking about in terms of practical experience." P.W. Boyd, "Catechetics 1970: European Perspectives." *America*, 25 July 1970, 123 (2), 40–41.
3. Joseph C. Neiman, *Coordinators: A New Focus in Parish Religious Education*. Winona, Minn.: St. Mary's College, 1971. Pp.2,5.
4. "New frontier" is from Neiman, *Coordinators*, p.1; "new ministry" from National Conference of Catholic Bishops, *National Catechetical Directory*. Washington, D.C.: United States Catholic Conference, 1974. Para.95; "new role" from Maria Harris, *The D.R.E.* [Director of Religious Education] *Book: Questions and Strategies for Parish Personnel*. Paulist, 1976. P.2.
5. Andrew M. Greeley and Peter H. Rossi, *The Education of Catholic Americans*. Aldine, 1966. Pp.24,285,288.
6. Greeley and Rossi, *Education of Catholic Americans*, p.2.
7. Here one is reminded of Urban Steinmetz's remark (after Thomas Szasz): "... *Anytime in recent history we have increased the number of 'trained and qualified' people to 'help' us with a particular problem, we have also increased the number of problems needing help*" (p.110). Urban G. Steinmetz, "A Return to Common Sense." *Notre Dame Journal of Education*, 1974, 5, 107–120.
8. For example: Neiman, *Coordinators;* Stephen C. Nevin, "Parish Coordinator: Evaluating Tasks and Roles." *Living Light*, 1972, 9 (1), 48–56.
9. Eric Berne, *Games People Play: The Psychology of Human Relationships*. Grove, 1964.
10. Cited in Moran, *Design for Religion*, pp.12–13.

Chapter 6. TO CONSTRUE A WORLD

1. The editions consulted and quoted for this book are as follows.
Sacred Congregation for the Clergy, General Catechetical Directory. Washington, D.C.: United States Catholic Conference, 1971. 2nd printing, 112pp., 134 paras. Frontispiece contains under the title: "This is the only English translation of the *Directorium Catechisticum Generale* approved by the Sacred Congregation of the Clergy."
National Conference of Catholic Bishops, National Catechetical Directory: For Catholics of the United States. Washington, D.C.: United States Catholic Confer-

ence, 1974. 48 pp., 237 paras., tabloid, printed by Our Sunday Visitor Press, Huntington, Indiana. Frontispiece contains as first sentence: "This is the first draft of the National Catechetical Directory." And a later: "Publication date is expected sometime in 1976."
National Conference of Catholic Bishops, *To Teach as Jesus Did: A Pastoral Message on Catholic Education*. November, 1972. Washington, D.C.: United States Catholic Conference, 1973. 57 pp., 155 paras.

2. Some examples of interesting discussions may be noted.
For the General Catechetical Directory:
Special Issue, *Living Light*, 1972, 9 (Whole No.3); Berard L. Marthaler, *Catechetics in Context: Notes & Commentary on the General Catechetical Directory Issued by the Sacred Congregation for the Clergy*. Huntington, Ind.: Our Sunday Visitor Press, 1973. [Gives the official text on left-hand pages and an erudite commentary on facing pages.]
For the National Catechetical Directory:
Wilfrid H. Paradis, "A Precedent-Making Project in the Catholic Church: The Preparation of a National Catechetical Directory." *Religious Education*, 1975, 70, 235–249.
For the Pastoral on Catholic Education:
Special Feature, "The U.S. Bishops on Religious Education." *Living Light*, 1973, 10 (2), 237–295.
Special Issues, "To Teach as Jesus Did: Educational Developments Since the Pastoral; Alternatives in Education." *Notre Dame Journal of Education*, 1975, 6 (Whole Nos. 3,4).

3. For example, two Protestant responses to the General Catechetical Directory may be cited.
C. Ellis Nelson, "A Protestant Response." *Living Light*. 1972, 9 (3), 85–93.
John H. Westerhoff III, "Protestants and Roman Catholics Together." In Westerhoff & Gwen Kennedy Neville, *Generation to Generation: Conversations on Religious Education and Culture*. Pilgrim, 1974. Chapter 1, pp.27–35.

Chapter 7. THE CHANGING CONSCIOUSNESS OF MAN

1. Peter L. Berger, *The Sacred Canopy: Elements of a Sociological Theory of Religion*. Doubleday, 1967. P.4.

2. Such is the sense made of this paragraph in Berger's *Canopy:*
"Externalization is the ongoing outpouring of human being into the world, both in the physical and the mental activities of man. Objectivation is the attainment by the products of this activity (again both physical and mental of a reality that confronts its original producers as a facticity external to and other than themselves. Internalization is the reappropriation by men of this same reality, transforming it once again from structures of the objective world into structures of the subjective consciousness. It is through externalization that society is a human product. It is through objectivation that society becomes a reality *sui generis*. It is through internalization that man is a product of society" (p.4).

3. Jan Hendrik van den Berg, *The Changing Nature of Man*. Norton, 1961. P.8.

4. Some examples to consult:
Charles A. Reich, *The Greening of America*. Random House, 1970; David Riesman, *The Lonely Crowd: A Study of the Changing American Character* (with Nathan Glazer & Reuel Denney). Yale, 1950 [abridged ed., 1961]; Alvin Toffler,

Future Shock. Random House, 1970; and Toffler (Ed.), *Learning for Tomorrow: The Role of the Future in Education.* Random House, 1974.

5. Bruno Bettelheim, "Parent and Child." *New York Times Magazine,* 13 April 1969, pp.125+; Walter J. Ong, *In the Human Grain: Further Explorations of Contemporary Culture.* Macmillan, 1967. P.11.

6. Wayne R. Rood, *On Nurturing Christians: Perhaps a Manifesto for Education.* Abingdon, 1972. P.29.

7. Walter J. Ong, "Knowledge in Time." In Ong (Ed.), *Knowledge and the Future of Man: An International Symposium.* Holt, Rinehart & Winston, 1968. Pp.3–38. P.7.

8. James Michael Lee, *The Shape of Religious Instruction.* Notre Dame, Ind.: Religious Education Press, 1971. P.20.

9. Dennis Gabor, *Inventing the Future.* London: Secker & Warburg, 1963. P. 180.

10. Rood, *Nurturing Christians,* p.49.

11. For explanation and examples from several spheres of activity, see Herbert A. Thelen, *Dynamics of Groups at Work. Chicago,* 1954.

12. Walter J. Ong, *The Barbarian Within.* Macmillan, 1962. Pp.225–226; see also his *The Presence of the Word.* Yale, 1967.

13. Reuel L. Howe, *The Miracle of Dialogue.* Seabury, 1963. P.65; Gregory Baum, *Man Becoming: God in Secular Experience.* Herder & Herder, 1970. P.41.

14. Lester R. Brown, *World Without Borders.* Random House, 1972.

15. Walter J. Ong, "The Barbarian Within: Outsiders Inside Society Today." In Ong, *The Barbarian Within,* pp.260–285. Talcott Parsons, as cited in E.Zigler & I.L. Child, "Socialization." In G.Lindzey & E.Aronson (Eds.), *Handbook of Social Psychology.* 2nd ed. Addison-Wesley, 1969. Vol.3, p.471.

16. Ong, *Human Grain,* pp.1–16 ("Breakthrough in Communications").

17. For example: Philippe Ariès, *Centuries of Childhood: A Social History of Family Life.* Random House, 1962; Margaret Mead, *From the South Seas: Studies of Adolescence and Sex in Primitive Societies.* Wm. Morrow, 1939.

18. Frederick Elkin and Gerald Handel, *The Child and Society: The Process of Socialization.* 2nd ed. Random House, 1972. P.54.

19. John Middleton (Ed.), *From Child to Adult: Studies in the Anthropology of Education.* University of Texas, 1970. P.xv.

20. Editorial, "Red, White, Blue—and Gray." *Chicago Tribune,* 13 June 1976.

21. For example: James E. Birren (Ed.), *The Handbooks of Aging; I, Biology of Aging; II, Psychology of Aging; III, Aging and the Social Sciences.* Van Nostrand Reinhold, 1976; Zena Smith Blau, *Old Age in a Changing Society.* N.Y.: New Viewpoints, 1973.

22. Edgar Z. Friedenberg, *The Vanishing Adolescent.* Dell, 1959. Pp.203,204.

23. Middleton, *From Child to Adult,* p.xv. The sense of the sentences that precede and follow this citation are also from Middleton.

24. Frank Musgrove, *Youth and the Social Order.* Indiana University, 1964. P.33 [as cited in Elkin & Handel, *Child and Society,* p.145].

25. "Tension and Growth: Annual Report of the Student Mental Health Clinic, 1974–75." *The University of Chicago Record,* 1976, 19 (3), 60–66. P.60.

26. *Time,* 26 July 1976, p.74.

Chapter 8. AN EMERGING CONCEPTION OF GOD

1. In addition to those quoted in the text, see the enlightening analysis by John S. Dunne, *Time and Myth.* Doubleday, 1973.

2. James T. Burtchaell, *Philemon's Problem: The Daily Dilemma of the Christian.* Chicago: Foundation for Adult Catechetical Teaching Aids, 1973. P.11.
3. Peter L. Berger, *The Sacred Canopy: Elements of a Sociological Theory of Religion.* Doubleday, 1967. Pp.1–6.
4. John R. McCall, "Excerpts from a Talk." In John R. McCall (Ed.), *Dimensions in Religious Education.* Havertown, Pa.: CIM Books, 1973. Pp. 145–148. P.145.
5. See for example: Peter L. Berger and Thomas Luckmann, *The Social Construction of Reality.* Doubleday, 1966; Thomas S. Kuhn, *The Structure of Scientific Revolutions.* Rev. ed. Chicago, 1970; Jean Piaget, *Biology and Knowledge: Relations between Organic Regulations and Cognitive Processes.* Chicago, 1971.
6. George McCauley, "Christ and Growth in Personality." In McCall, *Dimensions,* pp.149–153. P.151 [from *Worship,* 1969, 43].
7. For example, Langdon Gilkey, *Naming the Whirlwind: The Renewal of God-Language.* Bobbs-Merrill, 1969.
8. Albert Schweitzer, *The Quest of the Historical Jesus* [1906]. Macmillan, 1961.
9. Avery Dulles, "The Church, the Churches, and the Catholic Church." In McCall, *Dimensions,* pp.3–35 [from *Theological Studies,* 1972,33]. The doctrines mentioned in the text subsequently are from this article. See also Dulles' *Models of the Church.* Doubleday, 1974.
10. For proposals advanced by writers cited, see: Baum, *Man Becoming,* pp.61–93; Cox, *Snake,* p.315; Kenny, *Christian Future, passim;* and for McBrien, *The Remaking of the Church: An Agenda for Reform.* Harper & Row, 1973.
11. Maria Harris, "The Aesthetic and Religious Education." In McCall, *Dimensions,* pp.141–144 (from *The Ecumenist,* 1972, 10). P.142.
12. James Michael Lee, *The Flow of Religious Instruction.* Notre Dame, Ind.: Religious Education Press, 1973. Pp.180–188.
13. James Michael Lee, *The Shape of Religious Instruction.* Religious Education Press, 1971. Pp.85–86.
14. Reuel L. Howe, *The Miracle of Dialogue.* Seabury, 1963.
15. Daniel Callahan, as cited in Kenny, *Christian Future,* p.226 (from *National Catholic Reporter,* 9 August 1967).

Chapter 9. ALTERNATIVES TO SCHOOL

1. Didier J. Piveteau, "Illich: Enemy of Schools or School Systems?" [Trans. J.T. Dillon] *School Review,* 1974, 82, 393–412. P.398.
2. *Chicago Tribune,* 7 July 1975.
3. *South Bend Tribune,* 6 and 7 July 1975.
4. Lewis H. Lapham, "Received Ideas." *Harper's,* July 1976, p.10.
5. Andrew M. Greeley & William E. Brown, *Can Catholic Schools Survive?* Sheed & Ward, 1970; C. Albert Koob & Russell Shaw, *S.O.S. for Catholic Schools.* Holt, Rinehart & Winston, 1970; Martin A. Larson, *When Parochial Schools Close: A Study in Educational Financing.* New York: Robert B. Luce, 1972; Mary Perkins Ryan, *Are Parochial Schools the Answer?* Holt, Rinehart & Winston, 1963.
6. From 1966 to 1976, enrollment declined from 5.1 to 3.1 million, and the number of parochial schools from 12 to 9 thousand, according to figures in *The Official Catholic Directory. Anno Domini 1976.* P.J. Kenedy, 1976. A study by the National Opinion Research Center suggests that declining enrollment might be due largely to the lack of available_or accessible schools. Andrew M. Greeley,

William C. McCready & Kathleen McCourt, *Catholic Schools in a Declining Church*. Sheed & Ward, 1976.

7. Allen Graubard, "The Free School Movement." *Harvard Educational Review*, 1972, 42, 351–373. (This article reports an "official survey" funded by H.E.W.; all figures are approximate.) While it may surely be true that numbers of these schools would close within a few years, their significance to the narrative lies in the effort to open them.

8. Sara Little, "On the End of an Era." In John H. Westerhoff (Ed.), *A Colloquy on Christian Education*. Pilgrim, 1972. Pp.25–30; Wayne R. Rood, *On Nurturing Christians: Perhaps a Manifesto for Education*. Abingdon, 1972.

9. Piveteau, "Illich," pp.396–397.

10. Edgar B. Gumbert & Joel H. Spring, *The Superschool and the Superstate: American Education in the Twentieth Century, 1918–1970*. Wiley, 1974. Chap.5, "The Search for Alternatives"; Gerald Lee Gutek, *Philosophical Alternatives in Education*. Merrill, 1974. Chap.12, "Open Education and De-Schooling"; Michael B. Katz (Ed.), *School Reform: Past and Present*. Little, Brown, 1971.

11. Paulo Freire, *Pedagogy of the Oppressed*. Seabury, 1970; Paul Goodman, *Compulsory Mis-education*. Vintage, 1962; John Holt, *How Children Fail*. Pitman, 1964; Ivan Illich, *De-schooling Society*. Harper & Row, 1971; Herbert Kohl, *36 Children*. New American Library, 1967; Everett Reimer, *School is Dead: Alternatives in Education*. Doubleday, 1971.

12. Bicentennial Editorial, "The Freedom of the Educated." *Chicago Tribune*, 30 June 1976.

13. Arthur Bestor, "Education and the American Scene." In Brand Blanshard (Ed.), *Education in the Age of Science*. Basic Books, 1959. As exerpted in Katz, *School Reform*, p.105.

14. Rachel Henderlite, "Asking the Right Questions." In Westerhoff, *Colloquy*, pp.197–206. P.202.

15. Andrew M. Greeley and Peter H. Rossi, *The Education of Catholic Americans*. Aldine, 1966.

16. Robert Dreeben, *On What Is Learned in School*. Addison-Wesley, 1968.

17. Edgar Z. Friedenberg, *The Vanishing Adolescent*. Dell, 1959; *Coming of Age in America*. Vintage, 1963; *Society's Children: A Study of Ressentiment in the Secondary School* [with Carl Nordstrom & Hilary A. Gold]. Random House, 1967; *The Dignity of Youth & Other Atavisms*. Beacon, 1966.

18. Robert K. Merton, *Social Theory and Social Structure*. Free Press, 1968.

19. Paul B. Horton and Robert L. Horton, *Self Review in Introductory Sociology: Programmed Learning Aid*. Homewood, Ill.: Irwin, 1971.

20. Westerhoff, *Generation*, p.42.

21. Didier J. Piveteau, "The Christian School, Sign of Salvation." In J.T. Dillon (Ed.), *Catechetics Reconsidered: Readings in Catechetics for High School Teachers*. Winona, Minn.: St. Mary's College, 1968. Pp.68–75.

22. Christopher Jencks, "Is the Public School Obsolete?" *The Public Interest*, Winter 1966, 18–27. As excerpted in Katz, *School Reform*, pp.241,242.

23. David Rogers, *110 Livingstone Street*. Random House, 1968. As excerpted in Katz, *School Reform*, p.269.

24. Francis P. Rotsaert, "Confessions of a Straddler: Towards New Structures in Catholic Education." *Notre Dame Journal of Education*, 1973, 3, 330–337.

25. For more Freire, see his *Education for Critical Consciousness*. Seabury, 1973. For further implications for religious education, see William B. Kennedy, "Education for Liberation and Community." *Religious Education*, 1975, 70, 5–44.

26. The next few paragraphs in the text borrow from Piveteau, "Illich," pp.401 *sq.*

27. For recent formulations, see Mario D. Fantini (Ed.), *Alternative Education*. Doubleday, 1976.
28. Roger L. Shinn, "Education is a Mystery." In Westerhoff, *Colloquy*, pp.18–24.
29. Rotsaert, "Confessions of a Straddler," p.332.
30. Office of Education, World Council of Churches, *Seeing Education Whole*. Geneva, 1970. P.111. For full text of the Bergen proposals, see Appendix.
31. Richard H. Metzcus, Gregory M. Holtz and Jerry G. Florent, Guest Editorial, "New Directions in Catholic Education: An Empirical Approach." *Notre Dame Journal of Education*, 1975, 6, 5–12.
32. Westerhoff, *Generation to Generation*, p.42.
33. Henderlite, "Asking the Right Questions."
34. Wayne R. Rood, *Understanding Christian Education*. Abingdon, 1970; Westerhoff, *Colloquy*.
35. John H. Westerhoff, *Values for Tomorrow's Children: An Alternative Future for Education in the Church*. Pilgrim, 1970.
36. For more Illich, see his *Celebration of Awareness: A Call for Institutional Revolution*. Doubleday, 1970; also his (and others') essay in Alan Gartner, Colin Greer & Frank Riessmans (Eds.), *After Deschooling, What?* Harper & Row, 1973. For further implications for religious education, see Theodore A. McConnell, "Ivan Illich's Assault on Education." *Religious Education*, 1972, 67, 41–48; and Piveteau, "Illich."
37. James Michael Lee, *The Flow of Religious Instruction*. Notre Dame, Ind.: Religious Education Press, 1973. P.9.
38. John H. Westerhoff, "A Socialization Model." In Westerhoff, *Colloquy*, pp. 80–90. P.90.

Chapter 10. APPROACHES TO INSTRUCTION

1. For example: Robert R. Boehlke, *Theories of Learning in Christian Education*. Westminster, 1972; Iris V. Cully, *Change, Conflict, and Self-Determination: Next Steps in Religious Education*. Westminster, 1972; James R. Schaefer, *Program Planning for Adult Christian Education*. Newman, 1972; Mary Michael O'Shaughnessy, "B.F. Skinner Revisited: Implications for Religious Education." *Living Light*, 1973, 10 (3), 360–374; Gerard P. Weber, "Goal Analysis and Religious Education." *Living Light*, 1973, 10 (2), 200–212.
2. Notably by Harold Burgess, who analyzes Lee's system according to traditional categories of aim, content, teacher & student, environment, and evaluation. Harold W. Burgess, *An Invitation to Religious Education*. Notre Dame, Ind.: Religious Education Press, 1975. Pp.127–165; or his article, "James Michael Lee's Social-Science Approach to Religious Instruction." *Notre Dame Journal of Education*, 1974, 5, 293–312.
3. See Lee, "Prediction in Religious Instruction." *Living Light*, 1972, 9 (2), 43–54.
4. Nathaniel L. Gage (Ed.), *Handbook of Research on Teaching*. Rand McNally, 1963; Robert M.W. Travers (Ed.), *Second Handbook of Research on Teaching*. Rand McNally, 1973; Merton P. Strommen (Ed.), *Research on Religious Development: A Comprehensive Handbook*. Hawthorn, 1971.
5. Michael O'Neill, "Review of *The Shape of Religious Instruction* by James Michael Lee." *Living Light*, 1972, 9 (1), 143–145. P.143.
6. O'Neill, "Review," p.144.
7. The number of which may perhaps be indicated by the 422 footnotes in the chapter.

8. For two examples:

   "For religious instruction, value-freedom means that the teaching process itself can facilitate behavioral modification toward one system of values more or less as readily as toward a different system of values. In other words, the process of producing learning outcomes can take place regardless of the values the teacher wishes the individual to attain" (S, 207).

   "These three devices can be used as effectively in the teaching of religion as in the teaching of any other kind of content" (F, 268).

9. Among the "blocks to change" which Lee identifies in the effort to persuade Americans to the social-science approach is the European influence upon religious instruction in this country. The European mentality he characterizes as ignorant, uncomprehending, antagonistic, and prejudiced out-of-hand against the approach he urges. In his list of influential European writers there figures the name of Piveteau (S, 306).

10. For example, Westerhoff's coauthor, Gwen Kennedy Neville, is an anthropologist who studied a Presbyterian sect in North Carolina; see her chapter in *Generation to Generation,* "The Sacred Community—Kin and Congregation in the Transmission of Culture," pp.51–71.

11. Bruno Bettelheim, *A Home for the Heart.* Knopf, 1974; also his "A Therapeutic Milieu," *American Journal of Orthopsychiatry,* 1948, 8, 191–206 (with Emmy Sylvester); and his "Eriksonian" study of education in the kibbutzim, *Children of the Dream: Communal Child-Rearing and American Education.* Macmillan, 1969.

12. Wayne R. Rood, *On Nurturing Christians: Perhaps A Manifesto for Education.* Abingdon, 1972.

13. Lee: "A major focus of religious instruction is to consciously facilitate the socialization of the individual into the church community in particular, and into the Christian fellowship-community in general, and finally into God's special fellowship." (S, 24).

    Westerhoff: "While socialization includes education, education is a distinct aspect of socialization.... Schooling is a specific form of education, a much narrower phenomenon" (G, 38).

14. The distinction runs:

    "Education is a more limited concept. While socialization includes education, education is a distinct aspect of socialization.... Schooling is a specific form of education, a much narrower phenomenon. Socialization, on the other hand, while including all such specific efforts (schooling and education), also includes the formal and informal implicit means by which a people acquire and sustain their understandings and way of life" (GG, 38).

15. Rachel Henderlite, "Asking the Right Questions." In John H. Westerhoff (Ed.), *A Colloquy on Christian Education.* Pilgrim, 1972. Pp.197–206.

16. Wayne R. Rood, *The Art of Teaching Christianity: Enabling the Loving Revolution.* Abingdon, 1968; *Understanding Christian Education.* Abingdon, 1970; *On Nurturing Christians: Perhaps a Manifesto for Education.* Abingdon, 1972.

17. J.W. Getzels, "Socialization and Education: A Note on Discontinuities." *Teachers College Record,* 1974, 76, 218–225.

18. Other differences could be noted. For example, nurturing theorists, by and large, are Protestant, and nurturing has a longer tradition. The first edition of Horace Bushnell's *Christian Nurture* appeared in 1847: "no American book can with better right be deemed a religious and educational classic," says Luther A. Weigle in a reprint of the 1916 edition (Yale, 1947, p.xxxi).

19. Carter V. Good (Ed.), *Dictionary of Education*. 3rd ed. McGraw-Hill, 1973. P.542.

20. The point of the text is to review one particular conception rather than to represent "socialization theory." But interested readers will appreciate that the writers under review take only one of several options available among the manifold issues, viewpoints, and conceptualizations in the field. For comprehensive overviews, see the compendium by David A. Goslin (Ed.), *Handbook of Socialization Theory and Research*. Rand McNally, 1969; and two impressive shorter accounts: John A. Clausen (Ed.), *Socialization and Society*. Little, Brown, 1968; Edward Zigler and Irvin L. Child, *Socialization and Personality Development*. Addison-Wesley, 1973.

21. William J. Bouwsma, "Christian Adulthood." *Daedalus*, 1976, 105 (2), 77–92.

22. For a suggestive analysis, see Robert Dreeben, *On What is Learned in School*. Addison-Wesley, 1968. Dreeben views the school as a "transitional mechanism" linking the family life of children and the public life of adults; he studies social norms and behaviors, and does not limit himself to what is taught or to what is "teachable pedagogically." The demands of modern industrial society are such that, on Dreeben's hypothesis, "persons raised almost completely within conjugal or extended kinship units would be psychologically unprepared to cope with them" (p.94).

23. Orville G. Brim and Stanton S. Wheeler, *Socialization after Childhood: Two Essays*. Wiley, 1966. P.35.

24. Frances W. Eastman, "The Open Church School," pp.106–111; Charles C. Lemert, "Suburban Action," pp.127–132; Roger L. Shinn, "Education is a Mystery," pp.18–24.

25. Joseph Williamson, "A Pedagogy for Christians," pp.31–39.

26. Brim & Wheeler, *Socialization*, pp.25,45.

27. Henderlite, "Asking the Right Questions," pp.204–205.

28. Mary-Margaret Scobey and Grace Graham (Eds.), *To Nurture Humaneness: Commitment for the '70's*. Association for Supervision and Curriculum Development, 1970 Yearbook. Washington, D.C.: National Education Association, 1970.

29. John M. Larsen, "Learning Space for a Learning Community." In Westerhoff, *Colloquy*, pp. 112–126.

30. Andrew M. Greeley and Peter H. Rossi, *The Education of Catholic Americans*. Aldine, 1966, P.95.

31. Greeley and Rossi state their position as follows: "As social scientists, we maintain a skeptical view concerning the efficacy of formal schooling for the teaching of values. To the social scientist a view of formal education as an omnipotent socializing agent shows an exaggerated regard for education.... Most of the research literature available indicates that the changes in value orientations which do occur in the schools are limited and are conditioned by the previous experiences of the student in his family milieu" (p.7).

32. See for example James Coleman's celebrated study of the school's "informal culture," *The Adolescent Society: The Social Life of the Teenager and its Impact on Education*. Free Press, 1961. And, for an interesting closer look, Philip A. Cusick's participant-observation study, *Inside High School: The Student's World*. Holt, Rinehart & Winston, 1973. Cusick, a former teacher and administrator, discovered in mid-semester that he was in effect being socialized by the students with whom he was sitting in class (and subjects of his observations); among other developments, Cusick began to cut classes, avoid teachers, and spend group-

discussion periods huddling not over Beowulf but schemes to rob gas-stations, date girls, and, above all, to maintain active noninvolvement in academic matters.
33. Erik H. Erikson, "Identity and the Life Cycle." *Psychological Issues*, 1959, 1 (Whole No.1); *Childhood and Society*. 2nd ed. Norton, 1963.
34. Harriet L. Rheingold, "The Social and Socializing Infant." In Goslin, *Handbook of Socialization*, pp.779–790. P.785.
35. An intriguing question would be the extent to which, despite verbal disavowals, nurturing theorists actually seem to hold, and structuring theorists need to hold, a "passive" view of human nature.
36. Hans Peter Dreitzel (Ed.), *Childhood and Socialization*. Macmillan, 1973. P.5. This collection is designed to illustrate research and theory in line with the shift to an active or interactionist view. One early pertinent model is found in Talcott Parsons and Robert F. Bales, *Family, Socialization and Interaction Process*. Free Press, 1955.
37. Hope Jensen Leichter, "Some Perspectives on the Family as Educator." *Teachers College Record*, 1974, 76, 175–217; Rheingold, "The Social and Socializing Infant," p.779.
38. Edna Stumpf, "Learning Clusters." In Westerhoff, *Colloquy*, pp.152–157.

Chapter 11. CALL TO ACTION

1. For examples Protestant and Catholic: Michael G. Lawler, "Long Live Paradigms: Models of Religious Education." *Religious Education*, 1974, 69, 268–276; Randolph Crump Miller, "Predicaments and Pointers in Religious Education." In John H. Westerhoff (Ed.), *A Colloquy on Christian Education*. Pilgrim, 1972. Pp. 188–196; Gabriel Moran, "The Future of Catechetics." *Living Light*, 1968, 5 (1), 6–22; Gabriel Moran, Gerard Pottebaum, Mary Perkins Ryan and William J. Reedy, "Catechesis for Our Times." In J.T. Dillon (Ed.), *Catechetics Reconsidered*. Winona, Minn.: St. Mary's College, 1968. Pp. 6–13 (from *The Bible Today*, February 1967); John H. Westerhoff, "The Signs of the Times." In Westerhoff, *Colloquy*, pp.248–252; and Westerhoff, *Values for Tomorrow's Children: An Alternative Future for Education in the Church*. Pilgrim, 1970.
2. See Barian Bohen, "Catechesis in a Diaspora Situation." *Living Light*, 1968, 5 (1), 87–94.
3. Monika Hellwig, "Catechetics Here and Now: Thoughts on Moran's Article." *Living Light*, 1968, 5 (2), 62–70.
4. Henry J. Perkinson, "Education and the Open Society." *Notre Dame Journal of Education*, 1973, 4, 345–350. P.350.
5. Harvey Cox, "Pluralism and the Open Society." *Religious Education*, 1974, 69, 150–159.
6. For example: Mary S. Fasenmeyer, "Catholic Schools and Organizational Change." *Notre Dame Journal of Education*, 1973, 3, 324–329; John H. Westerhoff, "The Visionary: Planning for the Future." In Westerhoff, *Colloquy*, pp.236–245.
7. Howard Erickson, "What We Did with Our Empty School [Family Learning Center]." *U.S. Catholic*, January 1972, 37 (1), 6–13; Martin A. Lang, "Education through Availability: The Marist House Plan." *Living Light*, 1968, 5 (3), 36–41; Raymond A. Mack, "An Experiment 'En Rapport.'" *Living Light*, 1969, 6 (1), 118–123.

8. James Michael Lee, *The Flow of Religious Instruction*. Religious Education Press, 1973. Pp.19–20.
9. Theodore R. Sizer, "Values Education in the Schools: A Practitioner's Perspective." *Religious Education*, 1975, 70, 138-149. P.149.
10. Quoted by Patrick C. Rooney, "Religious Instruction in the Context of Catholic Schooling." In James Michael Lee and Rooney (Eds.), *Toward a Future for Religious Education*. Pflaum, 1970. Pp.5–29. P.9.
11. John H. Westerhoff and Gwen Kennedy Neville, *Generation to Generation: Conversations on Religious Education and Culture*. Pilgrim, 1974. P.42. On Lee, see for example *The Flow of Religious Instruction*, p.243.
12. Ellen Dunn and Gerald Dominiak, "Celebrating Change: Liturgy as an Educational Process." *Notre Dame Journal of Education*, 1973, 4, 177–188.

Chapter 12. ENHANCING THE FAMILY

1. The standard research compendium for this chapter and the next is Paul H. Mussen (Ed.), *Carmichael's Manual of Child Psychology*. 3rd ed. 2 vols. Wiley, 1970. Standard textbooks are: Paul H. Mussen, John J. Conger and Jerome Kagan, *Child Development and Personality*. 4th ed. Harper & Row, 1974; Joseph Stone and Joseph Church, *Childhood and Adolescence: A Psychology of the Growing Person*. 2nd ed. Random House, 1974. See note 11 for references particular to this chapter.
2. Burton L. White, *The First Three Years of Life*. Prentice-Hall, 1975.
3. Reference to White's somewhat sensational pronouncement. "Is it all over after three? [a parent will ask] . . . *to some extent* I really believe it is too late after age three" (p.257).
4. James Michael Lee, *The Flow of Religious Instruction*. Religious Education Press, 1973; John H. Westerhoff and Gwen Kennedy Neville, *Generation to Generation: Conversations on Religious Education and Culture*. Pilgrim, 1974.
5. This thesis was brilliantly demonstrated by Philippe Ariès in *Centuries of Childhood: A Social History of Family Life*. Knopf, 1962. For an assessment of Ariès' "immensely influential" contribution, see Lawrence Cremin, "The Family as Educator: Some Comments on the Recent Historiography." *Teachers College Record*, 1974, 76, 250–265.
6. Benjamin Spock, *The Common Sense Book of Baby and Child Care*. Duell, Sloan & Pearce, 1945. This remarkable combination of medicine and educational psychology has supposedly been read by more people than any other single volume in recent decades.
7. Understandably the text may appear to stretch a point. However, readers are invited to do some counting back to the days of their acquaintances' grandparents and parents, and then match them against these examples: William James' new professorship in "Psychology" at Harvard (1889); John Dewey's new "Department of Pedagogy" at Chicago (1894); the American publication of Sigmund Freud's first major work, *Interpretation of Dreams* (1913); and of Jean Piaget's first, *Language and Thought of the Child* (1926). Compute now the case of Dr. Anna Freud: *her* father was born in 1856, her grandfather in 1815; she herself was born [as was Piaget], and her grandfather *died*, some five years before Freud published [in 1900] his book on dreams. Dr. Anna Freud and Prof. Jean Piaget are alive today and doing research in child psychology and education. Thus were our

grandparents and parents, and even some of "us," required to endure life or a good part of it not only without T.V. but also, sadly, without knowledge of the "latest"—nor yet of the *first*—research in education and psychology, etc.

8. "The Family: First Instructor and Pervasive Guide." Special Issue, *Teachers College Record*, 1974, 76 (Whole No.2).

9. Lee, *Flow*, p.64; Westerhoff, *Generation*, p.45.

10. Hope Jensen Leichter, "Some Perspectives on the Family as Educator." *Teachers College Record*, 1974, 76, 175–217. This is an admirable and stimulating review.

11. For this chapter in particular readers might wish to consult: E.J. Anthony and J.M. Foley (Eds.), *The Child in His Family*. 3 vols. Wiley, 1970, 1973, 1974 (esp. vol. 1); T. Berry Brazelton, *Infants and Mothers: Individual Differences in Development*. Delacorte, 1969; also, *Toddlers and Parents: A Declaration of Independence*. Delacorte, 1974; Selma H. Fraiberg, *The Magic Years: Understanding and Handling The Problems of Early Childhood*. Scribner, 1968; Daniel G. Freedman, *Human Infancy: An Evolutionary Perspective*. Erlbaum, 1974; Lawrence Kohlberg and R. Mayer, *Early Education: The Cognitive View*. Holt, 1974; Margaret Mahler, Fred Pine and Anni Bergman, *The Psychological Birth of the Human Infant: Symbiosis and Individuation*. Basic Books, 1975; Burton L. White *et al.*, *Experience and Development: Major Influences on the Development of the Young Child*. Prentice-Hall, 1973. Not to omit an important contrasting viewpoint, see the "behavior-analysis" treatment in Sidney W. Bijou and Donald M. Baer, *Child Development*. 2 vols. Appleton-Century-Crofts, 1961, 1965.

12. For example, Fred Beauvais and Linda Beauvais, "Catechetics in Community: A Program with Growing Pains." *Living Light*, 1968, 5 (3), 30–35.

13. Maureen Gallagher, *Family: Parish Religious Education Program. Complete Cycle A, B*. Paulist, 1974, 1975; Margaret Sawin, "An Overall View of the Family Cluster Experience: Historically, Leadership-wise, and Family-wise." *Religious Education*, 1974, 69, 184–192.

14. Margaret M. Sawin, "A Family Cluster Approach to Learning: A Report of an Innovation in Church Education," 1971. P.O. Box 871, Nashville, Tennessee.

Chapter 13. AWAKENING TO THE WORLD

1. John H. Westerhoff, *Values for Tomorrow's Children: An Alternative Future for Education in the Church*. Pilgrim, 1970. Pp.89,90.

2. Charles Y. Glock, "On the Study of Religious Commitment." *Religious Education*, Research Supplement, 1962. As cited in James Michael Lee, *The Shape of Religious Instruction*. Religious Education Press, 1971. P.11.

3. Cited in Peter A. Bertocci, "Psychological Interpretations of Religious Experience." In Merton P. Strommen (Ed.), *Research on Religious Development: A Comprehensive Handbook*. Hawthorn, 1971. Pp.3–41. Pp.7,11,25.

4. A good example of the view proposed in the text is the stages of faith tentatively devised by James Fowler at Harvard, developing out of Lawrence Kohlberg's states of moral development. James W. Fowler, "Toward a Developmental Perspective on Faith." *Religious Education*, 1974, 69, 207–219. The chapter, "Faith of Children" in Westerhoff and Neville's *Generation to Generation* is an outcome of conversations between Westerhoff and Fowler: "His work is original and its implications for religious education immense" (p.186n).

5. Bertocci, "Psychological Interpretations," p.20.

6. Jean Piaget & Bärbel Inhelder, *The Psychology of the Child*. Basic Books, 1969; *The Growth of Logical Thinking from Childhood to Adolescence*. Basic Books, 1958.
7. Kurt Lewin, *Field Theory in Social Science*. New York: Harper, 1951.
8. André Godin, "Some Developmental Tasks in Christian Education." In Strommen, *Research on Religious Development*, pp.109–154. Pp.111–112.
9. John S. Dunne, *Time and Myth*. Doubleday, 1973.
10. See these articles by Claude Lagarde: "Une foi mal placée." *Catéchistes*, 1974, No.98, 279–305; "Foi et logique enfantine." *Catéchistes*, 1974, No.99, 409–429; and continuing in *Temps et Paroles* for 1975: "Initiation au langage symbolique." No.1, 18–25; "Approche d'une catéchèse de 5°." No.2, 14–23; "Détruire en catéchèse ou détruire la catéchèse?" No.3, 16–27; "Préparation à la vie communautaire en 6°." No.4, 16–23; "Sauver la Révélation." No.5, 20–25.
11. Ronald Goldman, *Religious Thinking from Childhood to Adolescence*. London: Routledge & Kegan Paul, 1964; Wayne R. Rood, *On Nurturing Christians: Perhaps a Manifesto for Education*. Abingdon, 1972. Pp.86–87.
12. The English rendering of this example is rather straightforward but with a restrained touch of scriptural rhetoric that, as noted, may or may not be discerned in the children's original.

Chapter 14. VENTURING ON CHANGE

1. For further considerations, readers might wish to consult: James S. Coleman, *Adolescents and the Schools*. Free Press, 1965; also, Coleman, *Youth: Transition to Adulthood*. Report of the Panel on Youth of the President's Science Advisory Committee. Chicago, 1974; S.E. Dragastin and G.H. Edler (Eds.), *Adolescence in the Life Cycle: Psychological Change and Social Context*. Wiley, 1975; Kenneth Keniston, *The Uncommitted: Alienated Youth in American Society*. Harcourt, Brace & World, 1965; Rolf E. Muuss, *Theories of Adolescence*. 3rd ed. Random House, 1976.
2. Walter H. Clark, "Intense Religious Experience." In Merton P. Strommen (Ed.), *Research on Religious Development: A Comprehensive Handbook*. Hawthorn, 1971. Pp.521–550.
3. Robert J. Havighurst and Barry Keating, "The Religion of Youth." In Strommen, *Research on Religious Development*, pp.686–723. For further references on adolescent religious growth, see note 22, chap. 3 herein.
4. A standard, and lively, reference is Robert F. Mager, *Preparing Instructional Objectives*. 2nd ed. Palo Alto, Calif.: Fearon, 1975.
5. "Venture" is the rhetoric chosen to express that which is perhaps more conventionally termed "pilgrimage" in the literature, "secular" as well as "religious"—the referent is the same in both cases; for example, the ideology of "pilgrimage as the essence of group experience" is elaborated by K.W. Back, *Beyond Words*, New York: Russell Sage Foundation, 1972.
6. Readers seeking further understanding of this type of group leadership in practice, as described in this and the following chapter, may find these especially helpful: Matthew B. Miles, *Learning to Work in Groups: A Program Guide for Educational Leaders*. Teachers College, 1959; Theodore M. Mills, *Group Transformation: An Analysis of a Learning Group*. Prentice-Hall, 1964; Carl R. Rogers, *Freedom to Learn*. Merrill, 1969. A masterly treatment is given by Herbert A. Thelen in chapter 2 of *Dynamics of Groups at Work*. Chicago, 1964; and his

Education and the Human Quest. 2nd ed., Chicago, 1972. One of many attractive summaries of this field is Arthur Blumberg and Robert T. Golembiewski, *Learning and Change in Groups.* Penguin, 1976.

7. For further details on this particular procedure, see Didier J. Piveteau, "Catéchèse, valeurs et valorisation (Parts I, II, III)." *Catéchistes;* (Part I): 1971, No.88, 75–86; (Part II): 1972, No.90, 363–373; (Part III): 1972, 92, 75–84.

Some acquaintance with Transactional Analysis ("T.A.") might be very helpful to working at the "third" level of language described in the text; of many popular introductions, one may cite the original, Eric Berne, *Games People Play: The Psychology of Human Relationships.* Grove, 1964; and an application to classrooms, Ken Ernst, *Games Students Play (and What to Do about Them).* Millbrae, Calif.: Celestial Arts Publishing, 1972.

Chapter 15. FLOURISHING THROUGH COMMUNITY

1. Elisabeth Kübler-Ross (Ed.), *Death: The Final Stage of Growth.* Prentice-Hall, 1975. For her scheme of stages in dying, see *On Death and Dying.* Macmillan, 1969. It is of poignant note that Kübler-Ross, long a professor of psychiatry at the University of Chicago, has publicly declared her conclusion—from clinical research, *not* from private meditations—that conscious existence does not terminate with bodily death; moreover she revealed that several of her patients have palpably visited her after their death in order to dissuade her from abandoning her now-famous studies; and, adding fire to the storm, she has espoused independent researches drawing the same conclusion, by prefacing the sleeper republication of Raymond A. Moody, M.D., *Life after Death* (Mockingbird, 1975), Bantam, 1976, with the warning that opposition to such inquiry will be met in the first place not by the scientific profession, but by "members of the clergy." For the *revenant* item, see "Doctor tells of visit from dead," *Chicago Tribune,* 7 November 1976 (a page-one headline).

2. Fred McMorrow, *Midolescence: The Dangerous Years.* Quadrangle, 1974.

3. Provoked in part by Herant A. Katchadourian's learned discussion—far more comprehensive than indicated by the adjective in the title—"Medical Perspectives on Adulthood." *Daedalus,* 1976, 105 (2), 29–56. There seems to be no medical definition of adulthood.

4. Stephen R. Graubard, "Preface to the Issue 'Adulthood.'" *Daedalus,* 1976, 105 (2), v–viii. This issue contains essays by Erik Erikson and one on "Christian Adulthood" by William J. Bouwsma.

5. Erik H. Erikson, "Identity and the Life Cycle." *Psychological Issues,* 1959, 1 (Whole No.1); James W. Fowler, "Toward a Developmental Perspective on Faith." *Religious Education,* 1974, 69, 207–219; Robert J. Havighurst, *Developmental Tasks and Education.* 3rd ed., rev. David McKay, 1972.

6. Representative of major studies are Roger L. Gould, "The Phases of Adult Life: A Study in Developmental Psychology." *American Journal of Psychiatry,* 1972, 129, 521–531; and Bernice L. Neugarten (Ed.), *Middle Age and Aging.* Chicago, 1968. See also note 7.

7. For current research on this aspect, see B.P. Dohrenwend and B.S. Dohrenwend (Eds.), *Stressful Life Events: Their Nature and Effects.* Wiley, 1974. Recent popular accounts, with interviews, include: Barbara Fried, *The Middle-Age Crisis.* Rev.ed. Harper & Row, 1976; Fred McMorrow, *Midolescence: The*

Dangerous Years. Quadrangle, 1974; Gail Sheehy, *Passages: The Predictable Crises of Adult Life.* Dutton, 1976.

8. René Daumal, *Mount Analogue.* Trans. Roger Shattuck. Pantheon, 1959. Pp.150–151.

9. Kevin Coughlin, "Adult Learning Research and Adult Religious Education: Some Implications." *Living Light,* 1973, 10 (2), 188–199.

10. See Robert M. Smith, George F. Aker and J.R. Kidd (Eds.), *Handbook of Adult Education.* Macmillan, 1970. Especially, Wayne L. Schroeder, "Adult Education Defined and Described," pp.25–43.

11. Malcolm S. Knowles, *The Modern Practice of Adult Education: Andragogy versus Pedagogy.* Association Press, 1970. P.39.

12. Paul Bergevin, *A Philosophy for Adult Education.* Seabury, 1967. Pp.166–170. See also Bergevin, "Adult Education: 'The Chief Form of Catechesis.' " *Living Light,* 1972, 9 (3), 105–114; Bergevin and John McKinley, *Adult Education for the Church.* St. Louis: Bethany Press, 1971; Bergevin, Dwight Morris and Robert M. Smith, *Adult Education Procedures.* Seabury, 1963.

13. On the categories labelled and defined by the Directory, percentage of total lines devoted has been computed to these approximate figures:

	Life-span 70 years	paras. 165–69 "Implications for Rel. Ed." 627 lines	paras. 221–26 "Organization & Structures for Rel. Ed." 466 lines
Infancy	7%	11%	3%
Childhood	7	15	32
Puberty	6	16	
Adolescence	10	31	58
Adulthood	70	27	7
	100%	100%	100%

A further discussion under "adults, youth and children" (172–79) does not permit such comparison.

14. *GED Annual Statistical Report, 1974.* Washington, D.C.: American Council on Education, 1975. To pass this test an adult must score at least 225, the level achieved by 70% of the high-school seniors who served as the norming population during development of the GED. *GED Manual.* American Council on Education, 1975. Information thanks to R. Cervero (see note 15).

15. The text here relies on a dissertation proposal by Ronald M. Cervero, "Assessing the Reliability and Validity of the Adult Performance Level [APL] Test." Unpublished manuscript, University of Chicago Department of Education, 1976.

16. Cyril O. Houle, *The Design of Education.* Jossey-Bass, 1972.

17. For example: Knowles, *Adult Education,* p.156.

18. One case in point occurred in the diocese of Detroit; see *National Catholic Reporter,* 1 August 1975, vol. 11, No.36. A dramatic neighborhood case in the early '50's is recounted by one of the leaders, Herbert A. Thelen, in *Dynamics of Groups at Work.* Chicago, 1954. Chap.1, "Rebuilding the Community through Citizen Action."

19. Judith Barnard, "If It Works, Stop It." *Chicago,* August 1976, 102–113. In

borrowing from this account, we have not named names and so forth, since our purpose and the source's may differ, and since factuality may be presumed or wholly ignored for our purposes, as well served if the whole were taken as a parable. No side-taking in this particularly explosive issue is intended, to apply to the city and personages in question.

20. Compare: M.C. Bryce, "The Catechumenate—Past, Present, and Future." *American Ecclesiastical Review,* 1969, 160, 262–273; François Coudreau, "The Catechumenate in France." *Worship,* 1968, 42, 223–241; Joseph V. Gallagher, *A Parish Catechumenate: Materials and Format for Adult Catechesis.* Newman, 1967.

21. Thierry Maertens, *Les Petits groupes et l'avenir de l'Eglise.* Editions du Centurion, 1971.

INDEX OF SUBJECTS

INDEX OF NAMES